Praise for *Breaking Infinity*

Breaking Infinity is a testament to the power of love and how it can save in the most trying of circumstances - it is the story of young girl who moves into adulthood surrounded by the most traumatic of circumstances. Poignantly written with great attention to detail, Dr. Utti shows us that even children can find the strength to save themselves and those around them. This emotionally powerful book pays tribute to family, transcendence, and the human spirit.

— Ayesha F. Hamid, MFA, MA,
author of *The Borderland Between Worlds: A Memoir*

Breaking Infinity is a heart wrenching account of stark anguish. You don't want to stop reading this compelling story which chronicles an experience with honesty and a sorrowful sensitivity. There is a description of self-loathing for a pre-teen (age 12 through the teen years to age 18) which is devastating. Lina and her brother share a painful intersection of loneliness that drives them to alcohol, drugs, addiction, and worse. This book leaves one with a haunting feeling of remorse.

— Joan Maguire RN, PhD, Professor Emeritus, Sage College, Albany, NY

More Praise for *Breaking Infinity*

Breaking Infinity isn't just a book—it is a deeply personal story that carries the reader along a life journey of someone who struggled with their mental health from a young age. It allows you to see the world through the eyes of loss, prostitution, and addiction...ultimately finding self-love and acceptance. This book has the beautiful capability of connecting to anyone!

— Amanda Hodge, Addictions Counselor, Cedar City, Utah

Breaking Infinity is a beautiful, haunting memoir with powerful themes that will stay with you long after you turn the last page.

— Heather Schugar, PhD, Professor of Literacy, West Chester University, West Chester, PA

Breaking Infinity
A Memoir

Cristina Utti, Ed.D.

www.auctuspublishers.com

Copyright© 2021 Cristina Utti

Cover photo by Angelina Utti-Hodge and James Lee
Book and Cover Design by Colleen J. Cummings

Published by Auctus Publishers
606 Merion Avenue, First Floor
Havertown, PA 19083
Printed in the United States of America

Breaking Infinity is a memoir. Characters names have been changed for anonymity. This is a true story.

All rights reserved. Scanning, uploading, and distribution of this book via the internet or via any other means without permission in writing from its publisher, Auctus Publishers, is illegal and punishable by law. Please purchase only authorized electronic edition.

ISBN 978-1-7368278-4-0 (Print)

ISBN 979-8-9868429-0-5 (Electronic)

Library of Congress Control Number: 2021950057

*Of all writings,
I love only that which is
written with blood. Write
with blood and you will
discover that blood is spirit.*
— Friedrich Nietzsche

Preface

This book was a long time coming. A deep need within me arose to write my story, not only for myself, but also for anyone who is going through or went through divorce, the death of a loved one, or addiction of any sort to show others that healing is possible. I wrote this with the thought that I wanted anyone to read this, adults and teenagers alike, and for them to realize that divorce cannot be blamed on one person. I wanted to share my experience so others would know that addiction can be overcome, or it could kill us. Healing is possible.

Memoir is written from memory, as the word itself states. This is the memory of the self as a little girl growing into adulthood. Sometimes our memory fails us. Sometimes it plays tricks on us. As young children we many times misinterpret intentions and words of adults. It is here that I would like to point out some of those misinterpretations.

While working on my MFA in Creative Writing and throughout the finalizing of this manuscript, my father was diagnosed with Alzheimer's and then with cancer. I had to take guardianship of his medical and financial affairs as his wife was gambling away his life savings. I saw him every day until the day he passed, April 13, 2016. Watching a man I loved and looked up to decline and wither down to a skeleton while his wife abused him was no easy feat. My writing was put aside during that time. After his death I came to realize that maybe he could have done more for me when I was a child. Everything was not as it seemed.

Right after I heard back from my publisher about the final edits necessary, my mother was diagnosed with cancer. I became her sole caretaker while holding full-time job as a 7th grade English teacher and working on my doctoral dissertation. Again, my writing was put aside during that period. The most important thing I learned while caring for my mother was that she loved me. She really did love me, and I love her more than I ever realized. One day, as I was sitting with her because she could not be left alone any longer due to constant vomiting and being too weak to get out of bed, I was holding her hand and brushing the hair form her face. She looked at me and told me that I was beautiful. I said, "You made me this way, Mom." To which she replied, "No, your father did." The realization of my misunderstanding when I was twelve years old swept over me like a tidal wave. I cried and cried that day. There is a time where my mother told me that I look just like my father. When she said that, I was twelve. They were going through a divorce, and she was leaving him. I took her words then to mean that I was ugly and that she did not like me, as I reminded her of the man she was divorcing. I thought then, in my adolescent brain, that if she no longer loved my father and if she thought that I looked just like him, then she no longer loved me either, as I look just like him.

I was gravely mistaken. My mother loved my father until the day she died. She thought he was handsome until the day she died. When she told me that he was the one who made me beautiful, my world came crashing down. My thoughts and feelings from the past were based on misconceptions. She was raised in poverty, sent to a convent for her entire childhood because her parents could not afford to raise her. She moved to this country at a young age, with no experience in how to be a mother or a wife. Her life was not easy. I realized a bit too late that she did her best, and that she loved me. She suffered greatly. I love my mother with all my heart. I was not ready for her to leave this earth on January 22, 2021. I hope that before she took her final breath, she was able to forgive my acting out as a teenager. I hope I made it up to her by being there for her and caring for her in those months, weeks, and days as she lay dying.

So, take this story as it is; told from the point of view of who I was then, not who I grew to become.

PART ONE

1976

Chapter 1
The Big Clean Up

The basement is where we play. It's a big room, with a black and brown tile floor and little bitty windows up high on the wall. It gets a bit chilly down here sometimes which feels nice in the summer. Mom sent us all down here to get us out of her hair while she cooks dinner. David set up all of his cowboys and Indians and wanted me to play with him, but I'm not interested. The book that I am reading, *The Little House on the Prairie*, is more interesting than having a war with little one-inch plastic people. Carmen is happily playing with his Lincoln Logs, and his Legos are all over the back corner of the basement floor. I don't know why, because he doesn't even play with them anymore. He probably dumped them out, got bored, and left them there. If there was a fire and we had to get out quickly, they would kill our feet. Stepping on a Lego with bare feet is no joke. The only person with shoes on is David because he never listens. One of Mom's rules is to take off our shoes as soon as we get in the back door.

"Clean up that mess down there," Mom yells down the steps.

I panic when I hear her anxious tone. I put down my book and look around. David has his whole zillion cowboys and Indians in a war, taking up the entire area rug in the center of the floor. Boys are so immature. David is the oldest, almost twelve years old. I can't believe he still plays with those toys. Anna and Lucy are playing with their rag dolls, having a tea party at their little yellow plastic table that sits in front of the closet. Their Barbies are on the floor along with a ton of outfits and shoes. The closet is to the right of the back door. Taking a glance back there, I can see that the back half of the basement is a big fat mess.

"C'mon guys, let's clean up," I tell them.

No one listens. No one ever listens to me, even though I'm the second oldest. I always have to clean up after everyone and I'm sick of it.

"C'mon David, pick 'em up before Mom comes down here and gets mad." I ask him first because he is the oldest. Maybe everyone will follow suit if they see him putting away his toys. For some reason, he is downstairs hanging with us today instead of upstairs in his room with the door locked.

"Anna and Lucia, put your dolls in the bin." Us girls are all two years apart. We are the insides of the sandwich; the boys are the bread. Funny how it all worked out biologically. David has the darkest, curliest hair, then mine is a little lighter and less curly. Anna has chestnut brown, wavy hair. Lucy's hair is blonde with slight leftover baby waves, and Carmen's is platinum blonde and straight. David is the darkest with the strongest Sicilian genes. I'm a bit lighter. Anna is olive color, Lucy is light, but can hold a tan, and Carmen's skin is milky. It's like the curl genes and color printer ran out as the kids kept coming. I'm not sure anyone else notices these things, but I do. That's me; always standing on the sidelines, watching. Anna's hearing problem must be contagious because now Lucy has it too. They act like I don't even exist, so I go clean up after Carmen. I pick up the logs and put them in the red bucket.

"Dinner is almost ready, is it cleaned up down there?" Mom shouts from the top of the steps again. "You better have everything put away and straightened up."

I pick up the Legos and put them in the Lego bucket. That is all I am doing. My mess is the book I left on the floor, so I go pick it up and put it back on the small bookshelf that sits under one of Dad's paintings. It's a painting of Uncle Freddy playing the piano. That's Dad's older brother. Dad is second in his family, like me.

"Carmen, put your cars away before Mom comes down," I tell him. He is old enough to know better.

I hear her yell again. She sounds angry. I don't care. I'm angry too. I'm not cleaning up their messes anymore. I sit down on the yellow bean bag chair and pick up the Barbie that's on the floor. I fix her clothes and smooth her hair. I hear Mom coming down the steps.

"I told you guys to clean up!" She has the belt out. We start moving fast, but not fast enough. I hear the leather swish through the air before it cracks on my back. I try to run. It strikes again. When this happens, I leave my body. I watch from above; it hurts less this way.

Her sky-blue eyes turn dark, just like the sky before a storm. Her face is bright red and splotches are breaking out on her neck. She's in a rage. David gets the buckle as he is escaping up the steps. It hits him on his thighs, and he tumbles back down. Anna and Lucy are huddled together in the corner crying. I want to help them. I move toward them.

"Don't you go near them!"

The leather strikes again. It pushes me forward onto the ground. I look for Carmen. I don't want her to hit him. He is only four years old. This mess isn't his fault. From the ground, I see him hunched in the corner near his blocks just across from my little sisters. Tears are rolling out of his brown eyes.

* * *

Somehow the basement is cleaned up. The floor is spotless, not a toy in sight. The giant plastic football toy container even has its lid on and the red chairs at the little table are pushed in, ready for the next tea party. The lights are off. Looking up at the little windows, I can see that it's getting dark outside. I guess they forgot about me.

I climb the basement stairs as quiet as a mouse. My back hurts. I want to go into the bathroom and check my back in the mirror, but I hear soft sobbing as I walk through the kitchen. I follow the sound into the dining room. Peeking around the corner of the entrance, I scan the room. The wooden table sits perfectly gleaming; the carpet is freshly vacuumed. I spot Mom. She is huddled in the corner under the window, hiding in the space between the china cabinet and the wall. Her face is on her knees; her shoulders shaking.

"I am so sorry," she repeats over and over. She is trembling. Even though I'm the one with the bloody welts across my back, she is crying. Looking at her like this, I begin to cry. I don't know if it's because my back hurts, or because my mother looks like a broken doll with tears streaming down her face. I go to her.

"It's okay Mom." I sit next to her and wrap my arms around her.

"I am so sorry Lina," she says between sniffles.

"I know. It's okay." I don't know if I feel worse for her or the kids. She scared the heck out of us down there, and now she is crying, they are all crying, and I have to hold it together when I was the one hurt the worst. Anger wells up inside of me, but I can't be irritated with Mom when she is so sad for what happened.

"I'll go check on the kids," I tell her and unwrap myself from her.

"*Mi dispiace*." She covers her eyes and cries harder. I don't want to leave her like this. I am scared when she loses her temper, and then afterward when she gets like this, I am scared that I will lose her completely.

"Mom, it's okay. It doesn't hurt," I lie.

"Let me see your back." She begins to lift my shirt.

"No, Mom. I'm okay, really." I don't know how bad it is, but I can feel my shirt sticking to the wounds on my back while I stare at the floor.

"Lina, let me see," she demands. I shift my body around on the floor so she can lift my shirt and take a look at my back.

"*Oh Madonna!*" She gasps, and I can feel her cover her mouth although I have my back to her. The dark clouds of gloom overtake my heart.

"Come into the kitchen so I can clean that for you."

I move silently out of the dining room into the kitchen, moving past the fridge and counters toward the table as if in a dream. I'm glad the kids aren't in here. I don't want them to see my back. Mom searches the kitchen drawers for a clean towel as if she can't remember where they are. My brain thinks *second drawer to the left*, but my mouth will not move. She finds them as if she heard me. She pulls out a blue hand towel and then a white one. She chooses the white one, and I'm glad because it looks softer.

"Lina, sit down," she says as she runs the towel under water. She doesn't make eye contact with me. I don't want to look at her either. Actually, this whole thing is quite uncomfortable. She comes closer to me and my pulse races. She lifts my shirt off over my head and lays it on the kitchen table. She drizzles the cool water over the damaged, broken skin. I flinch.

"I'm sorry," she says over and over as she goes through this process of fixing me up. She has hit me with the belt before, but it has never been this bad.

"I have to get some peroxide. You've got your shirt all in it," as if this is my fault, but I don't say a word. She leaves the kitchen as I sit exposed. I don't have much of a chest, but I am glad I'm wearing my training bra today in case

David or one of the kids walk in on me. Mom returns with the brown bottle, gauze, and Band-Aids. I want to shrink and shrink until I am not here anymore. I don't want my mom to cry. All of the cool water, peroxide, and I am sorrys can't fix the damage.

Chapter 2

Getting Fat in LaLa Land

I'm getting fat. Mom says that I'm just growing, that I am beautiful. I know she just tells me this because she's my mom. All moms think their kids are beautiful, even if they are uglier than a mangled sewer rat. That's their job, to love their kids no matter what. I don't feel beautiful. Not only did I get braces last week and my hair turned curly overnight since it got chopped off, but I also got my period two days ago. Mom says that I'm a woman now and we should celebrate. I don't want to be a woman, nor do I want to celebrate this disgusting thing. I want to hang out with Penney, have fun, and be a kid. I feel fat and yucky, and I'm afraid that everyone at school could see my pad.

"Mom, I need some new clothes. All of my pants are too small," I tell her as she is sorting the laundry in the living room. When we got in from school, David went right up to his room, as usual. Carmen, Anna, and Lucy aren't home from school yet because the elementary school lets out after the junior high.

"I just bought you clothes," she says, not looking at me.

"But they're already too tight," I whine. She takes her time folding Carmen's jeans. She smooths them neatly so they won't wrinkle, places them in the basket and looks up at me.

"Oh Lina, when I was your age, I was as thin as a rail. What do you mean they are tight? My clothes used to hang off my bones."

"Never mind." Why does she always have to remind me about how skinny she was at my age? It's quite obvious that all of my pants are too tight. I think she likes to watch me suffer. Now that I'm a woman and have to wear these pads, everyone can see the lump between my legs that goes up my butt crack. I am fat. She is right. How can my pants not fit me already? I think she is secretly happy that I am fat because she was so skinny but isn't anymore. I'll get babysitting jobs with Penney so I can buy my own clothes. I'm not asking her again so she can tell me how skinny she was at my age.

Beautiful. Yeah, right.

I try to give her a break. Maybe she is upset because Carmen started first grade two weeks ago, and because Dad has been away painting a church in Baltimore for almost three weeks now. She hasn't been herself lately.

When we were eating breakfast, she told us the story of when she met Dad, again. I've heard it a million times, but I just shut my mouth and listened. The story always begins the same. It all began at a funeral. I sure hope I meet my husband someplace more fun than at a funeral.

"We were at my uncle's funeral in Roma. There were a lot of sad people around, but it was hard for me to be sad. I never knew my aunts and uncles. Being in the convent all of those years, I did not get to know most of my family as I grew up," she started telling the story. "I saw a handsome man and asked my sister about him."

"What man?" Lucy asked her. I shot her the mean eye for leading Mom on, but she didn't even look at me.

"Your father," Mom told her. "He was standing by a tree. He was absolutely stunning. He was wearing a black suit and had a head of beautiful thick black curly hair."

"Daddy had a lot of hair?" Anna asked because now Dad has a bald spot right in the middle of his head. Mom had them in her grip.

"He sure did. Then Gulia, my sister, said '*Chi, lui?*' and pointed at him, making a spectacle."

"What's a spectacle?" Carmen piped in.

"She made me embarrassed by pointing at him," Mom explains. "I told her to stop pointing because I didn't want him to look over at us."

"Why not?" Anna asked.

"Because I never had a boyfriend, and I was nervous. Stop interrupting," Mom said, and then continued. "Gulia pointed at him and asked me if he was who I was staring at."

"Why were you staring at him?" Lucy cut in. I was getting nervous about the time and I didn't want her getting mad at me for leaving the table while she was speaking.

"*Oh Madonna*, I wasn't staring at him. I was just looking at him. I wondered if he was a cousin or family member I had never met. And that's what I told Gulia, too."

"Was he?" Carmen asked.

"No honey, he wasn't a cousin. He was your father," Mom told him.

"How did Daddy know you were in Rome?" Carmen asked.

"He didn't. That's when I saw him for the first time. So Gulia said, 'Nope, I never saw him before in my life,' in Italian of course, and I was so glad he wasn't my cousin. The luncheon was held at La Travata. I stayed close by Gulia, not only because she is my favorite sister, but also because I had never been to a funeral luncheon and wasn't sure what to do."

"What were you supposed to do?" Lucy asked.

"I didn't know," Mom laughed. "That's why I stayed close to my big sister. She liked to point a lot, which got on my nerves because in the convent the nuns would punish us for pointing."

Cristina Utti

"The nuns punished you?" Anna asked.

"Oh, yes. They would hit us and take any food that our parents brought for us. I was scrubbing floors on my hands and knees by the time I was eight years old. Those nuns were so mean. I jumped out the window a few times and tried to run away."

I couldn't imagine living with a bunch of nuns. It was bad enough having them for teachers at Sts. Cosmos and Damian. I'm glad Mom and Dad transferred us to public school this year. I think I'd kill myself if I had to live with nuns 24/7. I'm sure those mean nuns are the reason why Mom beats us with the belt or the wooden spoon. That is when I stopped listening to the story this morning. I know it by heart anyway. She droned on about how they met, and how Dad was with some guy that had a handle-bar moustache who ended up being a friend of her deceased uncle. They landed up sitting together for the luncheon, all the while Mom got flutters. I don't know what flutters feel like. Maybe someday I'll feel like that about a boy.

I looked at the clock. It was 7:05. I had to catch the bus. Dave and I are the first ones out the door. The bus comes at 7:10 every morning. I looked for Dave to see if he was ready to walk to the bus stop with me because I didn't know where he went. I watched as he chowed down three bowls of Corn Flakes without even chewing, then he was gone. I'd get yelled at if I left the table without excusing myself. I wish the same rules applied to everyone around here. I thought he left already, so I gave everyone a quick peck, and headed out the door feeling like the day would turn out okay since Mom was in a better mood.

But my day did not turn out so great. At lunch I heard Andrew and Silvio snickering behind me in line. I bet they could see my pad. My jeans were suffocating me all day. I had to suck in my stomach just to get them zipped and buttoned. Mom's no help. All she does is snap out or ignore me. Now, the minute I get back in from school, she has me all upset again. She ignores that my pants don't fit and asks about David.

After telling me how skinny she was, she asks, "What's your brother doing?" It sounds like an accusation. I'm not into getting in the middle of Mom and David's fights. I have my own problems, plus I want to get a snack and eat in peace before the kids get home.

"I don't know. I'm not his keeper." I say with my back toward her as I walk into the kitchen. I know what he is doing. He is listening to music and smoking weed. Then he'll light incense. His bedroom is right next to mine, so I know the game. Plus, I've asked him, and David doesn't lie. I don't think he knows how.

"Don't get fresh with me young lady, and look at me when I'm speaking to you."

I turn around and stare at her, and all of my anger dissolves and drips away. "Sorry." I hang my head, not looking her in the eye. I don't mean to be fresh. I know what he's doing but can't tell her. Unlike David, I do lie, but I'm not good at it, especially with Mom. She has radar vision that sees through me. So, giving her the attitude hides the lie. Besides, being snippy with her makes me feel a little bit better because she was so skinny at my age and won't let me forget it.

"Tell him to come down here."

"David," I yell, "Mom wants you." I scream with all my might so maybe he'll hear me above the music he is blaring. I open the cabinet under the toaster and begin rummaging for a snack. No potato chips left. Crumbs and broken pieces are all that's left at the bottom of a bag of pretzel sticks. No good cereal either, just Cheerios and Bran Flakes.

"Lina, I could have done that myself. Forget it." She is exasperated with me.

I'm exasperated with myself. Forget the snack. My pants are too tight anyway, and all the good stuff is gone. I better go upstairs and warn him that Snoopy Sniffer wants him. That's Mom's nickname between us. David, Callan, Penney and I sometimes smoke cigarettes that Penney gets from her mom's stash which she keeps in the cabinet above the refrigerator in her kitchen. When we came in the back door after the first time we smoked, Mom sniffed us like she was a hunting dog.

"Were you a'smoking, eh?" she asked us in a deep Italian accent. I was embarrassed in front of Penney and Callan when Mom acted like that, sniffing us.

Guilty as sin, we all said, "No," in unison. Except David. He just looked at the floor. After that we knew better. Now after we smoke, we grab pine needles from the trees that line the front yard to rub on our fingers and faces, then pop a piece of gum in our mouths to keep Snoopy Sniffer off our trail. I know if she goes upstairs to get him, she will smell his room and know what he's doing, then holy hell will break loose, so up I go. Guess I can use the exercise since my clothes don't fit.

"David," I knock on his door. No answer. "David," I knock harder.

"Hold on," he says. He's probably snuffing something out.

"Mom wants you." Even though I don't do drugs, I protect him. Mom can get a bit crazy.

"Okay," I hear him say through the door.

I hear her walking through the hall towards the steps. "David, hurry up, Mom's coming." I'm not in the mood for this today.

"Okay, okay." I hear the window opening. He is probably hoping the stench will float out the window, but that won't work. Snoopy Sniffer has canine qualities of smell. I open the door to my room nonchalantly as I see her coming up the steps. I don't want her to know I've given David a warning.

Breaking Infinity

Ever since I got into junior high, David has been cool with me. He lets me hang out with him and his friends. I like our new, more mature relationship because I get to hang out with older kids. He even took me to a keg party at Kane's house this summer. That night I tried beer for the first time. I don't know how people drink that stuff. It tastes gross. The Franklins live in Whitemarsh, right across from the police station. This must be the best place to drink and party underage because they never suspect, being right across the street. The Franklins are all boys, and Kane's the baby. They are all big drinkers, and the habit seemed to trickle right down to Kane, who resembles Baby Huey. He towers over the rest of us in height and weight. I even grew six inches last year and hit 5'9" which made me taller than most of the boys in my grade, so Kane must be about 6'2". The drinking part wasn't so good, but some of the guys there were checking me out. I could tell. I don't like any of them, but I felt pretty that night. So, to protect my relationship with my David, I do all I can to protect him from Snoopy Sniffer.

"David, open this door!" I can hear her pounding on his door. Now I'm the one with the volume turned up on the radio. I can still hear through the wall.

"Hold on." He stalls.

"Open up! What are you doing in there?" I hold my breath as I hear him open the door. She will really lose it if she knows he is getting high.

"What Mom?" he says as he opens his door. I can smell the incense burning. I'm sure Snoopy Sniffer can too.

"How many times do I have to tell you not to burn things in your room?" Maybe he wasn't smoking weed in there today because she would surely have smelled it.

"Sorry, Mom," I hear him say.

"Please come down and do your chores. The trash needs to go out." I hear her descend the stairs.

"I'm coming," David tells her. I turn down my radio to eavesdrop. I hear him close his bedroom door. "Thanks for the warning," he mumbles as he moves past my bedroom door. At least he knows I tried. My bedroom is the first bedroom on the right at the top of the stairs, so I get to hear all of the traffic. I know by the pattern of the feet and the heaviness or lightness of the sound who is going up or down the steps. I have it down to a science. I can tell who it is as soon as they hit the second step.

I hear him tumble down the stairs.

I whip open my bedroom door and fly down the steps behind him.

He is upside down on the steps. "You okay?" I ask as I help him get his foot out of the rail and detangle his boney limbs. His long, thick curls are stuck in the railing. Gently as I can, I detangle the dark locks. Maybe he should listen to Mom and get a haircut.

"Yeah, thanks," he says.

"You sure you aren't hurt?" He doesn't sound right. His eyes look round as quarters and his pupils are huge. David's eyes are almond-shaped and smile a bit upward at the corner, which makes him look like he is always happy. My eyes are big and round like a puppy's. They make me look like I am sad all of the time, or maybe they make me look serious, which I am. They are good for giving the innocent look. His eyes look like the shape of mine right now. Maybe it was the fright. Maybe he bumped his head and has a concussion. I read somewhere that a concussion can make your pupils dilate.

"Yeah, I'm okay." He tries to act cool. Mother Nature is not fair. David went through a growth spurt and got tall and lean. I went through a growth spurt and got my period and a layer of fat. My chest is budding, and I am scared to ask Mom to buy me a bra. She was probably so skinny at my age that she only sported ribs.

"Where's Mom?" Dave asks. Boy, something is wrong with him.

"I don't know, probably the kitchen. The kids just got home." It's our new thing to call them the kids; it differentiates us because we are the older two. Oh yeah, and because now I'm a woman.

"Mom just told you to put out the trash. Did you hit your head?" Something is definitely amiss. I'm sure Mom would've smelled it if he was smoking weed.

"Nah, nah, I'm okay." Off he goes to take out the trash. I'm glad Mom was busy with the kids. She didn't even hear him tumble down the steps or notice that his eyes looked weird. That's very odd because she notices everything. Usually, she is right up our butts, telling us to turn down the music, do this or do that. She even times how much television we watch. Usually, we can't get away with anything. She must be slipping.

Chapter 3
The Snack Wars

I found out why Mom has been so distracted. She's been looking for a job. I figured it out this morning. Usually by the time I'm in the kitchen packing my lunch I can hear the kids rustling upstairs. This morning all was a bit too quiet, so I went upstairs to find out why. Mom was in her room getting dressed. She had on snug white bell-bottom pants, a low-cut red bandana top, and was putting on mascara when I walked in on her. She looked at me like she was caught doing something wrong, and that's when I found out she had a job interview. I'm excited for her. It will do her good to get out of the house. To show my support, and since I am almost twelve years old now, I went ahead and got the kids ready for school.

Some mornings are better than others. This morning David didn't want to get up and go to school, which I don't understand because when he does go, he doesn't want to come home. He's not a morning person. Lucy woke with her hair matted on one side of her head, probably from drool dripping while she sucked her thumb, and it took about ten minutes to get the knots out. She wasn't too happy about that. She's lucky she doesn't have hair like mine or Anna's; ours is thick and the knots even thicker. Carmen spilled chocolate milk all down his shirt and I had to find him a clean one while he carried on crying. He gets as red as a cooked lobster when he gets upset, just like Mom. I had to calm him down and wipe the snot and tears. I told Anna to brush her teeth and hair after breakfast, but she refused. Her answer to everything is, "Why bother, they'll get dirty again anyway," or, "Why brush my hair? It will get knotty again anyway." I really don't understand her way of thinking at all. She doesn't like me to tell her what to do since she is only two years younger than I, so I told her if she wanted to go to school with bad breath, then go ahead. I think she refuses to do what I ask to spite me, which is pretty stupid. There are plenty of other ways to spite someone than not taking care of your own body. I totally understand why Mom wants to get a job. This is enough to make anyone crazy.

I was happy as a clam to get on the bus after the stress of the morning. School was pretty uneventful and boring. In most of my classes, I kept staring out the window, wondering if Mom got the job. She has always been home with us. I kept thinking about this and if I will have to get the kids ready every day if Mom has a job. That would really be the pits.

When the bell rings at 2:25, everyone stampedes out the door like the world is about to end. David and I sit together on the bus in the morning and on the ride home, but today there's no sign of him, so I sit alone with my thoughts. I sit in the middle of the seat hoping no one tries to sit next to me.

As soon as I walk in the back door, I see Mom in the kitchen washing the dishes that were left in the sink from breakfast. "Hi Mom, how was the interview?" I like when David goes out after school, so I can have Mom all to myself before the kids get home. She changed into her more comfortable clothes, jeans and a sweater, but the make-up remains. She looks pretty with blue eyeshadow; it brings out her eyes. I'd have to wear greenish-brown eye shadow to bring out my eyes. That doesn't sound pretty at all. I would probably look like a swamp creature.

"Oh Lina, it went great," Mom says, as she dries her hands on the towel that hangs from the oven door. "The owner of the agency is Italian. He is from Abruzzi, near where I grew up."

"That's cool, so what happened? Did you get the job?"

"*Oh Madonna*! Wait until I tell you what happened today," she exclaims. I feed into her energy.

"Tell me, tell me! What happened?"

"I got the job."

"Wow," is all I can say. Mom's never had a job in America. She only worked for a little while after she got out of the convent in Italy, before she met Dad.

"I start Monday. Anyway, listen. I was so excited that I got the job that I wasn't paying attention on my way home. Remember when I used to say I was so tired I wouldn't mind spending some time in jail, just to get some rest?"

"Yeah," I say, not really remembering.

"Well, it finally happened," she claims, then takes a breath.

"What happened? You went to jail?" I'm so confused.

"No, silly. I got pulled over. I wasn't paying attention and went through a stop sign." Then I remember. I remember how she had this great plan to get a bunch of speeding tickets and not pay them, so they could come get her and put her in jail for a night. The plan always seemed a bit far-fetched, but that's Mom. Dramatic.

"Did you get a ticket?"

"Nope. He was really nice. I told him my son was sick and I had to get him from school." She straightens out her shoulders and holds her head up stiffly. I hope if I ever get pulled over I can come up with a quick one like that, but I still have four years before I can get my license.

Breaking Infinity

"So, do you think you'll like the job?" I ask, so we can keep talking.

"Of course, what's not to like? I have to be there by 9 a.m. every day. That gives me time to get everyone on the bus, but I may need you to watch the kids after school sometimes. I'll be in training for a while, so I'm not sure what time I get done every day."

"What are you going to do there?" I have no idea what people in travel agencies actually do. Mom tells me that they help people make their travel plans. The owner, Saul, told her that all agents earn points on the vacations they book, and then they can use their points for their own traveling.

"Oh honey, I'm so excited. I can earn points to go back to Italy to see my family," she says, talking really fast. "I'm going to go upstairs and get the bedrooms cleaned up. I have to make sure everything is spic and span before I start my new job."

We headed up the steps together, me right behind her. "I'll clean my own room." I keep my room pretty clean, and I don't want her going through my things.

Mom starts in the girls' room. She picks up all of their dirty clothes from the floor and strips the beds. I see her carrying the laundry to the hamper in the bathroom. Then she heads into David's room. I'd be scared to clean in there. It always reeks like sweat, old moldy cheese, smoke, and burnt candles. While I dust my bureau, I can hear her cursing in Italian about a burn hole in the rug. She comes out with an armful of clothes.

"Lina, grab me a basket." I guess the hamper is full, so I stop what I'm doing and grab one from the master bedroom for her. I put it on the floor so she can dump her load into it, and then go back in my room to finish what I was doing. I hear her opening and closing drawers, like she is searching for something. "Lina, come here." I run because she sounds frantic. She is holding a pipe. *"Che diavolo e' questo?"*

"I have no idea, Mom." She speaks Italian when she is upset or doesn't want people to know what we are talking about. I knew Italian before I learned English since Mom was only in this country a few years before she had me. I don't even have to lie. I really have no idea what it is.

She sniffs the pipe. "What the hell is your brother doing with this?" she questions, and then begins hysterically murmuring in Italian while going through all of his bureau drawers and then all of his pants' pockets. A bottle of pills falls out of a pair of jeans. I stand here, frozen, watching her. In his sock drawer, she finds his weed. Oh crap.

"What is all of this? Your brother's not sick, why does he have a bottle of pills? *Cos'e' questo?*" She takes a deep whiff of the weed.

"*Non lo so.*" I say at the floor. David's in deep shit. It figures, today is Friday the thirteenth.

At this point all I can think of is getting the heck out of here and going to Penney's house. Her parents have "wine – o'clock" every night at 9 p.m. They sit together in the living room, reading their papers, enjoying each other and their wine. They've been doing this for years and I never noticed until last night. I'm all of a sudden more aware. I'm more aware of David's crazy eyes and more aware of other people's families. Maybe it is because I miss Dad. Maybe it is because I'm a woman now.

Mom is in her room, screaming at Dad on the phone, like it's his fault that Dave is smoking weed. Dad seems to be away more and more ever since we moved into this house from Turf Lane. This house took a lot of getting used to. First of all, this was the first house on the entire street. Second, we are surrounded by woods, which is a lot different from Turf Lane. Turf Lane was a neighborhood of small twin ranch homes, and all the neighbors were friends. Here there wasn't another home on our street until two years ago. On Turf Lane, I shared a bedroom with Lucy and Anna.

I hated it, and always complained that I wanted my own room, so when we moved here, because I'm the oldest girl, I got my own room.

I got what I wanted, then I was scared. I was so scared that for the longest time I had to pretend myself to sleep. I would pull the covers over my head and pretend there was a robber in the house. If I made one move, he would kill me. That's how I fell asleep every night. Or by memorizing my spelling words. That worked too.

All of the kids played in the street at our old home. I missed that for a long time, until I found Penney. I must be getting more mature because I never thought of all of this before. Watching Penney's parents made me miss seeing mine together and happy. Not that they drink wine. Neither of them drink, not really. The only time Dad drinks wine is when we have linguini and clams; he has a glass of wine with his pasta. Sometimes Dad treats us out to the Beef and Ale house. They are known for their hot roast beef sandwiches. Everyone orders a hot roast beef, and I order the cheese fries. Dad orders one beer, and we all get root beers with cherries. That's the extent of his drinking. Mom, she never drinks. They never hung out and drank wine together, but I do remember Mom and Dad making me embarrassed when they flirted and kissed in front of my friends. Funny, I actually miss those times now.

The memories fill my mind as I head downstairs, away from Mom, to wait for the kids to get home. I'll give them a snack and then head to Penney's. I look out the laundry room window for the kids and see that it looks like the clouds are going to open up and drench us in their tears. Perfect timing. I see them running from the bus stop, then down our long driveway. They whizz up the back steps, the cold chasing after them as they open the back door. I stand in the kitchen with my arms crossed, watching as they stumble into the laundry room, practically knocking each other over. Sometimes, when they aren't annoying, they're pretty cute. They take off their shoes at the door, toss them aside, and throw their coats that still smell of the outdoors onto the bench. They drop their book bags on the floor. They know better. This is what is annoying. I search the cabinets for something they can have for an after-school snack before I yell at them to pick up their stuff. Mom is usually in here to greet them, but since she's preoccupied, here I am.

"Hi Lina, where's Mom?" Lucy asks. Carmen comes into the kitchen and gives me a hug. I love how he smells of a little boy: a mix of crayons and trees. I ask them about school and pretend nothing just happened upstairs. I know she'll be down here any minute and nag at me for the shoes and coats being all over the floor even though none of them are mine. Today I decide not to even waste my energy by trying to get everyone to hang their coats and line up their shoes neatly. It's easier for me to just do it myself than to risk getting yelled at or worse, the belt. If I don't straighten up, the mess will be my fault, as usual. "Lina, why didn't you clean up?" Blah, blah, blah.

Before they get a snack, I pick up Anna's and Lucy's shoes and line them up nicely under the bench, which was really a church pew that Dad had brought home from Sts. Cosmos and Damian Church, which he then painted a deep indigo blue. I bang the mud out of Carmen's sneakers on the rug by the door and leave them there because they are still wet. He was probably walking in puddles. I hang everyone's coat on the rack. I pick up Lucy's pink book bag, put it on the right corner of the bench, and put Anna's right next to hers. Carmen has recently realized that he's a boy, and makes it known that he doesn't want his bag near girls' bags. He insists that his book bag gets put on the left corner of the bench. It is kind of adorable. David's stuff is on the floor from this morning. He didn't even take his book bag to school with him. I'm glad we're getting along better, but I'm not his maid. He should be here helping me, but he's always out with his friends.

While I am straightening up, they decide on their own snacks. "That's not fair! You got more!" Carmen yells at Lucy.

The snack war begins before I'm out of the laundry room. They are fighting over the last of the Doritos. I didn't think there were any good cereals left since yesterday there were only Cheerios in the cabinet. Mom must have gone shopping after her interview because I see cookies on the counter that weren't here yesterday, and there are boxes of Coco Puffs and Captain Crunch in the pantry.

I hear the freezer door open and don't even have to look to know what's going on. "You having ice cream?" I ask Anna sarcastically. I can't help myself. Anna is the lucky snack queen. Ever since her surgery, about a bazillion years ago, she gets to eat ice cream whenever she wants. Oh, and did I mention pudding, jello, and whipped cream? All she has to say is that her mouth hurts. I mean I know they removed her palate and drilled through her nostril so that she could breathe through both sides, but how bad could it really hurt after three, four, five years? And how could Mom fall for it every time? It just isn't fair. She has the reign over the ice cream in the house and lops scoops of mint chocolate chip in her bowl like there's no tomorrow. "There won't be any left for anyone else," I tell her, as if she cares.

What really gets me angry is when we have something really disgusting for dinner, like beef stew, and Anna's mouth suddenly hurts. She gets ice cream at the dinner table while us less fortunate ones have to plow through eating mammals. The vegetables aren't so bad, even if they were in mammal juice, but we can't leave the table until our plate is cleared and we get no dessert if we don't eat dinner. My trick is to chew the meat so it looks like I'm eating it, and then spit it into my napkin because I just can't bear to swallow an animal. I sure wish we had a dog so I could sneak him the meat under the table like the kids in the TV shows do. I have to go through all this nonsense without being caught just so I could get a measly scoop of ice cream for dessert. On the positive side, this excludes Anna from the ongoing snack wars. So, it's down to four of us most days, unless, of course, Penney or Callan are over. Those days are even worse because we have to try to act polite.

That or we get embarrassed. Like the time Dave and I were hanging out with Penney and Callan after school, and we came in the kitchen to grab a snack. Mom was starting dinner, and Rusty, our cat, kept rubbing on her legs while she was trying to cook. She got frustrated and blurted out, "This damn pussy, always in the middle of my legs," and shoved Rusty aside with her foot. At first, I giggled, thinking, *Where the heck do you expect it to be?* But when I turned around, Callan was staring at me and my face must have turned thirty shades of red. This is one of the problems with having a parent who was born in another country; they don't know the idioms of our language. Talk about embarrassing.

Anyway, most days, the early bird gets the worm. You have to get up early around here to get the good cereal and inconspicuously hide the good snacks after Mom does her weekly shopping trip. When she buys junk cereal, the first one that gets to it eats as much as they can because one box isn't enough for all of us. But, days like today, when Mom just did a shopping trip, it's a free for all.

Dave walks in the back door without saying a word and without taking off his wet sneakers.

I manage to straighten up the laundry room and zip back into the kitchen, grab a bowl, the box of Captain Crunch, and begin to pour the cereal in my bowl before Dave gets into the kitchen. I did all this at astonishing speed while he was still fumbling for a spoon and getting the milk out of the fridge. I don't have to waste any time on milk, since I hate milk. I use apple juice in my cereal, and the kids already have it out on the table. He must have seen me out of the corner of his eye, because quicker than Speedy Gonzalez he whips across the kitchen, and before I know it, he tears the box from my hand sending the entire box of cereal flying all over the table, into Anna's ice cream and hair, and onto the floor. Shrieking her high-pitched scream, Anna makes Lucy and Carmen fall silent and glare at us. I grab to get the box back, but Dave is taller and stronger. He holds the box up high and teases me with his height. I'm so frustrated I want to cry, and the tears well up under my lids like a volcano about to erupt, but I'm not going to give him the satisfaction.

"You can have the stupid cereal, it's stale anyway!" I storm out of the kitchen. I run up to my room, slam my door, and lock it. Second day minus an after-school snack. That's not even what bothers me the most. It's his meanness. I'm glad Mom found his weed and I don't care what kind of mess they leave down there. *He* can clean it up.

I put my Janis Joplin album on the turntable, stick my headphones on my head, and blast "Piece of My Heart" into my brain. It's probably frying my brain cells. Sometimes I hate David. He's so mean to me, like he resents the fact that I was born. It seems like every time I think we are getting close he reverts back to being mean.

I have an essay due Monday for English, so I try to brainstorm ideas, hoping this will help me take my mind off of David. I have no idea what to write about because as soon as I get into a flow of thought for a draft of my *Lord of the Flies* essay, I hear banging and yelling coming from David's bedroom. I take off my headphones to listen in. What the heck is wrong with him? Some days I'm not sure if I'm going crazy, or if it's him. He is nice, hangs out with me, then he treats me like dirt, or acts like an animal. I can't figure him out.

"Where's my stuff? Who was in my room?" He's ranting and raving, tearing his room apart. Oh, crap. I forgot about Mom looting his stuff. He starts banging on my door.

"Yo, give me my stuff back!" I leave my door locked and don't reply. Maybe this is part of acting like a woman and not like an animal, like him.

"Yo, Lina, open up!" I see him trying to turn the doorknob and shaking the door. I don't move an inch. I'm getting good at being invisible.

"Is this what you are looking for?" I hear Mom, and picture her dangling the pipe or the bag of weed under his nose.

"Gimme that back!"

"What are you, a drug addict? What is this stuff?"

"Yeah, I get high, so what?" Leave it to David to spurt out the truth. I would've denied it to the very end.

"It's mine, you had no right to be in my room!"

"It's my house, and I will not have drugs in this house!"

"What the fuck! Give it back!" I never heard him curse at Mom. He must have really lost his marbles.

More screaming and yelling. I want to turn up my music, but that might just make Mom angrier. Mom's awfully upset, but that's not unusual. She usually blows things out of proportion.

"Wait until your father gets home!"

"Big whoop, he's never even here. Fuck him and you too."

Yes. My brother has Lost. His. Mind.

The belt will be out any minute.

"I am going to leave here and never come back!" he yells, as if that is a threat.

"*Bene, ottenere l'inferno fuori, non sarà fare la droga in questa casa!*"

Uh-oh, there's the Italian. I stay in my room and hide in my music. I become one with my headphones. I don't want to be part of this. I don't want to see Mom or David's next move, and sure as heck don't want to believe he's doing drugs! Drugs? What was in the bottle?

* * *

Boy oh boy, do I need to talk to Penney. I'm going to crawl out of my skin if I just sit here with these headphones on my head. I definitely can't go down the steps and out the front door. If I do, I'll get caught up in the mayhem. Maybe I can escape through my window. Penney and I tried it before just for fun. It was two years ago. We were smaller. The dogwood tree looks tempting. I'm heavier now and hope it will hold my weight. I go to my window and open it.

    I thank God or whoever for my escape route. This tree grew right under my bedroom window with branches that serve as steps on the way to the ground. In this chaos, no one will even notice that I'm gone. All I want is to be in a normal household where moms don't hit their kids with belts, where brothers aren't doing drugs, and where dads have jobs where they can come home every night. Penney's house is right down the street. I send up a quick prayer hoping she's home and not at softball practice today. I can't call her unless I go down the steps to the phone, which is in the kitchen. If I go in the kitchen I will have to clean up after Anna, Lucy, and Carmen, which I don't feel like doing. Plus, I'll have to pass by Mom and David, which I sure as heck don't want to do either. I know she will yell at me to clean up their mess.

    I tie my hair up in a small ponytail to keep it out of my face and so it won't get tangled in the tree. I learned my lesson a few years ago. Penney and I were climbing pine trees, and I got sap caught in my hair. Mom couldn't get it out, so she had Uncle Johnny, who is a barber, give me a haircut—the Dorothy Hamill hairdo. My long straight hair that used to get caught in my pants was chopped off right up to my neck. I cried for three days. Penney cried too. It's just starting to get a bit long again, so I pin it up. Don't make the same mistake twice.

Out the window I go.

Planting my foot firmly in the crook of a branch, I gently shut the window. The tree is sturdy. It grew along with me. Stupidly, I didn't put on a coat so I'm freezing. My hands are already turning numb as I hold onto the branches and make my way to the ground. I have to stretch my leg as far as I can to reach the branch closest to the ground before I jump. I'm not scared. I jumped off of the balcony last summer. Hurt my butt really bad when I landed, but I did it. It was a dare. Now, I just want out of this crazy house.

I tiptoe around the side of the house, through the front yard, and past the front door. I don't know why I am tiptoeing; it's not like anyone can hear me with the yelling going on inside. I wonder what the kids are doing. I feel bad for them, but not bad enough to go back in there. Self-preservation. We learned about that in Science class. I make my way to the sidewalk and into the street. I'm not sure when I started walking in the street, but for some reason I'm uncomfortable walking on sidewalks. When I get to her house, I don't even have to knock; she opens the door as if she has been waiting for me.

"Hey, what's up?" She's wearing her favorite jeans, the ones with the rip in the right knee, her Rolling Stones t-shirt, and her wavy hair is pulled back into a ponytail, which makes her freckles even more prominent. She hates her freckles and I wish I had freckles. Funny how no one is ever happy with what they have. She still goes to Catholic school and has to wear a uniform. She must have gotten out of her school uniform and dressed in a hurry because her fly is down.

"How'd you know I was coming?" I ask her, quizzically, then look at her fly. "You're unzipped."

She pulls her zipper up and says, "Don't know, maybe I have E.S.P."

"Really?" Maybe she does. Maybe we both do. Sometimes when the phone rings, I just know it's her. More than once I have picked up the phone to dial her number, and she was already on the line. It's weird.

"Yeah, that and no one answered the phone when I called ten minutes ago, so I knew something was up." We both laugh. She always makes me feel better.

"Feel like taking a walk?"

"Sure, let me grab my sneaks." I wait at the door for her. I thought I wanted to be in a normal house, but all of a sudden I don't feel like going in and making small talk with her parents and her perfect family while mine is falling apart.

We head right down Pear Tree Lane, past the DiMarco's house. We are certain they are in the mob because we have seen them when they come out of the car in their black suits and black hats. But, that isn't conversation for today. We walk in silence down the block.

"So, what's going on?" she asks, finally.

"David's doing drugs. Mom found some stuff in his room and is freaking out. I had to get out of there."

"Wow," she says, almost speechless. Penney always has something to say. "What kind of drugs?" she asks me, as if I know.

Shrugging my shoulders, I tell her what Mom found: the pipe, the weed, the pills.

Penney nods but remains quiet. We walk all the way around the cul-d-sac, which is about a half mile, stuck within our own thoughts. Good friends are like that; we don't need idle chatter when there are no words. We can just be. When we reach the corner at the top of Pear

Cristina Utti

Tree Lane, the intersection with Scarlet Oak and Sugar Maple, we stop. This is our regular meeting point. It is the half-way marker between our homes. At this point we usually decide whether to go to her house or mine.

"Well, what do you want to do?" This has been our standard question when we don't know what to do. We've been asking each other this question since we met and became friends five years ago, when we were seven and eight years old.

"I don't know, what do you want to do?" We share tense laughter.

"I'm not ready to go home, want to go to your house?"

"Not really," she says.

"Okay," I answer, and we walk down Sugar Maple towards my house, both knowing we are not really going there either. "Penney," I say, not quite knowing how to verbalize what's on my mind.

"Yeah?"

I spit it right out. "Do you think you'll ever try drugs?"

"What do you mean?"

"Like, if someone offered, would you ever smoke weed or do pills or something?"

"I doubt it. Why would I ever do that? My dad would absolutely kill me!" She is right, he would.

He's a really nice man, but I would not want to cross him. He's a no-nonsense Irish/Englishman with piercing blue eyes that I wouldn't want looking at me with anything other than a smile on his face.

"I'm never going to do drugs." This is my statement to the world as I stare at the newly tarred street we are walking on. Penney doesn't like sidewalks either. She doesn't respond. "I'm never going to do what David does." I murmur, trying to convince the both of us with these words. Penney knows how he locks himself in his room and smokes, and God knows what else. I don't know what's gotten into him these past few months. Actually, although the confrontation between him and Mom was scary, I'm surprised she took this long to catch on.

"I guess I better head in," I say as we approach my house. "I don't want to get in trouble. I didn't tell her I was leaving, and she's not in a good mood with all of this crap going on. Want to come in and hang out for a while?"

"Nah, no thanks," she says. Yeah, why would she want to come over when I don't even want to go back in there?

"No prob, see you in the morning." Even though we go to different schools and therefore don't take the same bus, we always meet halfway before school to hang out a bit before our day starts.

"Good luck," she waves as she walks down the street.

I wish I could go home to her house. She's so lucky. Sometimes I'm envious, though I try not to be since she is my best friend. She doesn't realize how good she has it. She's the baby of five, so she doesn't have to worry about anyone but herself. I always have to help my little brother and sisters and watch out for them. Both in the world and within the confines of our home. I never asked for this position. I dread opening the door because I don't know what I'll find. Maybe they will be hiding in case Mom has the belt out. Maybe they are all in the kitchen cleaning up from their snack, or in the living room watching cartoons. We get what we get in life, so I make the best of it. I open the door, and all is silent.

I find Mom sitting in the living room, alone. "Is everything all right?"

"Nothing is all right Lina." I can tell she is holding back tears. I guess I would cry too if I had a kid that was doing drugs. "What have I done so wrong?" The tears let loose.

"You haven't done anything wrong Mom," I say to make her feel better. She's always so dramatic.

Cristina Utti

"Your father's never here, and when he is, he's painting, spending time with the kids, or sleeping. I don't even know why he married me, or why I even married him and left my family and my country. There has to be more to life than being alone with a bunch of kids. Every time I mention to him that we go out, or we go away, just us, he always has an excuse. I can't even remember the last time we made love. I don't even know if I want him to touch me anymore. It seems every time we have sex it ends with another baby. It's not that I don't love you and the children, I do, but five is enough. Now this problem with your brother. Your father doesn't even believe me." I don't know why she is telling me all this. I can't even think of her and Dad sleeping together, it grosses me out. I don't want to hear about their sex life. I was going to hug her, but now I feel a wall between us.

Speaking quietly, I tell her, "Everything will be okay Mom, you'll see." I try to believe my own words because if I don't, I will fall apart too.

"Lina, I don't know what to do with him anymore. He doesn't listen. I never know where he is, and when he is here, he locks himself in his room." I don't know what to say, so I look at the beige carpet. "I told your father he needs to come home," Mom says. That's the best thing I've heard in days.

Chapter 4
Denial, Denial, Denial

Dad is home. Mom made stuffed peppers for dinner, his favorite. Dad's happy to be home, and talks and talks during dinner, telling us all about the naked angels he painted and Father Dellesandro, the priest at Holy Trinity. He's acting like he doesn't have a care in the world; like he and Mom didn't argue on the phone two nights ago.

"I considered staying one more night to get some more work finished before I headed home, but Mom called and said she needed me home right away," Dad says. Mom shoots him a dirty look, and I pretend not to see. I guess this is how families are; we pretend. We pretend that everything is fine, ignoring the tension in the air that is so thick it can be sliced with a knife. "Friday evening traffic from Baltimore into Philadelphia is awful. I was going to come home tomorrow morning instead. Hopefully, I'll only have to stay overnight a few more times until I'm finished, but the cherubs put me behind schedule."

"What cherubs? The naked ones?" Carmen asks. I laugh to myself. Of course he is interested in the naked ones.

Dad loves telling stories. "Yes, Carmen. Father Dellessandro came up to me as I was ready to leave and said, 'Tony, you will return Monday, eh?' and I told him, of course, that I had a family emergency. I was taking my brushes out of the turpentine and getting ready to fold up my tarps." He smiles at Mom, but she is making sure not to look at him. Dad continues doing the imitation of Father Dellessandro and explaining what happened. "'No forget, next week, a funeral on Thursday.' He told me this because I must get the scaffolding out by then or at least move it out of the sanctuary. So I told him that I can be here early Monday to finish the cherubs behind the altar, no worries!"

"How are you getting the scaffolding out?" I ask, because I have no idea how he does that all by himself.

"Oh, I have Joe helping me with that," he says.

"My mouth hurts," Anna says, holding her hand over her mouth for dramatic effect.

"Can't you just be quiet? Dad's telling us what happened," I tell her before she gets to eat ice cream again. I'm not crazy about stuffed peppers, but you don't hear me saying my mouth hurts.

"When I was about to move the scaffolding to work on the steeple Monday, father stopped me. 'Tony, Tony, they are beautiful,' he said when he saw my work. 'But why they have no clothes?' So, I told him they are Michelangelo style cherubs." Dad is happy about his cherubs. I can tell because his eyes are sparkling as he tells us about them.

"But it does hurt," Anna whines. I'm going to ignore her, like we ignore everything else around here. I hope Mom and Dad do too. Enough is enough of that. Dad's into his story so he keeps talking over her.

"So, Father says, 'Oh, no, no, no. This is not the Sistine Chapel. They need clothes!' He was dead serious. 'We cannot have naked people in church,' he said. I thought he was joking. Painting from scaffolding directly on the ceiling is not easy. You guys know I paint all of my paintings in the studio, and then bring them to the church and paste them to the wall. I could not do that with the wall behind the altar. I did all of the work from scaffolding." I've never thought twice about naked cherubs because I have been looking at paintings of naked people all of my life.

"So, what did you do?" David asks. Everyone stops chewing and stares at him.

"I had to give them clothes," Dad laughs. "I had to, so I can give a second coat Monday, finish painting the background, and get the scaffolding out in time for Thursday's funeral. They are forty-five feet off the ground. I had to mix new colors. To paint loose robes over the cherubs that will cover some parts of their bodies but not ruin what I have already painted takes precision and patience." Dad tells us, and David listens intently.

"Can I work with you?" David asks in earnest. I never even thought he was interested in Dad's art. He shocks me daily.

"We'll see," Dad tells him.

"How did you make the new colors?" Dave questions.

"Well, there are three basic colors: red, blue, and yellow. Then you need white and black for making different shades. I mixed the white and blue until the hue was perfect for a light blue robe. For burnt sienna, I first mixed the red and yellow for orange. I then mixed in a dab of black to turn it a shade of brown. Next, I added a bit more red. If I add too much, I have to start all over. The lilac was not as difficult as the sienna. It's a simple mix of blue, red, and white. I robed the cherub on the left in light blue, the one on the right in a light burnt sienna, and the cherub closest to Christ I painted in faint lilac. The colors are very important, the lightness and texture of the lilac in the background makes the purple robe of Christ stand out. I managed to finish the first coat on all three today. Monday I'll give them the second coat, do the final touches of the clouds in the background, and hopefully move the scaffolding to the steeple to hang the paintings of St. Anthony and St. Francis that I painted in the studio."

David's eyes haven't left Dad's, all the while he continues eating. He takes a break, swallows, and says, "I wish

Cristina Utti

I could help," with a seriousness I've never seen in him. I wish I could help Dad too, but all I can draw is one good eyeball. When I draw two and try to sketch a face, the eyes are always crooked. David's so talented. He is a good writer, writes his own piano music, and can most likely paint and draw better than me too. All I am good at is watching kids. Maybe if David helps Dad, Dad can be home more.

"I brought two statues home that need work, how about we start with them?"

David stops shoveling food into his mouth and wipes the dribble of gravy off of his chin. "Wow, you'll really let me?"

"Sure, I have a few weeks to get them done. I'll show you how to mix colors and how to fix the broken plaster. The Blessed Mother has a chipped nose and Giovanni di Pietro di Bernardone lost a wing."

Anna pipes up, "He lost a wing? Is he an angel?" I guess her mouth stopped hurting.

"No, he's a saint. Giovanni di Petro di Bernadone was Saint Francis' real name. He is the patron saint for the animals. He believed that the animals are our brothers and sisters."

"Is that why he had wings?" Lucy now asks. The wings have everyone's attention.

"He didn't have wings. Flocks of birds would gather around him and would not fly away until he gave them a blessing. That's how he became known as the saint for animals."

"Did he wear the wings so the birds won't be scared?" Carmen asks. I'm glad the kids are asking Dad about this because I am really confused about the broken wings too.

Dad looks at Carmen, smiles, and takes another stuffed pepper. He sprinkles some Locatelli cheese and crushed red peppers on it, then continues. "He didn't have wings. All of the statues of him have birds or animals all around him. He has a bird on his shoulder. When they were moving the statue to the new church garden, they dropped it and broke the bird's wing."

"That's so cool. Not about the chips and broken wing, but knowing how to fix it," Dave says. I'm glad everyone is so engrossed in the conversation. Maybe no one will notice that I moved all of the meat out of my stuffed pepper and only ate the pepper.

I looked over at Mom, to see if she is watching my plate, and she's seething. I get it. She is here all of the time with us and Dave treats her like crap, then in walks Dad and he is all polite and interested in his work and puts him on a pedestal as if he were Giovanni di Pietro di Bernadone, or Saint Francis.

After dinner, while we are still doing our chores, Mom tells us to go to our rooms when we are finished so her and Dad can talk. I go into my room and close the door. I can't stand it, not knowing what they are talking about. Quiet as a mouse, I go down the steps and sit on the fourth to last step, right where the wall connects with the railing. It's far enough up so Mom and Dad won't see me unless they come around the corner, and far enough down so the kids won't see me here unless they are at the top of the steps. I feel guilty, but not guilty enough to go back to my room. Mom's Snoopy Sniffer and I'm Eerie Eavesdropper.

"What's wrong hon?" I hear Dad ask.

"I don't know where to begin. I know I called you to come home, but I don't want to burden you with all of these problems after you've worked so hard."

"What problems?" Dad asks, and I wonder if he is clueless or in denial. Or both. For a moment there is an uncomfortable silence.

"Your son is doing drugs. I told you on the phone."

"Oh Franca, he isn't doing drugs. Didn't you hear him at the table? He's interested in art. He's just trying to find himself." Yep, denial. And clueless. Mom stays silent, or says something that I can't hear because the next thing I hear Dad say is, "And why is he always my son when you think he has done something wrong?"

"I found drugs in his room," her voice trembles. Their voices get softer, and I have to strain to hear. "Oh, Tony, what are we going to do?"

I hear Dad move through the kitchen, shutting a cupboard. "Franca, he is not doing drugs, you are overreacting." Now I'm getting pissed off. Why can't he just listen to her?

"Haven't you heard a word I said? I found it in his room."

"You found what in his room? Where is it?" Dad obviously needs evidence. I know he has to work, but if he was home more maybe he'd know how David has been acting.

"I flushed the pills and the green stuff down the toilet." Mom tells him. I wondered what she did with the stuff.

"Why would you do that?"

"So the children don't find it laying around."

"Oh. Okay. He's fine Franca. He has a nice group of friends, and wants to spend time with me learning my art. What teenager wants to spend time with their parent? See? That's a sign that he's okay. Can we talk about this tomorrow? I've had a long day."

"Well, if you don't want to talk about your son being a drug addict, how about we talk about my job?" Mom's voice is getting louder and louder, which is scary because I've never heard them fight.

"Your job? It looks like you are doing a fine job. Don't worry about David. I'll talk to him tomorrow," Dad tells her. I can't believe she didn't tell Dad she got a job. I thought they talked every night on the phone when he's away from home.

"You never listen to me. I got a job. I start tomorrow."

"A job? You never asked me."

"Asked you? When should I ask you? You are never here!" I can barely hear Dad now because Mom is so loud, but he must have said something.

"Si. I had an interview this morning. He wants me to come in Monday to train."

"He? Train?" Dad sounds like an echo.

I wish he had a regular job, like Penney's dad. Then he could be home more often, and he would know what's happening in his family. Maybe Mom would be happier too and wouldn't have looked for a job. I'm so proud to show Dad's artwork to my friends, and there was nothing better than the feeling I had in third grade when Dad was painting Sts. Cosmos and Damian church. Actually, he was retouching some work because he did the original sixty-five paintings on the ceiling ten years ago. I told my friends that my Dad did all of those paintings. No one believed me. The nuns and teachers would walk us up the block to the church for mass once a week, like a class trip. I would just stare at all of the paintings Dad painted. While Dad was working, the teachers didn't take us to mass. Everyone knew there was an artist in there, but no one believed he was *my* dad. One morning, Dad told us (Dave, Anna, and me because we were the only ones in school) not get on the bus, that he would be finished early and give us a ride home. Boy, what a feeling I had that day. I held my head up high and told everyone that I was not getting the bus, my dad was giving me a ride. As I walked right out of the school yard towards the church, I could feel the eyes burning through my back.

"Yes, train," she repeats.

"Train for what?" Dad asks, and I feel a twinge of sadness. He has no idea what's been going on. Drugs, jobs, what next?

"It's a travel agency. I'll be training to help people with their vacation plans."

"Oh. You don't have to work, Franca. You have enough work around here." I silently nod my head because Dad is right. I don't want Mom to work either, but I honestly don't know how she does this every day without going nuts. The kids sure drive me crazy when I help out, that's why I'm never going to have a bunch of kids when I grow up.

"Tony, I want to work. I'm tired of being here alone. I'm alone all day now that the kids are all in school." She sounds sad. This makes me sad too.

Dad raises his voice, "Fine, go to work." Mom is silent. Dad's voice drops a few decibels. "If you want to work, then go ahead. I'm taking a shower and going to bed." I scamper back up the steps before he sees me.

Mom calls after him, "What about David? What are you going to do?"

Dad leaves her standing alone in the kitchen.

Chapter 5

No Party, Please

Yesterday was my birthday. The last year before I become a teenager. Mom wanted me to have a party; she said twelve is a big thing. I didn't want a party. Dad came home for the weekend, which made me happy, and Penney came over for dinner and cake. Mom made ravioli, my favorite, and chocolate chip cake. That's good enough for me. I don't like big parties and everyone making a fuss over me.

I've gotten into a routine after school. Mom was getting home by 3:30 the first two weeks, then it got to be later and later. I eat a snack in peace when I get home, usually a bowl of cereal or some fruit and peanut butter. When the kids get in, I give them a snack, and make them do their chores and their homework before they do anything else. Mom's late today. It's already past 4:30.

"Hi Mom," I greet her at the door. She's dressed up real snazzy. She's wearing a tight black leather skirt, black high heels, and a snug blue sweater the shows cleavage. I hope my boobs never get that big. The color of the sweater matches perfectly with her eye shadow. I can smell her perfume, Channel No. 5, which makes me nauseous because my stomach is empty. "What's for dinner?"

"Hi. Where is everyone? Can you give me a minute to get my shoes off?" She seems annoyed; she doesn't even give me a hug or a kiss. We *always* hug or kiss hello and goodbye.

I try to make her happy and proud of me. "The kids did their homework and chores and are in there watching cartoons." She peeks into the living room to see if what I said is true. They are so quiet that even I didn't hear them. "I gave them a snack when they got home and helped them with their homework. There's a paper from Lucy's teacher that you need to sign. I left it on the counter for you."

Now she gives me a hug. "Thanks, how was your day?"

"It was okay." She looks tired and distracted. I know that even though she asked how my day was, she really doesn't care or want to hear about it.

"Where is your brother?" Mom asks. This is her real concern.

"Which one?" Of course I know which one she is talking about because Carmen is sitting right there watching television. This tests her patience. She glares at me. "He's in his room, where else?"

These days I don't know too much about my brother. I don't know where he goes when he leaves the house. He doesn't come home on time, which is by 9 p.m. on school nights and 10 p.m. on the weekends. He came in smelling like beer two nights ago, but I kept it to myself. Mom smelled it too, and she told Dad about it. Dad did nothing. David blamed me for telling on him which made me angry because I would never do that. I always cover for him. This being Mom's first full-time job outside of the home, I really try to mind my mouth with her, the kids, and Dave. Not like that matters, or changes anything.

The interrogation begins. "How did he look after school?" I hate when she puts me on the spot or expects me to tattle on him. I'm so past tattling now.

I shrug my shoulders. "I don't know. I guess he looked okay. He didn't have a snack with us, he just went upstairs and has been up there 'til now."

"Okay." Mom says while she walks through the living room toward the hallway closet to hang her jacket. The kids run up to her.

"Mommy!" I guess she walked through during a commercial because they didn't budge from the television when she first walked in. Carmen clings to her leg as Lucy hugs her around the waist and Anna greets her with a kiss that does not touch skin. Sometimes I think that she was adopted. Anna is the only one out of the five of us that isn't all huggy and emotional.

"I'm hungry, what's for dinner?" Lucy asks.

"I'm not sure yet, can you be a big girl and help Lina set the table?" Lucy gets right to it. She loves to be a big girl and help out. Anna is another story. Whenever I ask her to help, she pretends not to hear me. Three years ago, when she was seven years old, Mom took her to a doctor to have her hearing checked. She explained to Dr. Castelano that when she called Anna, or even sometimes when she spoke directly to her, she would just stare off into space. We thought she couldn't hear us or had some kind of mental block. He checked her ears. He checked her reflexes. He ran some tests. The conclusion was there is nothing wrong with her hearing. Selective hearing was the diagnosis. I guess Mom chooses her battles too and never asks her to help.

"Lina, put on some water for rice and take a container of chicken soup out of the freezer." Mom heads up the steps to get changed out of her skirt and pantyhose. There's always looming dread whenever heading up the steps. I fear smelling the odor of smoke that is not from cigarettes when I reach the landing at the top of the steps, so I'm sure Mom feels the same way. I can hear Mom banging on his door from down here and want to run up there to see what's going on. I hold myself back and keep busy in the kitchen.

"David, open this door right now." I hear her yelling above his music.

"Mom? Yo, I ate already. I'm not hungry." I hear him through the ceiling.

"Come down for dinner. Lina said you didn't eat when you got home," Mom says back to him. I hate when she puts me in the middle.

"I'm not hungry! I'm doing homework!" This is what it always leads to—yelling. And slamming doors.

"I am not going to feed into this mess today, I have four other children to take care of and if you want to kill yourself, so be it," Mom yells back. I hear her bedroom door slam.

A little while later, Dave slips this under my door:

Let me Die

Let me die
a child
inside a tender heart
that aches of joy
and the struggles of insignificance

Chapter 6

The Fake is Upon Us

Dad was home the entire month of December, so the holidays were nice. Mom's job is going well, and Saul has become a friend of the family. We were at his house for a Christmas party, and he and his wife have been over a few times for dinner. They all speak Italian together, but I can feel him putting on airs. He always dresses in suits and wears too much cologne. He looks like he has a fake tan, which matches his fake smile. His hair is slicked back like he is trying to be thirty again, when he is probably ten years older than Dad, who is ten years older than Mom. Whenever he comes over, Mom has the adults eat in the dining room like it's all fancy, and us kids have to eat in the kitchen. I don't like him. He gives me bad vibes.

Dad starts a new church in Camden, New Jersey tomorrow, so back to babysitting.

Chapter 7
The Great Burp

Dave must not like Saul either. I went to his room to wake him up for school this morning because I didn't want him to miss the bus. He's not a morning person, so when I see he isn't getting out of bed, I make sure he's up. That's how I found this on his desk. I didn't mean to be snoopy and read it, but the title caught my eye.

Saul Gave me a Burp, March 2, 1978

Do you know my name?
Do you want the fame?
Do you know the truth?
I'll tell it to you…

Saul gave me a burp.
He gave me a burp.
He just looked at me,
And gave me a burp.
He went slurp, slurp, slurp.
He gave me a burp.
I asked him why,
he gave me the news.
I looked at him,
He said, "Please excuse?"

Breaking Infinity

I asked him to stop.
He'll go to the top.
He went down to say.
"Alright, yea, no way!"

Chapter 8
Poor Lucy

I have to practice the piano after we finish dinner, but David's already there, banging on the piano with all his might as he plays "It's My Life" by Billy Joel. If this isn't a hint for Mom, I don't know what is. I wonder if she even gets it.

"When are you gonna be done? I need to practice too," I scream above his banging. When we started taking lessons in third and fourth grade, he did all he could to make me cry almost every day. Every time I sat down to practice, he would come in the room, sit on the piano bench next to me and bang on the keys, making me mess up my piece. Every time I messed up, I had to start all over from the beginning. Most days ended in tears.

One day, I decided I wouldn't let him bother me anymore. Enough was enough. Mom told me stories about how mean he was to me when I was little, but I don't remember much. The clearest memory I have from when I was a baby was the day David slammed the gate of the metal fence at the end of the driveway right into my little face and cracked my head open. That was the day we were leaving for Italy. Mom picked me up and ran me into the house, sitting me on the kitchen counter. I remember there being a lot of blood. I remember crying. I remember Dad in the background shouting, "We are going to miss the plane!" I was two years old. I guess David was jealous of me for being born. Maybe it is a first child thing. When I got to the point that I had enough of his taunting and teasing, I came up with a plan.

I was practicing Tchaikovsky's Symphony No 5. I was so proud that Sister Rose, our piano teacher at St. Matthew's convent that we went to every Tuesday after school, gave me this piece to learn. It's one of Dad's favorites and I was proud to be able to play it. I started with my scales, C, G, F, A, E, up and down the keys for a warm-up, then started on the symphony.

The way I learn new pieces on the piano is by first learning the treble clef, which is the melody and played with the right hand. Then, when I have that down pretty well, I learn the bass clef which is played with the left hand. This is always a challenge for me because even after taking lessons for four years, I still can't remember the darn notes for the bass clef keys. Once I know how to play both hands separately, I put it together, stopping each time I mess up and starting from the beginning until I can play it perfectly. Then I memorize the piece. I was into the second page when David came, as usual, to torment me. He sat to my right hitting the high keys all out of tune, obviously not doing a duet.

"Wow! That sounds great!" I told him, while I kept on playing. He abruptly stopped. So I stopped playing. "C'mon, let's do that again! It sounds good!" I was as enthusiastic as could be, showing him that he did not bother me one bit. He looked at me like I had lost my mind, got up and stormed out of the room. I could see smoke coming from his ears. Since that day, he has never bothered me again while I practiced.

I push that memory back, "David, can you even hear me?" I told Penney I'd meet her halfway after dinner and Mom won't let me go out until I practice. He has been at it for a while and he isn't even practicing. He is banging out his anger. He ignores me. "Hey, I need to practice too. When are ya gonna be done?" I feel like banging on the keys like he used to do to me, but I'm not stooping to his level. He bangs louder on the lower, alto keys, looks at me silently, scornfully. He closes the lid over the keys, gets up and leaves the room. Okay, that wasn't too bad.

I get through my scales and begin on my new piece. My mind drifts away while my fingers play. David can play just about anything by ear. I know I shouldn't be, but I'm jealous of that. I also don't know why he used to torment me when he plays better. I have to have the sheet music in front of me to play. Last week, Sister Rose whacked David's hands with her stick because he was looking down. She forbids that. Our eyes are always to be straight ahead, never on the keys. I was angry at her for hitting my brother, while at the same time happy that it wasn't me. That will probably never happen to me because I have to read the music while I play, so my eyes are always on the sheet in front of me, not on my hands. Maybe not being able to play by ear is a blessing.

"Heading to Penney's!" I yell down the foyer. Mom's in the kitchen, so I know she hears me. I don't wait for an answer; if I wait too long, she will probably find something else for me to do before I go out. I head right out the front door. She said practice first, so I did. I'm out of here.

We meet at our halfway spot under the enormous oak tree on the corner of Pear Tree Lane. I always thought that was quite ironic. Shouldn't there be pear trees on Pear Tree Lane? Then again, I live on Sugar Maple Lane, and have never seen a sugar maple tree in my life. Penney lives on Scarlet Oak Drive. Why does she live on a drive, and we live on a lane when it is all the same street? Why do we park on a driveway and drive on a parkway? There are no scarlet oaks on her street either. My brain just never shuts up.

"What's up?" She looks up, taking a break from whistling with a blade of grass. My grandpop taught me how to do that, and I taught Penney. The blade of grass has to be a certain thickness and held really tight between the thumbs and forefingers of both hands. I showed her how to blow air just right to make it whistle.

"Ah, nothin', same ole, same ole."

"So, what do you want to do?" she asks.

"I don't know, what do you want to do?" Like I said, same ole, same ole. At least we have each other. "Are your parents home from work yet?" I ask, because if they aren't, we can hang at her house in the living room and watch MTV. She has cable; we don't.

"Yeah, my mom's cooking dinner and not in a good mood. I've been waiting here for you for a while. Had to get outta there." I've never seen her mom in a bad mood.

"Okay, want to head to my house? We can hang out and play backgammon." We go through phases with board games, last month was *Life*. She agrees, and we walk to my house.

We head up the steps to my room, and David calls us into his bedroom.

"Hey guys, come listen to this," he entices us, playing on our curiosity.

"Listen to what?" Penney asks him. I jab her in the ribs with my elbow. "What?" she says as she looks at me wondering why I did that.

"Backgammon?" I really don't feel like listening to whatever he is talking about.

"Led Zeppelin," he says. Penney walks into his room. Kane is here too. I'm not going to let my best friend hang out with my brother and his friend and leave me all alone. Anyway, I can't play backgammon by myself. Having no choice, I follow.

We take a seat on his bed because the only other two seats are the desk chair, and a foldable chair that Dad brought home from one of the churches. Kane is sitting in the metal folding chair, looking out the window, ignoring us. David is sitting in the desk chair. He rolls himself in front of the bedroom door.

I cross my arms over my chest and tap my foot. "Well?"

"Ready?" he asks, and without waiting for our answer starts singing "Stairway to Heaven" and playing air guitar. Penney and I look at each other wondering if he's for real. He sings the whole song, completely. Penney claps. Ugh. He's actually pretty good, but I wish she wouldn't feed into this.

"That was great. Ready, Penney?" I head toward the door. He's still sitting on that stupid chair, blocking the door. Her clapping fed his ego, and now he is playing Ted Nugent's "Cat Scratch Fever." I don't even like this tune sung by the real singer. Penney seems to be enjoying the show, so I sit back down next to her on the bed. He goes right into the next song, "Goodbye Yellow Brick Road" by Elton John, then "Big Balls" by ACDC. He sucks me in with that one. I find myself laughing right along with Penney.

We get up to leave after that, but he won't let us out. He's serenading us with his off-key voice and air guitar. Holding us hostage, he's now onto Pink Floyd's "Money." Actually, he sounds pretty good singing this one, but we are laughing so hard we can barely hear him. My stomach hurts and tears are rolling down my face. Penney is doubled over holding her stomach. Faintly, we hear a knock.

"What're you guys doing in there?" It's Lucy.

"Hey, open the door David, I think Lucy wants us." At this, he finally rolls aside and opens the door. Penney and I sprint out and give Lucy a hug for setting us free.

"We were dying in there!" I tell her. She has no idea what was going on, but the look on her face made us laugh even harder.

I look at Penney. "Backgammon?"

"How about Scrabble?" Penney suggests. She knows she owes me for getting us into that mess. Scrabble is my favorite. We hear David close his door, and he is singing again. I guess Lucy is his next victim. We listen and laugh; grateful we were freed.

* * *

After I walk Penney halfway home, I come back home and start in on my homework. Lucy comes to me with tears in her eyes. She seems smaller and younger than her eight years. Her hair still holds the baby curls and lightness of a blonde, almost platinum, color. She looks up at me, eyes huge and round, like a deer in headlights.

"Lucy, what's wrong?" I quietly ask her. She cannot talk. She looks up at me with her big blue eyes. I softly move the hair out of her face. Her bangs are getting too long. She hands me a piece of paper with three words written in blue crayon.

Yucky.
Scared.
Licked.

I don't know what all of this means. Her eyes are wide with fear. Her head hangs with shame.

"Lucia, what happened?"

"I, I, he, I," and she wraps her small arms around my waist. I lift her into my arms even though she is too old to be held like a baby.

"It's okay," I whisper, as I hold her weight with my right arm, the stronger one, and I smooth the hair that flows down her back. She is sobbing uncontrollably into my shoulder.

"Hey," I hold her with both hands under her arms and look in her eyes.

"Hey, what's all of this about?" I ask her again. She is getting heavy, so I sit on the corner of my bed with her, making her comfortable on my lap.

"What's the matter?" I wipe the tears from her face. "Did something bad happen at school?" She looks at the floor and sniffles great gobs of snot and wipes her nose with the sleeve of her shirt.

"Here," I hand her a tissue from the tissue box that is always on my night table. I keep a steady supply there because not only am I a crier, but I also have allergies. She takes the tissue and wipes her nose.

"No, not school."

"Did someone hurt you?" She shrugs her shoulders and stares at the floor again. I look down to see what she is looking at so intensely, thinking that maybe there is a spot or something that keeps catching her eye.

Nothing.

"Someone must have hurt you." I don't know if this is the right thing to say because I don't want to put words in her mouth. She's still little and impressionable.

She shrugs her shoulders again.

"Do you want to talk to Mommy?"

"No."

Thinking fast, I come up with a plan. I look at each word she wrote. They obviously mean something.

"Okay, how about we play a game?" She nods her head and cracks a tiny smile.

"Alright, I'm going to read what you wrote, and you tell me the first thing that you think of, okay?" She nods in anticipation.

"Don't think too much, just say the first word that comes to mind or you will ruin the game,

okay?" She agrees. "Ready?" She nods.

"Yucky," I say.

"Boys." She is not looking at me.

"Scared."

"Kane." Kane? I can see why she would be scared of him. He's taller than Dad. I hope they weren't bullying her.

Quickly I move on.
"Licked."
"Kane."
Oh. My. God. The only thing that I can think of is so disgusting that I can't even think of it. I hold her until her tears run dry.

Chapter 9

Where is my Mother?

I've held it in for almost a week. The fake has been here for dinner every night. I'm glad Mom has a friend, but she is always preoccupied, and I have no one to tell because Dad has been away the past few weeks. I haven't told Mom yet because it's none of Saul's damn business what happened to my sister, and Mom's always either at work or with Saul. I'm not telling Penney either, because it's too embarrassing, and I don't want Lucy's business out there like that. Plus, I'm not really sure exactly what happened. I didn't mention it again to Lucy because I don't want to give her bad memories or anything. Maybe she put it out of her mind. I really want to tell Mom but every time I try, *he* is hanging around.

The kids are outside playing kickball in the back yard today when Mom walked in from work. I take the opportunity to tell her what Lucia said about the licking and stuff. She looks shocked. I don't think she believes me. She gives me the mom stare, like I'm making it all up, checking to see if there are lies in my eyes. I must have passed the test because then she gets real upset.

After dinner, her and Saul go in the front room and put Italian music on the record player. We never use that room, except to practice the piano. That's where the stereo is, and I guess they want some privacy. She sends us to bed early. I think she is embarrassed by her own kids.

Chapter 10
The Pictures that Ruined my Life

We spend our days at the swim club since school let out. In the past, I would grab the kids, meet up with Penney, and we would cut through the woods behind her house. Andorra Swim Club is right off Barren Hill Road if you take a car, but the woods behind Penney's yard lead directly to the back parking lot. Things changed this summer. Suddenly, Mom wants to go with us, and Saul is there. I don't remember him being a member last year. Maybe I didn't notice him because we didn't know him then. It's not like I go around checking out old farts.

The latest excitement is that Mom finally got enough points selling vacations that she earned enough to go to Italy to see her family. She left this morning. Even though we lived in Sicily when I was little and went back to visit there and Rome a few years ago, I still can't remember all of the relatives I've met. Mom is from a family of fifteen kids. There are so many of them that I can't keep count. I remember Zia Guliana, Zia Maria, Zio Mario, and some of my cousins, Emilio, Roberta, Carlo, Letitzia, and Stephano. Mrs. Salkowski, our babysitter, came this morning when Dad took Mom to the airport, and is going to stay with us during the day while Mom is away. She really doesn't do much except fall asleep all day on the recliner in the corner of the living room while I watch the kids. I should get paid, not her.

I'm not very good at holding things in when they bother me. Today, I just can't keep it in anymore. It has been bothering me for a long time and now that Mom isn't here, I can tell Dad. The notion popped in my head the moment I knew Mom was on the 9:13 flight from Philadelphia to Leonardo di Vinci Airport in Rome. Something just isn't right about all of this. *He* was coming over at night while Dad was away in Camden and when Dad did the church in Maryland. Every night *they* sat in the front room singing along to Italian songs while we got sent to bed early. It started with the dinners, then the Italian music, then sending us to bed early. Something stinks. I don't like Saul. I see right through him. He's a fake. Even his accent gets on my last nerve.

"Spinach-rice soup okay, guys?" Dad asks from the kitchen. I'm pretending to do homework in the living room. The TV is blaring. Lucy and Carmen are arguing over whether to watch Tom and Jerry or The Flintstones. It is impossible to get anything done with them in the room, plus my mind is definitely not on homework right now. I've a ton of math to do and I hate math, so anything is a good distraction from that.

"Sounds yummy!" I say because no one else answered him, and because it is good. Mom makes her chicken soup from a chicken carcass. Sometimes we find bones in the soup which grosses me out. Dad makes his from a can of broth. No bones. "Do you need some help, Dad?" I ask as I'm already headed into the kitchen.

"Grab an egg for me, hon," he says as he is chopping up fresh spinach to add to the broth. While that cooks down, he has the rice boiling in a separate pot so that it doesn't suck up all of the broth. I grab a bowl from the cupboard and beat the egg.

"Can I add it in?" It's the best part of the process of making this soup. After he combines the rice into the spinach-chicken broth, he gets it back to a boiling point, and then it's time to beat in the raw egg. If I don't keep beating it while the soup boils, it ends up being a scrambled egg instead of egg-drop. When it's done just right, it adds a finalizing touch to the soup. No, actually, it's the grated Locatelli cheese sprinkled on top that completes it.

"Sure, just remember to keep beating it," he says as he hands me the long two-pronged metal fork.

"Anna, call David down for dinner," Dad yells from the kitchen. There is a hierarchy in every family. I learned this in Social Studies class. Usually, the oldest has the most responsibility, but since David isn't here even when he is here, it falls on me. Since I'm helping in the kitchen, next in line is Anna. Of course, she doesn't hear him. She doesn't even acknowledge that he is talking to her.

"Anna!" his voice gets louder. I beat the egg in just right.

"I'll get him, Dad." I cut through the dining room into the foyer and stand at the bottom of the staircase, cupping my hands around my mouth. "David, it's time for dinner." No response. He's so annoying. He acts like he doesn't even want to be part of our family. I raise my voice a few more decibels. "David! Dad said come down for dinner!"

"Be right down," he yells through his door. Good enough answer for me. I walk down the foyer into the living room.

"C'mon guys, dinner." They act like I'm invisible. I march right past them and turn off the TV.

"Aw, c'mon!" says Anna. Oh, she saw that!

Dinner runs pretty smoothly. No spills. No arguments between Lucy and Carmen. They are constantly instigating each other, but today they are quiet during dinner. It's a blessing. They give me agita when they act up during dinner. Afterwards, we all know what our chores are. We get a week for each clean-up duty: dishes, wipe table and chairs, or sweep. It's my week for the dishes. I can feel Dad moving around behind me while I'm doing them, putting away the leftovers.

"Dad, you got a minute when I'm done here?"

"Sure, hon," he answers absent-mindedly.

"I have something to show you." My heart is beating so fast it feels like it will pop out of my chest and I'm beginning to feel nauseous. My palms are probably sweating too, but I can't tell because they are soaked in dishwater. This is definitely a sign that this will be bad.

"What is it? I've some work to do in the studio."

"It's okay, it can wait 'til later." I'm such a chicken. It's been on my mind all week, to show him. It sucked up all my brain cells. He puts his warm hand on my shoulder and gently urges me to face him. I look at the countertop behind him.

"Lina, what is it?"

I turn back toward the faucet, washing the last glass and spoons as slowly as humanly possible. If I don't do it now, I never will. "It's upstairs, I'll get it soon as I finish here." I inspect them for any stuck bits of food. I rinse them twice before putting them in the dish rack. When I dry my hands, Dad is standing by the edge of the counter, waiting.

"I'll be right down," I say, not facing him, already heading to my bedroom to dig under my mattress. As I head up the stairs, my belly turns into a rock. I shouldn't have had that second bowl of soup. I feel sick. I grab the sandwich baggie that I have shoved between my mattress and box spring. It's been here for a few weeks. I found these in Mom and Dad's room when I snuck in there to use Mom's makeup. They were under the decorated mirror that she lines her perfumes upon. I saw it sticking out, and my curiosity got the best of me. I've been scared to death that she would find them missing and freak out. But then again, what would she say?

Dad is standing by the little black and white TV that

sits at the end of the kitchen counter. He looks as nervous as I feel. I lay the bag on the counter in front of him. He picks it up to inspect it. I say nothing, knowing that he will see soon enough. I continue to look at the floor. I count how many tiles from one cabinet to the other. There are six and a half.

"What the…? Where did you get these?"

"They were in your room, under Mom's perfumes. I'm sorry." I feel so guilty giving him those pictures. There are photos of Mom and Saul at the swim club kissing, photos of a smiling Mom with her arm around his shoulder at a restaurant. Why is she so happy there? What the heck was she doing with these pictures, and what is she doing kissing his ugly face? That should be Dad in those pictures. I feel so guilty that my brain is about to explode with all of these thoughts, and then there's Lucy. Mom never did a thing to see if Lucy was okay. How do I tell him about Lucy?

Dad looks right in my eyes and says, "This is not your fault." After that, he is silent. I just broke his heart. He gathers up the pictures, puts them back into the baggie and sulks into his studio. I head up the steps to my room, but instead barely make it to the bathroom, my stomach exploding into the toilet.

Strangely, it feels good to be empty. I don't deserve to be full of the comforting food.

Chapter 11
Leaving on a Jet Plane

Dad's been moping around since I showed him those pictures.

"Lina, can you come in here for a minute?" he calls from his bedroom. We usually have talks in his studio, not in his bedroom, so my radar goes up and my heart starts thumping.

"What's up?" I ask, standing at his door trying to act calm. He is opening and closing drawers, scavenging through clothes. His hair is sticking up on the sides and he looks like a mad scientist. "What are you doing?"

"I'm looking for my passport," he says as he opens his closet door. "That's what I want to talk with you about." I take a seat on the edge of their bed. Dad comes and sits next to me.

"Did I ever tell you how I became an artist?" I realize this is a story I have never heard. I have no idea what this has to do with his passport.

"No, how?" I really do want to know because he is amazing and not just because he is my dad. Dad starts telling me about Mr. Hale, his eighth-grade art teacher. Mr. Hale called him to stay after class and told him about an artist that was working in a nearby church. He gave Dad an assignment to meet with the artist and watch the way he works for a few days, then write a short paper about what he learned. He was also the teacher who gave Dad an art scholarship to Fleisher Memorial Art School in Philadelphia. This is a happy story, yet there's desolation in his tone and in his facial gestures. Dad always bites his cheeks when he is worried, and he is biting away.

"My Uncle Petey was the sexton at St. Mary of the Eternal, where my teacher assigned me to observe. When I told him of my assignment, he said, 'no problem.' Mario Sgambati was the artist doing the restoration." He continues to tell the story in a monotone voice. Usually, his deep voice is full of inflection. It sounds like an alien took over his voice box. I'm being as patient as possible as he drones on. I'm still wondering what this has to do with looking for his passport. He catches me drifting, puts his hand over mine, and says, "You have to understand how excited I was Lina."

"Sgambati was a legend. He studied under Vincenzo Volpe, who studied at the Academy of Fine Arts in Naples. Volpe was the painter who was known for servicing the Royal Family. He painted all of their portraits. Volpe studied under Dominico Morelli, another legend, dating back to the 1800s."

"Wow, that's pretty impressive," I add to show him that I am still listening. Dad loves to tell long stories, but I can't listen for too long. My mind drifts. I'm not an auditory learner. I hope he gets to the point soon.

"So, the very next Monday after school, I didn't have the patience to wait for Uncle Petey. I went directly to the church. I had to see the great master in action, not only for my assignment from Mr. Hale, but also for myself. I headed straight there after school. I couldn't believe I would see the master in the flesh. I thought my heart would pound right out of my chest."

Then he tells me about the massive oak door of the vestibule, and how it creaked as he pushed it to let himself in. The first things he noticed were plain white marble protrusions from the wall, the Stations of the Cross. Then his eyes averted directly to the ceiling as if by magnetic force. Well, that's how he tells it. He goes on and on about how magnificent it looked, how the paintings looked so realistic. How the emotion in Mary's features as she held Jesus in her arms as he lay bound to the crucifix could be felt through his soul. For a moment I can see the Blessed Mother and I'm captivated.

"That woman's sadness brought tears to my eyes. It took a minute to remember why I was there." Dad said, which makes me wonder why I'm here, listening to this. I notice a suitcase at the foot of the bed.

"What's the suitcase for?"

"I'm getting to that, Lina." The sadness in his eyes is so clear that I shut my trap and listen. "To the left, I saw the scaffolding. There at the very top of it was Mario. I held my breath and stared, wondering if my eyes were playing tricks on me. He lay across the very top, painting directly on the ceiling. The painting he was working on was St. Lucy. I'll never forget that moment. I recognized it because she is the patron saint of the eyes, and the lady in the painting held a plate with eyeballs upon it. That moment is the reason for your sister's name. Silently, I slipped into the back pew and watched, trying to absorb his talent into the fiber of my soul. As I concentrated on his fluid movements, his every stroke upon the canvas, every cell in my body pricked alive."

"Then Mario saw me watching him. He came down off of the scaffolding and we began to talk. I told him of my assignment to observe him at work, and he offered to show me how to paint with oils. Grandmom and Grandpop didn't have money to buy me oil paints, so at that time all I had painted with were watercolors."

"So, what happened?" I ask, wondering how he got so good at painting with oils.

Breaking Infinity

"Sgambati made me a deal. If I came after school to help him clean up, he would give me lessons in oils. And that was the day I met my true love, my calling, my art."

"Oh," I say, and pick at my nails. I'm not sure what he's getting at with all of this about true love and his art, but I've a feeling that it has something to do with Mom.

"So, you see Lina, I've been so caught up with my art, that I may have lost my other love, your mother. I'm leaving for Italy in the morning to go be with her."

I'm stunned, then excited. They should have gone to Italy together in the first place. I'm so happy Dad is doing this that I can barely contain myself. Then, the worry wart rears its ugly head. "How long will you be gone? Who's gonna stay with us?" Even though I babysit all of the time, I'm scared to stay here all alone with the kids at night.

"Mrs. Salkowsky will be staying with you guys until I get home. I asked her this morning and she said it was fine. I'm just asking you to help her, she's no spring chicken you know," Dad says, and chuckles. I laugh too. If not, I'll cry.

PART TWO

1978

Chapter 1

Insignificant Frogs

Happy Independence Day. They got back from Italy about an hour ago. I'm hiding out in my room because I'm not sure I want to know what happened. I hope they made up. My insides churn as I hear Mom's footsteps on the stairs. She opens my door without knocking.

"These are for you!" She throws a package at me that lands on the bed right in front of me. "And remember, this is all your fault!" She then slams my bedroom door.

I feel like crap. I betrayed my mother. I stare at the package, not sure if I should look at what is inside. Tears prick my eyes, but I force them back. I decide to study to block out whatever is going on in my family. I know I'm a nerd for studying in the summer, but I don't have a good book to read right now.

I take out my old science textbook. We dissected frogs last year. When Mr. Kinkead told us that we would be dissecting frogs, I almost puked right there on the spot. It was disgusting. Tina Cabrina was my lab partner. She wasn't as grossed out as I was, so she was a good partner. Not only did we have to cut the frog open to look at its guts, we also had to study the insides of the mouth.

I never knew that frogs had teeth. The vomerine teeth and maxillary teeth are directly underneath between the eyes. I didn't see any teeth in our frog, but that's where they would've been. I still remember the other parts we memorized: the right and left atrium, the heart, the small intestine, the gallbladder, the liver (which was practically under its throat), the anus, and the cloaca. Girls giggled and the guys made crude jokes when we discussed the last body part. Me, I just felt uncomfortable, like we shouldn't be discussing these dead frogs' personal parts.

Personal. Which reminds me of my gift lying on the bed. I open it and find a leather wallet and a pair of gold heart earrings. They are post earrings with two fine chains dangling from a gold heart. There are five chain links holding a smaller heart on each end. Three hearts. Mine, Mom's and Dad's.

"Lina, you in there?" David calls from his room. I don't answer. A moment later, he knocks gently on the wall between our rooms. This is our code when we want to have private talks.

"Yeah," I say, barely audible.

"Can you talk?"

"Sure," I mumble. "Be there in a minute." I set aside the science test I was making up for myself, just to keep up with remembering stuff before I start high school this September. I started doing this a few years ago to get better grades. Before a test or quiz, I'd make one up for myself, put it aside, and take it the next day. This study technique has worked out pretty well; I was on honor roll all throughout elementary school. The only thing that really stinks is that I always, always came in third place in my class. Anthony Valerio always came in first place, Nancy Scialano came in second, and then me. I always came in third, no matter how hard I tried. I was never good enough to be first honors. I made myself quizzes, fell asleep to spelling words swirling in my head, woke in the middle of the night to study math. It was this way for all of my years at Sts. Cosmos and Damian School. Now that

Breaking Infinity

I am entering high school, my rank is going to change. I'm not going to be third anymore. There are a lot more kids to compete against. If I want to be the top student in 9th grade, I have to study all summer.

I close my books and go into Dave's room. "What's the matter?" I ask him. He is sitting at his desk writing. I look around and notice his bed is made, there are no clothes on the floor, and the tops of his bureau and desk are shining like they were just polished.

"Something's wrong," he says. Something must definitely be wrong for his room to look like this without Mom bugging him to clean up.

"What are you talking about?" I ask him, kind of knowing what he is referring to but not wanting to jump to conclusions. "With Mom and Dad. Do you know what's going on?" He looks at me with sad brown eyes. I don't know how to answer him.

"I heard them fighting. Do you think something happened when Dad went to Italy?" Dave knows about the pictures, I told him. I'm wondering what happened in Italy.

"I don't know, probably. I hate that Saul dude. What do you think about him?"

"I think he's creepy. He gives me the willies." I say. Just thinking of that guy makes my stomach turn, and those pictures keep flashing through my brain camera.

Dave scribbles ferociously on the open page of his notebook. "I don't know what Mom sees in him," he mumbles.

"Me neither. Don't worry, everything will be okay." I say this because I have to believe it. I know my brother. He's sensitive, even though he tries to hide it under his weed and beer and stuff. "Let's go make some sandwiches," I suggest. "If you make them, I'll make the fries." Sandwiches always cheer him up. Plus, I'd rather eat fries than study science right now anyway.

As we head down the steps, we are brought to a halt by screaming voices.

"I'm sorry," we hear Mom say to Dad. "I wished it hadn't turned out this way." I look at David. He looks as stiff and as cold as the statues Dad brings home.

"Sorry? For what?" Dad's voice is raised. "Going to Italy with another man?" Oh my God. I look at David. He looks at me.

"Tony? Can we talk?" Dave and I are frozen on the steps, listening, barely breathing.

"About what? How much you were enjoying your trip to Italy with Saul?"

"This is always the problem," Mom mumbles under her breath, but I hear her because I have bionic hearing.

"What?" Dad says back to her.

"This is always the problem. You never talk to me," Mom repeats.

"Well, what should we talk about? Did you enjoy it? Did he give you orgasms? Did you like leaving your children and ruining our marriage?" I don't know what he is talking about. I don't know what that 'o' word means. I look at David, who avoids eye contact, just shrugs his shoulders and then looks at his feet.

"No," Mom mutters again. I feel sorry for her. "I'm sorry."

"We have to tell the kids," Dad insists.

"Tony, please stop. I'm trying to talk to you. I don't love him. I made a mistake."

"Yes, you sure did." These words hit like a brick. That saying, 'sticks and stones may break your bones, but words will never hurt you' is wrong. Words do hurt. Words cleave your soul while sticks and stones only break your bones. Bones heal. "I'm going to call Lina and David down here so we can talk to them." I've never heard Dad speak to anyone in the tone he is using. I hope to hell that they do not call us down there.

"Talk to them about what?" I can hear her crying.

"To tell them that we are getting divorced." The words cut through my heart. David and I stare at each other in disbelief.

"Divorced?" Mom sounds as shocked as we are. I try to head back up to our rooms so we can pretend we didn't hear anything, but David doesn't budge.

I nudge his leg and look up the steps. He shakes his head and puts his finger to his lips, shushing me.

"Obviously, you don't want me or this family anymore." Dad says.

"That's not true." Mom is sobbing now.

"Really?" Dad laughs at her. His meanness is breaking my heart. My face and armpits are getting sweaty and my stomach hurts.

"You never listen to me. I told you your son had a drug problem and you ignored me. I told you I was lonely, that we should do things together, and you kept going away."

"Jesus Christ, Franca. I was working!" He yells even louder.

Now Mom is blubbering and explaining herself. "He made me feel attractive, made me feel like I was smart and had something to offer someone besides being a mother. I felt like I failed as a mother with all that has been going on with David. I tried to talk to you, but you're always too busy with your art to pay attention. I've been struggling for a long time to be a good mom, to be a good wife. But I'm lonely Tony." I wish we didn't hear this and had gone to our rooms when I motioned Dave to go back up.

"So you went out with another man?"

"All I wanted was your attention." I can picture her eyeballs doing that twitching thing they do when she is nervous.

"Well, you sure got it," Dad says. He's not budging an inch. I don't know who to feel sorrier for, Mom or Dad.

I look at David for help. His head is between his knees and his shoulders are shuddering. I shake his shoulder gently.
"Hey, let's go upstairs," I whisper. He knocks my arm away.
"Franca, did you hear me?" I hear Dad yell as I go up the steps and leave Dave behind.
"Do you want to explain it to the kids or should I?" I hear him from my room. I wonder what the kids are doing, if they can hear them too. I hear Dave come back up the steps and slam his door.
I look at my science book and realize just how insignificant frogs really are.

Twenty Minutes Later...

"Lina! David! Come down here!" Dad yells from the bottom of the steps. "Your mother and I have something to tell you."
I am paralyzed. David knocks on my door and opens it a crack. Sticking his head in, he tells me that he is heading downstairs. His eyes are swollen and red. He wipes his nose. He hands me a paper with this written on it:

Tears

Wearily I lay on my bed
Trying to comfort my bewildered head
Trying to distress all of the stress
I'm sadly confronted with being fed
Taking the calling direction of this sled
Sailing and failing the path where it has led
Leaving me abandoned herds
Of animal tears in my loneliness

I get it. Sometimes it is easier to write our feelings than to speak them.

"I'll be right down," I tell him. My body feels like lead on my bed. Slowly, I make my way to the door. I turn back, glancing at my earrings and wonder what's going to hit me next. I take my time going downstairs.

Mom and Dad are in the studio and tell David and me to come in. I wonder exactly how they are going to tell us. I barely even said hello to Mom when they got back because I felt so guilty. Walking through the kitchen into the studio I paid no mind to the clock. It must be past 9 because the kids are in bed. I'd rather be studying, or reading, or writing. Anything besides standing right here right now.

"Your mother and I want to talk to you two."

"Oh," I say, and stand at the door to his studio. David stands next to me, slumping his shoulders.

"Come in, sit down," Dad motions for us to join them. I look at Mom, but she doesn't look at me. Dave and I remain standing by the door.

"Well, what's up?" David asks, looking from Mom to Dad, back to Mom, acting like we didn't hear a thing. Heavy silence fills the air.

Mom's head nudges in Dad's direction. "Your father has something to tell you."

"Your mother and I want to tell you something," Dad says as he looks at the floor. My chest is closing in on me and it is hard to breathe in the thickness of the stale cigarette smoke-filled air. We look at him in anticipation, acting like we don't know, hoping not to hear the words.

"We want to tell you that we are getting divorced," he finally states.

"Divorced?" David asks like he never heard the word. I just stare. My heart stops beating. Divorced? They never even argue. Until recently.

"Well, we can talk more about it tomorrow," Dad says.

"We just wanted to tell you two because you are the oldest." All of us are engulfed in our own worlds of shock and pain. Dave and I head back to our rooms. Mom and Dad continue talking, standing there together, yet apart.

As I'm walking through the kitchen, I hear Dad say, "I bought you a ticket to the Dominican Republic. Divorces are quick and easy there. You can file there, then you will be free to be with your lover." I want to shut my bionic hearing off. I want to cover my ears, and shout *lalalalala*, like a little kid. I can't bear to listen to another word of this. I move faster to get away from them.

"Tony," is all I hear Mom say before I'm through the kitchen and halfway up the steps.

I hold back the flood until I get to my room. I turn on the radio so no one can hear me. Cat Stevens' "Wild World" plays on WFIL, and I bury my head on the pillow and cry.

This is all my fault.

Chapter 2

The Rat's Nest

After Mom and Dad told us that they were getting a divorce, I knew my whole life would change into a before and after.

Divorced?

I just don't get it. I thought people divorced because they didn't love each other anymore, or because they fought a lot. Mom and Dad never fought. Everything was fine until that Saul came into our lives. I don't even know what all of this means except one of them will leave and the pain is so deep that I don't know what to do with it.

The only good thing so far about this year is that Penney and I are in the same school. Dave got sent to Plymouth-Whitemarsh, and I got sent to Archbishop Kennedy for 9th grade. Even though Penney's in 10th grade like David, now when we meet halfway in the morning before school we can get on the same bus. As a matter of fact, we are the only two kids in this neighborhood that go to Kennedy, everyone else gets the bus to the public high school. I'm so glad I get to be with Penney every morning because I'm not sure how to get through my days with all that's going on at home. The house is creepily quiet this morning for it being the first day of school. Dad has been away most of the time since that night they told me and Dave the news. I never mentioned it again to Mom, because she already told me it was my fault. I pretend nothing ever happened. I'm not sure if the kids know yet, so I say nothing to them, and pretend it is just another regular beginning of the school year.

"Good morning," I say as I enter the kitchen. Carmen, Lucy and Anna are eating cereal. Mom is by the sink, making herself busy not looking at me.

"'Mornin'," Carmen says, mouth full.

"You all ready for your first day of school?" I can't help but be the little mommy, even if Mom is standing right there. No one answers me. The kitchen is quiet and tense.

"Are you excited?" I ask, looking for some life, something to break this mood.

"I am!" Carmen is the first to speak. "I hope my teacher is nice." It's his first day of third grade. I remember how excited I was the first day of my third-grade year. That was the year we moved into this house. My third-grade teacher gave me a ride home one day when I missed the bus because I was confused when my bus changed. Ms. Kelly was my favorite teacher. I hope this year Carmen's teacher will end up being his favorite so far too. Mom turns and looks at me, drying her hands on a kitchen towel that is decorated with snowflakes. She never puts out seasonal towels before the season. She folds the damp towel, puts it in the towel drawer, and goes into the dining room. There are a bunch of boxes in there. I'm not sure what she's doing. I get the feeling that she doesn't either.

"Oh! It's 6:52, I have to go," I say nervously, afraid I'll miss the bus the first day at my new school. "Don't forget to brush your teeth, guys." I grab my backpack and make my way around the table giving goodbye kisses to everyone. On my way out the front door, I give Mom a hug. We are both stiff and awkward, but it would feel worse leaving without saying goodbye.

"Have a good day at school, Lina."

"I will, you have a good day too." The sadness comes and tears well up in my eyes. I'm back to thinking about the divorce and which one will leave us. I am too scared to ask.

As I head to the corner, I see Penney coming up the street. It will be a cool sort of strange being on the same bus. "Hey," I say, looking at the asphalt. I haven't had a chance to really talk to her because she was visiting her cousins in England for six weeks over the summer. She has no idea about all that's happened over the summer.

"Hi," she says, all smiles, and gives me a great big hug. We match. The uniforms are plain dark navy blue. This is the only time you'd ever catch Penney in a dress. I'm not thrilled about having to wear a dress to school every day, but these uniforms sure beat the maroon plaid of my elementary days.

After not seeing her for weeks, the first thing out of my mouth is, "Do you have practice after school today?" and I feel like an idiot. I'm not sure when softball starts, or if it ever ended. She's on a team for the township. I'm hoping she doesn't have practice because I really need her right now.

"Nah, we don't have practice on Mondays. You okay?"

"My parents are getting divorced," rolls right out of my heart and off of my tongue. She just looks at me like I have two heads. "Can you hang out after school?"

"Yeah, sure." She looks as sad as I feel at this news. She gives me another hug.

"Thanks. I'm kind of nervous about school too," I say, not looking her in the eye, making excuses for the way I feel. If I look at her, it will be real, and I will cry again. Then I will have puffy eyes and look terrible all day. My eyes are still puffy from crying last night.

"Take it easy, man. This school's no biggie; it's way smaller than P-W. You'll fit right in. After we get home today, we can smoke and have some laughs. I'll snag a few from my mom's stash."

Cristina Utti

"Cool, some laughs." I force a smile. Although there is nothing funny at all going on in my life right now, smoking a cigarette and laughing sounds good. That thought gives me strength to face my day. I try to force some positive thoughts in my head as I see the bus coming around the corner. We get on and share a seat in the back with the cool kids.

* * *

At school, my day just gets worse and worse. I bum a smoke from some girl in the bathroom and smoke it, hoping it would calm my nerves, thinking I would not get busted because of the way the girls' bathroom is set up. There's a heavy door, with the sign "Girls" on it. Upon opening that door, there's another heavy metal door that leads into the bathroom. When I hear the bell ring, I run to my homeroom class, room 203. The teacher, who looks like a mean little rat, must've smelled the smoke because when I try to get a seat in the back of class, she yells, "Right here, Missy," as if that was my actual name, and points to the seat directly in front of her desk. Wonderful. This is my seat for the year, staring at rat face.

First class is math, to start my day off just right. My math teacher is mean and scary looking. He has big, thick hands that match his big fat face and big thick glasses. All he talks about for the entire forty-five minutes is the demerit system. Second period is English. A nun teaches this class. Sister Maria. She is younger than the nuns that taught at Sts. Cosmos. She leaves a bit of hair out of her habit so that it covers her forehead and forms dark ringlets around her face, just like my hair does. She has soft honey-brown eyes and a nice smile. She explains to us how much she loves reading books and how much she dreads teaching grammar. She promises to try to make grammar as interesting as possible, and we all giggle nervously. She actually seems pretty cool. I think I'll like this class.

Science class is right before lunch. Alan Esposito sits near me. He is the cutest boy ever. We were in elementary school together, but I never noticed him. He grew a lot during the summer. Now he's in with the cool crowd. I'm kind of a loner, only ever had a few school friends. I don't really fit in with any of the cliques and don't really care. There are more important things in life than acting all girly and stupid just to fit in with people I don't like anyway. I cut him a look out of the corner of my eye as we lined up to sign out our lab supplies and textbooks. He was with some of the guys, joking about something. Unfortunately, my bionic ears kicked in.

"Look at her hair," Gabe elbows Alan and they both laugh.

"Yeah, looks like a rat's nest." I could feel the heat of their eyes burn through my back. My face gets hot, and feel like I'm going to throw up, or cry. They must be talking about my stupid curly hair. I can't even get a brush through it. I bet they are laughing at how fat I'm getting too. For them to be laughing and pointing at me, I now know for sure that I am the ugliest girl in the class. Devastation two days in a row. Could my life get any worse?

Chapter 3
The Move Out

Mom moved out today right on Penney's fourteenth birthday. I guess they were keeping it from us to not ruin our Christmas. It makes no sense to save Christmas only to ruin our lives. Dad said that he can't afford Catholic school anymore, that I'll have to transfer back to public school.

I don't care. I hated that uniform anyway.

Chapter 4
Happy Valentine's

I got a Valentine today from Mark Lane. It's my first Valentine. All last week they were selling candy heart chocolates with a little card as a fundraiser for something. I wasn't paying attention because I had no intention of buying one. Today they gave them out in homeroom and that's when I got one from Mark. I'm not sure how to feel about it.

The past six weeks have been extra busy since Mom left. Now I have to do *everything* at home, including cooking, helping Dad grocery shop, and making sure the kids get to bed on time. School is easy. I hardly ever have homework, which is good because I don't know when I'd find the time for it after taking care of everyone else. The two main problems that I have lately are: 1. School bores the crap out of me since I already learned what they are teaching in the public school two years ago at my old school; 2. The kids are angry. Every time I ask them to do something, they come at me with smart remarks.

Dave's lucky he is never home. I wish I could run away from all of this like he does.

Not only does Mom blame me for the divorce, but I guess the entire family does too.

Chapter 5

What's the Big Deal?

I call Penney to tell her I got some weed. "So, you want to try it?" I ask. I've been dying to find out what the big deal is with this stuff and why everyone smokes it. Dave has been smoking it for a while now and his brain cells don't seem dead. That's what they tell us in school; that weed kills brain cells, but it makes no sense because David is the smartest person I know. I figure, what the hell? Why not see what the deal is with this stuff?

"What are we supposed to do with it?"

"Smoke it, silly," I tell her. I spent ten dollars of my babysitting money to buy it and felt too stupid to ask my friend Irv what to do with it. Irv and Mark smoke all the time.

"How?" she asks, like I'm the expert.

"I don't know. You have any ideas?"

"Maybe we can put it in a cigarette. I can get some from my Mom's stash."

"Sounds good, leaving now." I put the phone back on the receiver and slip on my blue suede clogs to meet at our halfway point. Since Mom left, I have no one breathing down my back after school. I wait for the kids, make sure they have a snack and do their homework, then head out to hang out with Penney for a bit before I have to get back to make dinner. Excited, I jog there in my blue suede clogs.

"Hey," Penney says as she approaches the corner. She looks nervous. My heart's skipping beats too. "Where should we go?" she asks.

"I don't know. Maybe we can just go in the woods behind my house. Dad's not home yet." We have a favorite tree back there. About twenty feet into the woods, there's a tree that has a trunk that's split in two. Half of it grew out like a branch, then grew back into the truck. We climb up, sit on it, and dangle our legs. We haven't been here since last summer. It's still strong enough to hold both of us without bending in the least.

"I got the cigarettes," she says, and takes them out of her flannel shirt pocket to show me.

"Cool," I say, trying to act blasé while feeling a bit nervous.

"How's school?" Penney asks sincerely. Even though we see each other every day, I try not to talk about school. I have acquaintances, but no friends there. All of my friends are in the next grade up, tenth grade.

"It's stupid. They're doing stuff I learned two years ago. It's freakin' Mickey Mouse work," I tell her. I don't fit in. Not like I ever cared about fitting in, it's just that now I *feel* like I don't fit in. "How's it going for you?"

"The usual, boring as hell." School is always boring for her. She likes sports better than studying. I actually like learning. I liked how I worked hard to maintain my grades in Catholic school. Now school feels like a joke. Penney takes a cigarette out of the pack and lightly squishes and rolls it between her fingers. It takes me a minute to figure out what she is doing. She's dumping the tobacco out of it.

"Guess we can put the stuff in here."

"Sounds like a plan." I'm not even sure why I'm doing this. I made a few new friends, if that's what you call them, when I found out that Mark liked me. He kept throwing papers at me in Social Studies class. At first I thought he was teasing me, like Alan Esposito did, but then I figured out that boys are just immature. Actually, I already knew that. This is the way they get a girl's attention. Mark is so cute that I can't concentrate in class. He's tall and thin with wavy hair and green eyes. Probably has a six-pack. In class I pretend I'm reading the textbook, doing the work the teacher asks us to do, but my main concern is stealing glances at Mark. His friend Irv told me that he likes me and wants to go out with me. I know for sure that Mark smokes weed because Irv and I are in the same homeroom and talk.

I wouldn't really call Irv a friend; we sit next to each other by alphabetical order. Some stinky kid with greasy hair used to sit next to him until I came to the school, then the teacher redid the seating chart. Irv broke the ice by telling me I smelled better than the last kid he was sitting next to. We've been talking ever since. I bought the weed from Irv, acting like I did this all the time. I take out the little baggie of stuff and we gingerly fill the empty cigarette.

"Here, you can go first," Penney says. I'm not sure what to do, so I take it and try to smoke it like a cigarette. After a drag, I cough my lungs out. She laughs at me.

"You take it," I tell her.

"You're supposed to hold the smoke in," she says, and takes a long pull on it. I watch what she does. She holds it in her lungs until she can't anymore, then she coughs, and hands it back to me. I wonder how she knows how to smoke weed. We pass it back and forth, taking turns choking on the stuff. By the time we get to the filter, my left clog falls off from swinging my legs, and we are cracking up. We almost fall right off the limb.

"I can't go home like this," Penney tells me.

"That's okay, just hang out. Dad won't be home for a while." My head feels as loose as my legs.

"Okay. So, what do you want to do?" We immediately start laughing again. I jump down to find my clog.

"How 'bout we go make something to eat?" All of a sudden, I'm craving some homemade French fries, or maybe a milkshake, or maybe dip French fries in a milkshake. I have homework to do, and a chapter test in Algebra tomorrow, but push that thought right out of my head. Algebra gives me anxiety; all of those formulas make no sense to me. I mean, when will I ever need that? I'm not planning on becoming a mathematician or scientist. French fries are calling. Wow, now I know why David smokes. For the first time in a long time, I'm happy.

Chapter 6
Reflection of Nina

It's Friday night. Penney and I go to the softball game to meet up with Nina and Simone. They are in Penney's grade and go to Archbishop Kennedy too. I knew Nina from my old neighborhood even before Penney knew her. She went to Sts. Cosmos and Damian school and was at our bus stop on Turf Lane. She was in class with Dave. Simone is from Roxborough. A lot of girls from Roxborough go to Kennedy. I guess there is no Catholic high school where they live. We all used to eat lunch together when I went to their school. We know Simone smokes, so I bring the weed with me.

"Hey, what's up?" I say when we spot them near the bleachers.

"Hey," they answer in unison.

"What're you guys up to?" Nina asks.

"Wondering where we can go smoke before the game," Penney answers. She knows them better than I do. I'm sure they all still eat lunch together every day. I feel like a fourth wheel. I'm glad I have the weed to smoke because it helps me not to worry what other people think of me.

"I got my bowl," Simone claims.

"Cool," Penney replies, as if she already knew this fact.

By the beginning of the fifth inning, we decide to ditch the game. We walk over to Burger King to get some food since we all have the munchies. I order a vanilla shake and large fries. Penney gets a chocolate shake, burger, and fries. Simone and Nina both order whoppers, fries, and shakes.

We use the empty wrappers to make designs with the ketchup, mustard, and salt. After some jokes and gossip, my bladder calls so I head to the restroom. Nina's already in there.

"You in here?" I ask as I open the bathroom door. I hear someone vomiting. There are two stalls, and the one on the far end of the bathroom has the door closed. She doesn't answer. I peek under the stall to see if it's Nina. I remember she was wearing white Nikes with a blue stripe. Yep, it's her. I hear the toilet flush. When she comes out, her face is red, and her eyes are tearing and slinty.

"Hey, you ok?"

"Yeah, yeah, fine. Just getting rid of all those calories," she answers in between swishing out her mouth. She fixes her eye make-up as if this is something she does all the time.

Maybe she does.

Maybe this is a good way to get rid of calories, like she says.

Chapter 7
The Little Pill that Could

Smoking weed helps me to be happy for a while, but then the feelings come rushing back like a tsunami. Even though Mom and I talk on the phone a few times a week and spend time together when she isn't working weekends, it's not the same. I feel so empty since Mom left. So, I eat. It's the only thing that makes me feel better. Then I can't stop. My filled valve is broken. So now I do what Nina does. I did manage to make a few friends at school this year. My friend Dee gave me some little pills called Black Beauties. I'm not sure if I want to take them. She said they helped her to lose weight. Something has to be better than constantly puking. I didn't want to take them at school and be all messed up, so I waited until I got home today. I'm going to skip my after-school snack. I grab a glass of iced tea and pop two of them.

Nothing.

I don't know what I was expecting. I head up to my room to do my English homework. We have a presentation due Friday and finals next week. Mrs. Renniger gave us the assignment two weeks ago. I procrastinated, thinking I'd work on it on the weekend. But then I spent the weekend at Penney's, mostly smoking weed, talking, and listening to music. At least I was happy for a while. When I got home Sunday night, I binged, then took laxatives so I wouldn't have to vomit again. I was so sick that I stayed home from school Monday. Nina was wrong, the puking doesn't help the weight come off. I'm still 127 pounds, no matter how much I throw up.

   I don't know how to fill this emptiness. I miss Mom. She doesn't live too far; just a few miles away in Whitemarsh Apartments. I know she still blames me for everything, because she won't let me forget it. When I told her that I missed her, her reply was, "Well, we could have all still been living together…" This is always her reply. Rubbing it in, pushing the knife deeper and deeper. Dad got back late from work that night. The kids weren't listening to me. I was frustrated and feeling guilty as hell for ruining our family, so I grabbed a bowl of ice cream to make myself feel better. Then I couldn't stop eating. I don't know what's happening to me. Now I have two days to get this done.

   I open the book *Graphology* that I borrowed from the library last week. We got to pick our own topics. I chose graphology for my presentation. Since everyone writes, everyone in class should be able to relate. There are all types of handwriting. There are all sizes: small, average-sized, large, and huge. It says that small handwriting means that the person is intellectual and pays attention to details. I guess I'm not too smart. Average-sized means the person is well balanced and has a great deal of ability. Large says the person is active and restless; that they want constant change or want to control others. Huge writing means you are conceited. It is not a sign of honesty. Hmm. I think my writing is average-sized, but I don't feel well balanced or like I have the ability to do much of anything at all.

   I couldn't keep my mom here. I can't take care of the kids. They never listen to me. When they get on my nerves when I am babysitting, I play a game with them. I chase them around the house, then tie them to the railing on the staircase. It's just for fun. It takes them all of about fifteen minutes to get out of the ties, and then they run around waiting for me to do it again. Oh well, it gives me a little break. And I miss David. Sometimes when he does come home after school, we'll smoke a bowl together and hang out and talk, listen to music, or jam on the piano together. Those times are awesome. The thing that's not right is that he's always out with his friends so I have to do everything around here. It isn't fair.

My head is starting to buzz. My stomach isn't feeling too well either. I shouldn't have taken those things, but I guess they are working; I'm not hungry. I feel queasy. Okay, concentrate. I make up flashcards about strokes. Flashcards, short attention span. A thick stroke is a sign of greediness; a thin stroke means the person isn't interested in love. What kind of person isn't interested in love? I'm going to keep my eye out for those thin stroke people. A medium, firm stroke signifies energy, and the person can be temperamental. I'm not sure what that word means, so I look it up. I like learning new words. Temperamental - easily upset, moody, highly strung. Yep, that's me. I'm feeling very temperamental these days. Guess I have a medium stroke.

Next, there are different angles and spacing. I stop to brush my hair because it feels cool with this buzz in my head. I give my hair fifty strokes to get the oils through it since it is always dry. I wonder how many different kinds of strokes there are. There are hair-brushing strokes, swimming strokes, writing strokes, brain strokes, you can stroke your pet, and if you strike out in baseball and talk about it in past tense, is that a stroke? Stroke. Now the word looks like it is not even spelled correctly. I better move on. Angles are next. How many different types of angles are there? Someone can have an angle when they have a point of view. There are angles in triangles and in geometry. I have to stop myself, or I will never be ready for my presentation. *Focus on writing angles, Lina.* My favorite is the so-called normal angle. It is slightly upright and slightly to the right. These people are easygoing, calm, friendly, and sensitive. Who gets to say what is normal? I wonder if we change our handwriting on purpose if we can then become like what this book says the people with that handwriting are like. Maybe I'll try it. The forward angle, which is a right angle, is a person who is ruled by their heart and can be easily taken advantage of. Geeze. I study all of these traits and promise myself I'm going to change my handwriting so I can become the person that I want to be. Only, I don't know who that is.

"Lina, what's for dinner?" Lucy asks through my bedroom door as I'm finishing up my flashcards.

"I don't know. You can come in, the door's open." My brain is all cluttered with strokes and angles and I'm feeling jittery.

"I'm hungry," she tells me, and gives me the pout that she knows kills me.

"How was school? Is Dad home yet?" That is a dumb question, because if he were, she wouldn't be standing here asking *me* what's for dinner.

"School's okay. Are we having dinner soon?" She looks up and pushes her blonde hair out of her face. Those blue eyes just get me every time. She needs a haircut, and I just remembered that I forgot to brush her hair before I left for school this morning. This is the kind of stuff dads just don't think about. Poor kid. Looks like she doesn't have a mother. I don't remember the last time I brushed her hair for her. It's down past her shoulders now. Maybe shorter hair would be easier for the both of us.

"Soon as you do your homework," I tell her, giving her a little tap on the butt as I nudge her out of my room, realizing this is the end of mine for now. Off I go for mommy duty.

"C'mon, let's get your homework done, then you can help me with dinner," I tell her as we head down the steps. She likes to help me with dinner; it makes her feel like a big girl. "What do you think about a haircut soon?"

"Awe, Lina, I don't want no haircut."

"I don't want *a* haircut," I tell her. Lately improper English really irks me.

"You don't want no haircut either?" she asks, and I can't help but smile.

"No, silly. We say, 'I don't want *a* haircut,' not 'I don't want *no* haircut.'"

"What's the difference? If I don't want no haircut, I don't want no haircut!"

"Aw, forget it," I say. "C'mon, let's make dinner. You can do your homework after we eat."

Today I make grilled cheese sandwiches and homemade mashed potatoes. The kids love them. Lucy spreads the margarine on the bread for the sandwiches as I put the American cheese on them. She likes to watch the cheese melt.

"Be careful near the stove," I tell her as I head to the living room to turn off the television.

"Did you guys get your homework done?" I ask Carmen and Anna. Carmen is proud of doing his homework. I usually don't have a problem with him. Anna is aloof. And she needs her hair brushed too. Hers is thick and curly and a mess.

"I did all mine, Lina!" Carmen proudly states.

"Good job, show it to me so we can eat dinner soon." He goes to fetch his backpack from the laundry room and brings it to me.

"Anna, get your homework out so I can check it."

"Why? You're not my mom," she says, staring straight ahead at the TV. This is her favorite line lately. She is pissed off that Mom left, but who isn't?

"And did you even brush your hair today? If I'm not your mom, then I shouldn't have to remind you to brush your hair." She gets me so angry. She's only two years younger than me; I shouldn't have to tell her this stuff.

"Shut up," she mumbles, and her shoulders sag. Now I made her feel bad. I didn't mean to. When the kids feel bad, I feel bad.

"Just get it out so we can eat, okay?" I'm trying not to argue with her. I know she misses Mom too. Carmen's backpack is a mess. There are crumpled papers shoved in and squished, half eaten sandwiches in baggies at the bottom. Two are moldy. Gross. I pull the papers out along with half empty potato chip bags and cookie crumbs. Looks like he doesn't have a mother either. Poor kid. Sometimes I forget he is only eight and needs overseeing and help with keeping organized. While we clean out his backpack, I keep my eye on Anna. She just sits there.

"C'mon. Just get your homework out and show me you did it." She doesn't answer; her eyes are distant. "Anna, what's wrong with you? We have to eat dinner, just get out your homework so I can check it!" She gets up and goes to the laundry room to get her backpack. I'm kind of surprised she didn't put up more of a fuss. Thank God for small miracles.

Dad gets home as we are cleaning up from dinner. Miraculously, everyone is doing their after-dinner chores without complaint. Carmen helps clear the table, Lucy wipes the table and chairs, Anna's sweeping, and I do the dishes. David's not home. I saved him a sandwich and potatoes and saved two sandwiches for Dad.

"I made the grilled cheese for you Daddy!" Lucy tells Dad proudly as soon as he walks in.

"That's my big girl," he picks her up and she wraps her legs around his waist. I don't ever remember doing that. I probably stopped getting picked up when I was two and Anna came along. Dad looks around the kitchen. "Where's David?"

"I don't know. He didn't come home after school." Dad's smile turns upside down. I feel bad because I didn't think too much about where David was when he wasn't home when I got in from school. I was busy with my homework and the kids and my head just stopped buzzing from those Black Beauties. They worked. I wasn't hungry at all. I didn't even eat dinner. I'm getting some more of them from Dee tomorrow.

"Did everyone do their homework?"

"Yep," I tell him proudly.

"Thanks hon," he gives me a peck on the cheek. He has bags under his eyes. I feel sorry for him. I wonder what kind of handwriting shows feeling sorry for people. I bet it's mine. I'm always feeling sorry for everybody. I feel sorry for David too. I miss my brother. I know I smoke weed now, but whatever he's doing is way worse. When we get to school in the mornings, he gets off the bus and heads straight for the front lawn. I think he's been skipping classes. I see who he hangs out with—the crowd at school that's known as the 'dead heads.'

I change the subject. "How was work?"

"Good, I finished the chapel today," he tells me. His eyebrows go up and lips turn down. He starts biting his lip and chewing on his cheek. He's probably worried about David.

"I'll finish cleaning up, just go ahead and eat before your sandwiches get cold." I've got plenty of energy. I feel like I can clean the entire house. After I finish the dishes, I head into the living room to check on the kids while Dad eats his dinner. Carmen and Lucy are sitting in the dark, watching *The Brady Bunch*. As I flick on the light switch, I hear a big bang and look up to the ceiling where the noise came from. I look around.

"Where's Anna?"

"Upstairs," Carmen states, eyes glued to the television. It sounds like she's dropping stuff. When I listen harder, I hear the shower running. More stuff dropping, more banging. What is she doing? I head to the bottom of the staircase.

"Anna, you okay?" More banging. "Anna?" I run up the steps two at a time and knock on the bathroom door. The shower is running. "Anna, you all right?" I turn the knob, it's locked. I bang on the door. She doesn't answer. I bang harder. "Anna? Open the door!" I bang again. My hand hurts. I run down the steps.

"Dad! Help!" I run into the kitchen. He's eating his sandwiches. "Dad, something's wrong with Anna." We can hear the banging from the kitchen now.

"What? What's going on? Where is she?" Dad asks with a mouthful of grilled cheese.

"In the shower," I say, catching my breath as we are both running up the steps. "I don't know what she's doing in there, she won't answer." The banging is getting louder.

"Anna?" He knocks on the door then grabs the knob. "Anna, open this door." Dad yells as his eyes go wild. Last time I saw him like this was when Lucy was little and had the Croup. She couldn't breathe and we had to rush her to the hospital. Mom sent me upstairs to her room to give her cough medicine. I gave it to her, and she started choking. Then, she couldn't breathe. I got so scared that I could barely scream for Mom. All the kids were in bed already because it was a school night. David stayed here with them while I went to the hospital with Mom, Dad, and Lucy. Dad ran all the red lights. I'm surprised that we didn't get pulled over by the cops. I was so scared but didn't cry because I was the big girl. They put her in an oxygen tent, and almost had to cut a hole in her throat so she could breathe because she kept sucking her thumb. All this goes through my mind while we are standing in front of the bathroom door. It feels like we've been banging on the door forever. We hear more banging going on in there.

"Anna!" Dad is furiously turning the knob.

"Do something!" I yell at him. Without even looking

at me, he backs up a couple feet, turns to his side, and busts the door in. Anna is convulsing on the floor of the shower. He lifts her out. I'm horrified. She's totally naked, and too old to be naked in Dad's arms. I notice that her boobs are bigger than mine, and that she's starting to get hair down there, and look away. I'm embarrassed at myself for looking and embarrassed for her. I move past Dad and turn off the shower water. I run to grab a towel from the hallway closet to cover her private parts because I don't know what else to do. Her whole body is shaking and twitching. Her eyes are rolled up in her head. I'm too scared to cry. The kids are coming up the steps.

"Is Anna okay?" Lucy calls.

"Yeah, just stay down there. We'll be right down." I don't want them to see her like this. They'll get scared. I don't know what's happening. Dad lays her on the floor. She is still trembling, but it's slowing down. Her eyes have rolled back into place and she is staring at nothing without blinking. If her arms weren't twitching, I'd think she was dead. I've never seen a dead person, except in the movies, so I wouldn't know what one looked like for real. My heart's pounding. Lucy and Carmen aren't listening. They're coming up the steps.

"Go down there with them," Dad yells at me. I don't want to go down there with them, I want to stay here with Anna until I know she's okay. I'm pissed off that they won't listen. Taking a deep breath, I head down the steps so their view of naked Anna dripping on the floor is blocked. Just as I say, "Don't come up, everything's okay," Dave walks through the front door.

"What's going on?"

I shoo Carmen and Lucia away from the bottom of the steps. "Something's wrong with Anna."

David bolts right past me, ripping up the steps. I tell the kids to go back in the living room. My bionic ears kick in. Dad tells Dave to grab another towel for her. I hear them carry her to her room.

   I wanted to help.
   I'm the one who heard her.
   I always get stuck watching the kids.

Chapter 8
Nothing is Fine

"Bye Dad," I yell up the steps. I pretend I'm going out the front door. I open and close the door loudly. Then, moving silently back up the steps, I sneak back into my room and into the closet and gently close the door, encasing myself in the dark.

I am not going to school today. When I look in the mirror, I can see my legs are huge, my stomach is sticking out, and my face is puffy. I am too embarrassed of myself to be seen in public. So, I wait in dark silence, in the safety of my closet until everyone has left the house.

I hear the kids leave for school, then I hear Dad coming back upstairs. He opens my bedroom door. My heart beats so loudly that I am sure he can hear it. I realize that I've been holding my breath when I hear the door close and his footsteps heading into his bedroom. I exhale. I've been crouched in the same position for I don't know how long. It doesn't take long for my legs to get stiff. The thought hits that I could be sitting here all day. He's his own boss, so he's not on a time schedule. He may just work from home today.

I think I've dozed off because when I open my eyes, all is silent. I gently open the closet door and listen. The silence is eerie. I tiptoe to my bedroom door and listen. Nothing. I open my bedroom door as softly as possible, poking my head out just a tad to get a listen for any possible sounds. All seems safe, so I head down the steps.

First, I go to the laundry room window which overlooks the driveway. I peek between the blinds just to be sure that he left. His car is gone. The driveway is empty, which makes me think of my stomach which is growling. I only ate a banana for lunch at school and a salad for dinner last night after my run. I can afford a little breakfast. I'll drink a lot of water to fill my stomach. Matter of fact, I drink a big glass of water before I eat.

I pop a piece of whole wheat bread in the toaster, and decide I need a little protein, so I get out the peanut butter. While I wait for the toast, I have a teaspoonful. It tastes delicious, so I have another.

That's about 100 calories. When the toast pops up, I smooth some peanut butter over it and bring it to the table. I eat it slowly, making sure to chew each piece thirty times. When I get close to the last few bites, my stomach is feeling full, but I keep eating. I decide on another piece of toast, with more peanut butter and a smidge of Nutella. But that will be overdoing it. I'll be okay, I tell myself. No one will be home for hours, so I'll just go for a run to get rid of all the calories.

The plotting takes hold as I eat the second piece. Next I'll have cereal, the junk kind. I find Cocoa Pebbles. These are small and will come up easy. I use a lot of milk, even though I hate milk, so there is liquid in my stomach. It is a lot easier to get rid of it that way. After eating three bowls, I make myself a sandwich with potato chips. I make sure I cut up a tomato into thick slices to add to it because that will help the sandwich come up. I use the rest of the American cheese and sliced turkey and slather it with mayo. My stomach hurts, but I can't stop. I look in the freezer and find ice cream. Before I know it, half of the container is gone. It's chocolate. I don't even like chocolate ice cream, or turkey.

Cristina Utti

I feel as though I'm about to burst and can't believe I've done this to myself again. I look for some soda that Dad keeps in the bottom shelf of the pantry. Orange soda. Disgusting. Chugging down as much as I can as fast as I can helps it to come up faster. I feel like I'm going crazy. My stomach hurts as I make my way to the bathroom to get rid of all of the damage I've just done. I know I can't undo all the damage. I know that I didn't get it all out. My throat is sore, and my knuckles are bleeding.

It is only 8:30 in the morning.

I have no control over anything. I head back to my room, sink my disgusting body onto my bed and cry. I can feel my legs getting even fatter. All I wanted was a piece of toast and to lose ten pounds so I can be skinny like Mom was. Then I'll be happy.

"Lina, are you home?" Anna is calling me. I can't believe I've slept all day. Startled, I jump up. I feel guilty as hell, but I'm always home before them anyway, so they don't know the difference. David never even comes home after school. I wish he would. We used to hang out and talk about books and even make our own bookmarkers. I'm always alone here. Now I know how Mom felt.

"Yeah, be right down," I yell down to her as I'm already heading down for mommy duty. Downstairs, I greet them and give them a snack. While I'm filling them each a bowl of chips, I munch on a few, just to get the nasty taste out of my mouth. Even though I brushed my teeth, my mouth still tastes horrible. "You guys have homework?"

"Nope, did it at school," Carmen answers as he heads into the living room with his yellow plastic bowl filled to the rim with sour cream and onion potato chips.

"Sure you did. Let me see it. And you know there's no eating in the living room." He doesn't listen. I raise my voice a bit and try to sound mean. "Carmen, get back in here and show me your work." It's hard for me to be mean to him. No one is around to check up on him, so I have to do it. He comes back into the kitchen with his bowl of chips and plops into a seat at the table. He takes out a paper of addition problems that is half complete. "I thought you said you did it."

"I did most of it," he mumbles.

"C'mon, here's a pencil." I make him finish his worksheet.

"How 'bout you two? Where's your homework?" Lucy gets hers out, and Anna fumbles through her backpack. She's very disorganized. I sit down to help her sort through her papers and munch on a few more chips.

While I'm helping them and making sure their work gets done, I'm planning what to make for dinner. The way it works lately is if Dad isn't home by 4:30, I start dinner for everyone. I've already screwed up my day with those chips, so now I'll have to take laxatives because chips are a no-no.

Dad gets home a bit after dark. I made ravioli for dinner for everyone and ate two huge bowls. I figured I already messed up today, so what the heck? He's in his studio and the kids are in the living room, so now is a good time to ask him.

"Dad, can you take me to the store?"

"Hmm?" He's in a world of his own when he is painting.

"I need to go to the store; I have my thing." This excuse always works. He hates talking about women stuff.

"Oh, okay hon."

He lets me go into the store alone because he is old-fashioned and gets embarrassed when I have to buy pads. But I don't use the five dollars he gave me for that. I buy laxatives. I don't have enough for a box of 60, so I buy a box of 30 and save the change.

I'm feeling anxious and can't wait to get home to take them and get rid of all of this food. As soon as we get in, I head into the kitchen to grab a big glass of iced tea and bring it up to my room. I down the whole box, fifteen pills, then the other fifteen, and hide the empty pill packets and the empty pink box in the bottom of the bathroom trash can.

"C'mon, up to bed," I hear can hear what's going on in the living room right through my bedroom floor.

"Awe Dad, can't we have ten more minutes?" Lucia begs.

"Okay, then that's it." He is such a sucker, but they are so darn cute sometimes that I can see why he can't help himself. "Where's David?"

"In his room, like usual," Carmen chimes.

"I'm heading up for a shower. By the time I'm out, I want you guys to be in your rooms."

"Okay," Lucy and Carmen say in harmony. I don't hear Anna say a word. I hope she is feeling okay. She's been having seizures more frequently.

"Anna, you too," Dad tells her.

"What?" Of course, her ears don't work.

"Brush your teeth and head up to bed in ten minutes," he repeats as he heads up the steps. She does not respond. I wonder if she even heard what he said. He took her to the doctor after that first seizure. I went with them. The doctor couldn't come up with anything conclusive, all he told Dad was that they have to run more tests to see what is going on with her.

I hear Dad's footsteps on the stairs. He passes my room and stops at David's door. Dad knocks on his door, and Dave doesn't answer.

Dad knocks harder. "Are you in there?"

"Hey Dad, what's up?" he says as he opens the door. A puff of smoke flies out of his room, contaminating the air. I can smell it and my door is only opened about an inch. I smoke now too but would never do it right under Dad's roof. That's just wrong. I hope he's burning incense. I don't know if Dad can't smell the smoke, or if he chooses to ignore it.

"Just wanted to say hi. I just got home. Did you eat?" Dad says to him.

"Yeah. Just writing now." He has sadness in his voice.

"Are you okay?" Dad asks him. No one *ever* asks if I am okay.

"Yeah, sure. I'm fine. Just writing."

"Okay then. If you want to talk, I'm here." The words sound traitorous even to me. Dad never really wants to talk. I mean, he will talk to us if we start the conversation, but he never just comes to us and wants to talk. Unless it is bad, like when he went to Italy and when they got divorced. I feel safer if Dad doesn't want to talk. I get up from my bed to go take a shower. The bathroom is right across the hall from Dave's bedroom.

"I'm fine Dad, really," Dave says. From the corner of my eye, I can just see him trying not to make eye contact with Dad as he looks at the floor, the staircase, and back into his room. I know he is not fine because he is not making eye contact, but I let it go because I wouldn't even know what to say to Dad about it. I caused enough grief in this family when I told him about Mom. I can feel his unhappiness and everyone else's sorrow, and it is just eating me up that I can't help anyone to feel better. Not even my own self.

My bleeding heart is about to let loose. It is easy to cry in the shower because the tears and water blend together. I can't help my brother. My mom left. I can't help Anna to not have seizures. I can't help Lucy overcome whatever happened to her last year. I'm sure that's why she still sucks her thumb. And Carmen, all I can do for him is to be a mommy.

I find myself on my knees in the shower asking God to help me. I hope everyone is in bed by now, so they don't hear me. If I fall apart, who do they have left? I hear the phone ring as I dry off and wrap a towel around my head. I'd run to Dad's room to get it, but I'm in a towel so I stop at the door. I hear a bunch of sniffling. Dad's dam broke too. This makes my faucet spring back to life. I hear him answer the phone. I wait here a second to see if it's for me. Maybe it's Penney.

"Franca," I hear him say, and then there's uncomfortable silence. After sixteen years together, they now have nothing to say to each other as if they are total strangers. I understand because I don't know what to say to her either. Mom and I keep our conversations superficial and safe. I go into my room but leave it ajar so I can hear what he's saying to Mom. I'm so nosy I can't stand it, but I'm glad for my bionic hearing. I wonder if there is a handwriting type for nosiness or bionic hearing ability.

"They are okay. Lina's been a big help." I guess she asked how we are doing. If she really cared, she wouldn't have dated that creep.

"He's okay, I guess. The same." Dad says, and then there is more silence. And a sniffle. I get into a t-shirt and some shorts and stand by the door to hear. Dad isn't saying anything. I wonder if they are still on the phone.

"Yes," he says, so I presume she has been talking. Mom sure can talk a lot when she wants to, which is all the time. Dad is quiet again for what feels like forever.

"Yes. Yes, you can come home." In our lowest times, when we are most vulnerable, the decisions we make are not always the best. As soon as I hear those words, I feel sick to my stomach.

Chapter 9
Round Two

The laxatives made me sick as heck.
"Lina, are you okay?" Dad asks as he stands outside the bathroom door. No doubt he can hear me throwing up.

"I don't feel good." Which is the truth.

"Just rest today, hon. I'll call you out of school after I get the kids up. Mom's coming home today."

"Mom's coming home?" I ask as I come out of the bathroom. I almost forgot. This makes me feel sicker.

Dad looks at me. "You look pale." I must look like crap. I sure feel like it. "Yes, she'll be here in about an hour," he informs me. I'm pissed off at myself that I'm so sick that I can't go to school and get the hell out of this house.

"Anna, Lucy, Carmen," I call them from the hallway. "Time to get up." Immediately after I speak, I hear they are already awake and moving. My mind is elsewhere. I go back to the bathroom, then back to bed. I hear the little ones leave for school and I head back to the bathroom.

"Lina, can I do anything for you?" Dad calls from the bottom of the steps.

"I'm so sick," I tell him through the bathroom door and puke again. My stomach is cramping up.

"You want some tea?"

"No thanks," I tell him as I hear Mom come in the front door. I'm glad I'm already back in my room with the door closed.

I hear Dad say, "I thought we may be able to talk, but Lina is upstairs. She isn't feeling well. I'm worried about her. She's been having a lot of stomach trouble lately. I think it's girl stuff, maybe you can talk to her," and that's all I hear because they went into the kitchen, or maybe the studio.

My feelings are on a rollercoaster ride. Anger from being betrayed. Happy I won't have to be the mom anymore if she is back. Scared she will leave again. Confused. Not sure I want her to stay. Not sure if I even care if she leaves again. Not sure of anything, except that I need to lose at least ten pounds.

Chapter 10

The Invasion

Happy end of the school year. I get to share my room with my mother. Now she is trying to be my friend. But everything has changed since those stupid pictures. I should have never shown them to Dad. None of this would've ever happened and her and Dad would still be together, and she would be in her own room, not mine. She set up some of her stuff on my bureau and plugged in her fancy white and gold phone and put it on my night table. I feel totally invaded, but it's cool to have a phone in my room. That is the only plus in this whole mess.

Mom's sitting on my bed, checking out her makeup in the mirror that sits on my bureau. She fishes around in her makeup case for her lipstick. She finds bright red, smoothens it on her lips, smacks her lips together, and says in the mirror at me, "Dad said you haven't been feeling well."

"I'm fine." I love my life. It's been wonderful since you threw the wallet at me and blamed me for everything. I can't stop eating. Today I left school after the last final exam and went directly to the drug store. I'm sick and just want to be left alone.

"Are you having girl problems?"

"Girl problems?" What does that even *mean*? The kids don't listen to when I'm watching them, I barely passed my stupid classes because they were so stupid that I stopped going, and I caused my parents to get a divorce. To top it off, when I eat, I can't stop. I am a girl, and these are my problems. My whole life is a problem. "No, I'm not having girl problems."

"You sure? We can talk about it." I remain silent. Yeah, talk. I am not in the mood to talk about how everything is my fault. Now she is doing her eyes, applying blue eyeshadow. "So, how was your last day of school?" she asks, still staring at her own reflection.

"It was fine. I have to go to the bathroom." I go to the bathroom again.

"Do you have a boyfriend?" She continues when I come back into my room. A boyfriend? Even if I did, I wouldn't tell her. I wish she would leave me alone. I just want to sleep. Forever.

"No."

"My first boyfriend was your father. Oh, there was a boy with blond hair who used to serenade me at the convent. He used to ride a white horse to come see me. He was so handsome, but the nuns would never allow that."

"Oh," I say, not really caring about the blonde serenader.

"My mother never talked to me about boys. I don't want to be like her." I guess she is trying to make up with me. I like hearing stories about her and Dad. It puts a curtain over all the wrongs. "What was the name of the church where you and Dad got married?" I ask, even though I already know. She told me a thousand times.

"Oh, it was Santa Maria, in Roma." Her eyes shine when she says this, and it makes me happy. Maybe they will make up and life will go back to normal.

"I don't think I've ever told you what happened on our wedding day."

"What happened?" We are stuck here in this room together because I can't go far from the bathroom. I have no way out.

"Your father was late for the wedding. I thought he wasn't going to show up. I was about to pass out from embarrassment when he finally came through the doors."

I laugh. "Really? I can't believe he was late for his own wedding." This is a story I haven't heard.

"*Si*, the town was so full because of all of my family that your father couldn't find a place to park. His Italian was not so good, and he was shy. It took him forever to get through all the people." We both laugh. I picture Mom in her wedding gown, standing at the altar, alone. "I thought he wasn't going to show up. I stood there for a half hour before he came. I could hear my brothers laughing, saying that he wasn't going to show up."

"They were laughing?" That's pretty mean.

"I thought they were when I looked at them. I thought I would die right there, then your father finally came through the door," she said, her eyes sparkling.

"Thank God."

"I was so scared on our honeymoon," she continues. "I had never been with a man, you know." I am wondering why she is telling me this. "When I saw his thing, I got scared and started crying." Okay, this is getting awkward. I don't want to think about my Dad's thing. I can feel my face getting red. I wish she would just shut up. I get off the bed and start organizing my side of the bureau, trying not to listen. "When we made love, it hurt so bad, I wanted to jump off of the hotel room's balcony." I turn around and stare at her. I've never even kissed a boy yet. She doesn't get the hint that I don't want to hear this story anymore. She just keeps yapping. "I didn't have my sisters around to tell me about things. If I asked my mother about boys, she would slap my face. That's why I am telling you."

"Oh," is all I can say. This entire thing has been very weird. First, they get divorced, then, she comes home, moves into my room, and tells me this crap.

Cristina Utti

* * *

When my alarm goes off at 5:30 a.m., I hit Mom on the head instead of my alarm clock. I forgot she was sleeping next to me and she took my favorite side. Now I have to sleep next to the wall instead of next to my night table. That's where all of my stuff is, my clock, my glasses, my lamp, and my books. I read myself to sleep at night, or else I won't sleep at all because my brain never shuts up. I guess it takes after Mom. Then, when my eyes are tired and my brain is quiet, I lay my book on the nightstand next to my bed and turn off the light. Now Mom is here, sharing my bed, and I'm all thrown off. She's next to my stuff. My book, *Little Women*, is on the floor on the other side of the room.

"Sorry, Mom!"

"Hmm." Thankfully she's not awake. I dress quickly so she doesn't see me naked and head down to the kitchen. Just as I'm about to get some cereal, I remember not to eat before I run. David isn't up, so I head back up the steps to wake him because he has to go to work with Dad. I don't want to scream up the steps and wake the kids on their first day of summer vacation.

I softly open his door and see him still in bed. I go over and softly shake his shoulder. "David, get up, it's 5:45." He rolls over and pulls the blanket over his head. "Dave," I shake him again. "C'mon, wake up. Don't get Mom mad, she just got home."

"Okay, okay, I'm up," he mumbles, and pulls the covers over his head. I head back down to start my day. Mom must've heard the commotion because I find her in the kitchen, making coffee.

"Good morning," she gives me a kiss. Anna is sitting on the couch in the living room.

"What are you doing up so early?" I ask her.

Breaking Infinity

"None of your business! You're not my mother. Mom is home now," she snaps.

"Thank God." Like I would ever want to be *her* mother.

"I guess you're Mom's favorite now." She glares at me.

"What are you talking about?"

"She always wants to be with you," she says. I'm guessing she's referring to her moving in my room. I have a lot I want to spit back at her, like, 'yeah, I sure am the lucky one', and 'I wish she moved in with you', and 'I'll trade places with you', but I just keep my mouth shut because Mom is right there and I don't want to hurt her feelings, or worse, start my day with fingerprints across my face. I can't wait to get out of this house today. I'm glad Mom's home. I just wish she was back in her own room, not mine. I hope they make up soon. I want my room back. I feel full again with her here, but I'm also confused and sad and don't know how to make things better. I get on my sneakers and head out for a run.

When I get back from my run, Dave is in the kitchen making scrambled eggs. Dad's car is gone, so I guess he got tired of waiting for Dave to get his butt moving this morning.

"You hungry?" He always asks if I'm hungry. I'm starving, but not for food. I lie and tell him I already ate and ask him if he wants to go for a walk with me when he's finished his breakfast.

We walk down the dirt path that's to the left of our property. There's a huge weeping willow tree. We push through the branches to get to the trunk. Safely in our willow cave, we smoke. "Did you know what happened to Lucy that day Kane was over?"

"What day?" he asks. I explain about what she wrote on the paper that day he was singing to us.

Dave looks shocked. "What the fuck, Lina. Why didn't you tell me earlier? What exactly happened?" I tell him as much as I know, and we discuss what to do about it; whether we should talk to Lucy, kill Kane, or what. I don't think I've seen Dave this angry since the day Mom took his weed.

"I was pretty proud of you the day you helped Anna." I tell him, because I was, and to change the subject. "I thought you didn't care about us."

"What? Why would you think that?"

"Because you are never home."

"That's because Mom and Dad hate me because I caused the divorce."

"What?" comes out of my mouth at the same exact time I get a flashback of that night on the steps, when they were arguing about Dad never listening and Dave doing drugs. "It's not your fault, it's mine, with those stupid pictures." We sit in silence for a while.

"Want to see a poem I'm working on?" Before I can answer, he pulls a piece of paper out of the back pocket of his jeans and unfolds it.

"Do you keep your poems in your back pocket all the time?" I ask, laughing.

"Actually, I do. I never know when an idea will pop in my head. I keep a pen, too." I feel honored that he is sharing his poem with me. I love him so much. Spontaneously, I wrap my arms around him and tell him. Then, together we read "Not Mine."

Not Mine
June 14, 1980

Is it not mine
The merry yonder
With the earth and stars to ponder
The lands afar the ocean deep
And mind to keep a temple
In the sadness and the pleasure

Breaking Infinity

A life soft-spoken in the brokenness
Come what may
And my thought is but a ripple
In the mainstream of a blindness
Washed away
Inside a kindness

Chapter 11
Intuition is Calling

David and Dad have been working together all summer, so that has been going well. I've got a handle on the food thing now. I run five miles every morning and keep calories to no more than 1000 a day. I've lost eleven pounds since school let out and haven't had to make myself sick; I couldn't do that anyway with Snoopy Sniffer back in town. My relationship with Mom has stayed surface level, which is better than being blamed. I pretend that I am asleep when she comes into the room at night because I don't want to hear any more horror stories. Most nights she isn't here because she got a new job working at Dunkin' Donuts doing the 11 p.m. to 7 a.m. shift. But something's not right. My intuition is working overtime.

I'm in the kitchen playing a game of Go Fish with Carmen when Dad and Dave get in from work. Dad heads straight into his studio, no hello or anything. Dave takes off his work sneakers, comes into the kitchen, grabs a glass of iced tea and sits with us, swirling the cubes in his glass. Something is definitely wrong; he usually heads straight for food when he gets in. I ask Carmen for 5s. He tells me to go fish. I fish my wish, which ends the game.

"Hey, what's up? Is everything okay?" I ask Dave as he stares into his tea.

He comes out of his trance for a moment. "Hmm?"

"How was your day?"

"Oh, all right," he says, rubbing the skin under his chin as if he has a beard.

"I was going to take a walk to Wawa before dinner, want to come?"

"Can I come?" asks Carmen at the same time Dave says, "Yeah, sure. Give me a few minutes to jump in the shower," as he heads out of the kitchen.

"Can I come too?" Carmen tugs on my shirt sleeve as I put a rubber band around the deck of cards.

"How about you come with us next time?" He clenches his jaw and then looks at the floor. "I want you to come, but David didn't seem too happy, did he?"

"Uh-uh."

"Well, if you weren't happy about something, wouldn't you want me to take a walk with you?" He shrugs his shoulders, swings his legs, and bites his lip. "We won't be long, promise."

"But no one ever plays with me," he pouts.

"It's nice out, I bet if you go ride your bike, we'll be back before you know it."

He stares at me with those golden-brown eyes looking like he's about to cry. "But you guys always take too long." I melt. I put him on my lap and give him a hug.

"You know I love you lots and lots, right?" He nods. "What kind of candy bar do you want? I'll get you one from Wawa, then we can sneak downstairs and play a game so you can eat it before dinner." His face lights up.

"Really? Can you get me a Marathon bar?"

"You bet," I tell him as he is already squirming off of my lap. Dave walks in, hair still dripping wet. We head out the back door and walk in silence until we are past the house. "I guess we do have to go to Wawa now; I promised Carmen a candy bar." Dave says nothing. One of the reasons why I love taking walks with him is because our legs are just about the same length, so we walk in tandem.

Cristina Utti

Penney's much shorter than I am, so she slows me down. "What's wrong?"

"I don't know," he shakes his head, and then runs his hand down the back of his head, trying to flatten his hair. He's gotten into this habit as his hair grew longer. It's useless though, his hair is too curly and too thick to ever be flat. "Dad got all of his colors mixed up today." I have no idea what he is talking about, so I wait for him to continue. I'm working hard on becoming a better listener. "He mixed sepia with raw umber to paint the crucifix behind the altar. The colors didn't match, and he painted it anyway. Then he threw a fit because the color was off."

"I've noticed he's acting weird, too."

"What do you mean?"

"This morning he came in my room without knocking. I guess he thought I was out for my run, but I got back early this morning. I was on my bed, reading *Fahrenheit 451* because it's on my summer reading list. He stood there and just looked at me. No 'Good morning, Lina' or anything. He looked at Mom's phone and shut the door like he never saw me there at all."

"Yeah, that's weird," Dave agrees.

"What do you think is going on? You work with him all day." He shrugs and puts his hair into a ponytail. It's hot as heck today. Mine's been in a ponytail since my run this morning. The reason I left so early is because I watched the news last night and they said today would be the beginning of a heat wave. I hate pulling my hair back. My forehead is too big and my eyebrows are too bushy, but in this heat I don't care. Dave doesn't have those worries. He has a nice forehead and perfect eyebrows.

"I think it has something to do with Mom. You're with her all day, how's *she* acting?" This makes me think.

"To tell you the truth, I do my best to stay out of her way. After we pack up lunch for the kids, I usually take them to the pool. Penney comes with, and we stay there as long as we can stand them," I laugh. Dave does not laugh, which makes me nervous, so I keep blabbing. "Rainy days suck. Lucy and Anna get on my nerves, so I go to Penney's, or play games with Carmen, or read. I can't even chill in my own room because Mom naps in there since she started working that night shift."

"Yeah, that must suck. You can use my room when I'm at work if you need a place to chill." That's one of the nicest things he's ever said to me. I thank him as we walk through Wawa's door. We get Carmen his Marathon bar, Dave buys a Milky Way, and I buy a pack of Bubble Yum. Intuition, consciousness, soul, these words are not quite definable. These places are where we hear God if we just take the time to listen closely. God is telling me that something's not right.

Chapter 12
Loneliness

The heat wave is over. We woke to storms this morning. I can't run in this, so I decide to take Dave up on his offer. After breakfast is all cleaned up, I grab my book and head to his room to read in peace and quiet. I didn't want to sit at his desk because he has papers and notebooks on it, and I don't want to disturb whatever he's working on. I just want to lounge on the bed and read. The bed isn't made because he woke up late, again. Being the neurotic that I am, I can't sit on crumpled up sheets and covers. I pull the sheets taut and pick up the light blue blanket from the floor to put over them so I'm not sitting directly on his sheets.

As I shake the wrinkles out of it, a piece of crumpled paper falls to the floor. I put the blanket on the bed and pick up the paper. At first, I was going to toss it into the trash. I stop myself, remembering how he carries his poems in his pockets. Maybe it's important. I put it on the desk and smooth it out. It's a poem about loneliness. I know I shouldn't be reading his stuff without asking, but I can't help it.

Now I have two choices. I can either tell him the truth, that it fell out from his blanket and I read it or crumple it back up. I can't bear to crumple it, so the truth it is. I hope he doesn't get mad at me.

Loneliness, August 17, 1980

Sometimes I feel like crying
Cause this feelin' keeps goin' away

Sometimes I feel like crying
Cause this feeling keeps fading away
Ain't no use in tryin'
When I gotta move on
And just can't stay here anymore

Sometimes I feel like dyin'
All the dues I gotta pay
Just can't keep away anymore

Where is that kind-hearted woman
I keep thinkin' about?

Sometimes I feel like cryin'
Cause this feelin' keeps goin' away
Ain't no use in trying anymore
The lovin's gone and I must
get back to the shore

When my life was mine
I made a happy time
Findin' someone to love and cherish
She was sweet and made my life complete
Now there's only discontent and memories
Distress and loneliness

Chapter 13
The Fake Strikes Again

I'm sitting in my room, minding my own business, preparing for this school year, trying on clothes to see what fits. No matter how many miles I run, my thighs are still huge and have fat on them. Shooting for another five pounds before school starts. I'm trying on an old pair of Dave's jeans, when in walks Mom. I'm in my underwear. I hate this crap.

"You know Lina, I have no one to guide me through this divorce," she starts in on me, like it's my fault. "Now we are legally divorced, but this isn't what I wanted. I'm so confused; all I wanted was your father to love me. All he ever does is work, work, work."

I get my left leg in the other side, slide the jeans on, suck in my gut, zip and button them, and start organizing my clothes. Mom keeps talking.

"I'm trying to make things better, I really am," she says.

"I know Mom," I respond, and take the drawer out of the bureau and dump it on the bed. She sits down next to my pile, oblivious.

"I feel so alone. All of my sisters are in Italy," she tells me. I don't get it. I wish my sisters were in Italy. All they do is annoy me. Lucy narked me out about smoking weed and I had to kick her butt, then lie to Mom. "You children are all I have," she tells me. I flatten the wrinkles out of my shorts and put them in a pile. I'll leave two out for running and pack the rest in the closet. I put the two in the drawer and slide it back into its empty spot in the bureau. I pull out my shirt drawer and dump it next to Mom. She doesn't even flinch as I start making neat color-coded piles with my shirts.

"I'm working at Dunkin' Donuts because Saul suggested I get another job when I quit the agency. I know I embarrass you," she says.

"You still talk to him?" is all that comes out of my mouth. I'm not embarrassed about Dunkin Donuts. I keep folding as my blood boils. I take a deep breath.

"I have no skills. My education was in Italy. All I've done in this country was raise kids," she continues like I am not even here, and I wonder why I am.

"Why are you even talking to him?"

"Saul tells me to get a lawyer, tells me that I'm entitled to half of the house and to custody of my children. I don't want to fight with your father, Lina. I just want him to love me again, to pay attention to me, and to make me feel special, the way Saul did."

I can't listen to this one more millisecond. "Why are you telling me all this shit?" I grab my shirts, shove them back in the drawer, and slam it back into the bureau. I storm down the steps and out the front door and run. I run and run and run until the pain moves from my heart to my thighs.

I see Dad's car in the driveway when I get back. He should have left for work by now.

Sweat is dripping off my face when I get back home. That's the funny thing about running, I don't feel the sweat until I stop. "Good morning," I say to Carmen as I walk into the kitchen to grab a tall glass of water. It's probably already ninety-five degrees out there today.

"Can I have a donut?"

"How about a hug first? And, no, that's not a healthy breakfast."

"Please?" He is so hard to resist, even his morning breath is cute. Dad and Dave kid around and call him Chicken Little. I know he hates that. It bruises his pride.

"Tell you what, look in the bag and pick two of your favorites. I'll save them for you for after lunch," I tell him while taking out oatmeal for him. Mom brings home donuts some mornings because they would've just gone in the trash. Every twelve hours they make new batches and throw out whatever donuts are left from the last batch. As he attacks the bag of donuts, Dad enters the kitchen from the studio at the same time Mom walks in from the dining room. Eyes lock. Dead stare.

"You're not going to work today?" Mom asks him.

"Nope." I feel the ice in his voice and don't want to stare, so I busy myself getting out bowls for cereal for Anna and Lucy because they will be in here any minute. Carmen is already eating the oatmeal I made for him.

"Oh, okay," Mom says. We all pretend there's no tension in the air. I hold a knife in my hand and visualize slicing the tension, chopping it into little teeny-tiny pieces and putting it down the garbage disposal until it vanishes, and we are one big happy family again. "Tony, what's wrong?"

"What is wrong? Why don't you tell me?" Tension can't be sliced, diced, or disposed of. It has to air out.

"What?" Mom says. They don't even acknowledge us.

"C'mon guys, let's go upstairs. I've a surprise for you," I tell the kids to get them out of here before the explosion.

"But I'm hungry," Anna complains.

"Let's go," I say as I grab her arm.

"I'm not stupid, Franca. I know all about your phone calls," we hear Dad say as I'm trying to get the kids out of the kitchen.

"What are you talking about?" Mom asks. He stares at her, venom shooting from his eyes. We all stare at her, too, wondering what he is talking about. I come back to my senses within a few seconds.

"C'mon, I'll give you a treat," I tell them, and push them out of the kitchen.

"You, you and him. I heard it all. I thought you came home for us to work things out, but you are still talking to him," Dad's yelling now. The kids get scared and finally move their butts up the steps. I've no idea where Dave is. I wish he were here with me so we could figure out what the heck's going on.

"It's not what you think," I hear Mom murmur. "Tony, please don't. I've been trying to talk with you." I get the kids into my room as soon as possible. I tell them to set up the game Memory with the deck of cards that I keep in my nightstand for playing solitaire. I split the deck into thirds so they all have some cards and don't fight over them.

"I have to go to the bathroom. If the game is set up by the time I come back, I'll give you all a piece of gum," I tell them. I close the bedroom door behind me and stand at the top of the steps, tuning in my bionic ears. I hope Mom doesn't think I said something to Dad again about Saul.

"Trying to talk to me? When? When you were planning to take my house? When you were planning to take my children?" Dad screams at her. I catch bits and pieces.

"It's rightfully half mine! They're my kids too! He is just a friend!"

"I heard everything, I have it all recorded!" So, she *has* been talking to that jerk all along. She didn't lie to me about it, I just didn't want to listen. I hear something crash into the wall. It takes all I have not to run down there.

I hear Mom say, "Please stop." I wonder if the kids can hear too.

"No, you stop!" I hear stuff crashing around. "Get the hell out of my house! You will never take my children or get anything from me! If you take them, I'll move to Rome and you won't get a dime!" I've never heard Dad curse. That scares me more than anything.

"I'm not leaving without my children."

"I let you move back in thinking you wanted our life back, and you still talk to that asshole who ruined our marriage? You wanted to leave us, now get out!" I hear a door slam. "Pack your shit and get the hell out of my house!" My heart is thumping out of control and I get my butt back in my room. "We got it all set up," Carmen whispers to the floor.

I get the pack of Bubble Yum out of my purse, hands shaky. I hear a car door slam and one of them is pulling out of the driveway. I keep the kids in my safe haven.

Chapter 14

Partners

Dad's birthday is in a few days and we are trying to do something special to cheer him up. Even though he's the one who told Mom to leave, he's been moping around ever since she left. I haven't seen him eat in days. All he does is drink coffee, smoke cigarettes, and stay in his studio. I'm not sure of all of the details but there was a lot of phone arguing over the past few weeks. I've done my best to turn off the bionic ears. I don't want to know.

Dave and I stay out most of the time, hanging with friends in Plymouth or Conshy. Neither one of us likes to be home. We are sticking together through this. We've been hanging out a lot since that talk under the willow. We hang out at Marywood Park, or we walk to Callan's or Brandon's house. The Plymouth Meeting Mall is always the last resort, just for someplace to go. Dave's been kind of distant. I'm kind of glad he wasn't there to witness that fight. He doesn't like to talk about what's going on; he is like Dad in that aspect. Maybe he is better off that way. Every single little thing bothers me. I'm hoping that if I hang out with Dave enough, some of his attitude will rub off on me and I won't be such a worry wart.

Off to another great school year.

Chapter 15
Lookin' Good
While Feelin' Bad

One hundred and sixteen. Day five. Nothing but water, diet soda, and protein pills. Minus two pounds a day. Ten more pounds to go and all will be perfect. I'm proud of myself for my willpower not to eat, not a single morsel. I can cook for the kids, keep up with my homework, run five miles every day, and not eat a thing.

I got up all of my courage and told Dad I had a problem with food. He told me I am fine, that I'm just going through a growth spurt. He has enough to worry about, so I figured it out for myself. If I can't fill this emptiness inside of me, and my filled meter is broken, I just won't eat at all. I won't have to tell Dad about my problems again and worry him. While I'm getting my vitamins out of the cabinet, Dave and Callan walk in.

"Hi Lina, you look great," Callan says as soon as he sees me. David's busy getting out the ingredients for cheesesteaks. The three of us were hanging out all the time in the summer, but I haven't seen Callan since school began. This compliment makes me feel good about myself. I can finally do something right.

"Thanks," I say. Callan looks great too. I never noticed how green his eyes are. I've never looked at him like *that*.

He's my brother's best friend. The only people who tell me I'm pretty are Mom and Dad.

"Brandon's having a party. You wanna go?" David asks, knowing that I do. "We're gonna split before Dad gets home," he says.

"Uh, sure." I'd rather be chilling out with them, listening to music, and smoking some weed than sitting here in this house listening to complaining kids all day. Suddenly, I remember Lucy. "Is Kane gonna be there?" I'm not going if he's going to be there. Dave and I only ever spoke about what happened that day when we were under the willow. Lucy has never mentioned it again, but I haven't forgotten.

"I doubt it. We don't hang with him anymore." Dave says while chopping up some onions.

"What about the kids?"

"They're old enough. Anna's twelve now." She seems so young. That's how old I was when Mom left the first time.

"Yeah, you're right. Let's just wait for them to get home from school. I'm not sure if they have their keys." He is stuffing his face and not listening. He can eat four cheese steaks a day and never get fat. Callan, too. He's almost six feet tall and those pretty greenish-blue eyes and brownish-blonde hair that curls around his face are just killing me. It's like I'm seeing him for the first time. He eats as if he hasn't eaten in days, always has, and he doesn't gain a pound. He probably weighs less than me and I had to literally starve to get to this weight.

"What time you guys headin' over there?" They are totally absorbed in their food. "Hey, David, can I still go if I wait for the kids to get home?"

"Huh?" He looks up from his food. "Want some?" He offers me some sandwich. No one knows about my fast. I just say I'm not hungry or tell the kids and Dad that I already ate. Five days and going strong.

"Nah, I'm not hungry. What time you guys goin' to Brandon's?" I ask again.

"Oh," he grabs a napkin and wipes the cheese that stuck to his lips. "We'll wait for you."

"I'm gonna get changed. Don't forget to clean up, okay?" I head upstairs to try to find something decent to wear. I try on some jeans; size three. Still too tight. Anna gave me some shirts that were too tight for her. Lucky for her, she has a chest and a shape, at twelve. Life's not fair. I get hand-me-ups. I try on a few of my hand-me-up shirts. We really don't have the same style. I'm good with my jeans, flannels and boots. She gave me some tight-fitting cotton shirts that she can't fit her chest into anymore. I kept the plain ones and tossed anything with bows or sequins. I'm not that jazzy. We are opposites. She needs to be the center of attention and I like to be invisible. I try on the blue shirt, then the red one. The red one shows off my flat stomach and looks good. I turn to try to see the fit from the back, then the side. Nah, red's too flashy, and my stomach bulges out a little. I'll stick with the blue, it's a little looser and my little bulge should be gone in a few more days, then I may be in shape for a tighter shirt. I try on another pair of jeans that were too tight three days ago and they fit me again. This makes me happy. I'm good to go.

We head out with Callan. We cut through the front yard, ducking under the pine trees. We pass the house at the corner and hang a right on Joshua Road.

"What time does the party start?" I ask, mostly just to have some conversation.

"When we get there," Callan answers.

"Ain't that the truth." I try to sound cool, but probably sound stupid. At least I'm looking a little better. I've hung out with David and his buddies a lot throughout the summer, but suddenly I feel nervous. In the summer, Dave and I showed Penney and Callan the weeping willow tree.

They loved it. Our house is a corner lot. At the corner, there is a dirt path that leads to the school at the bottom of Joshua Road. The kids go to school there, at Spring Mill Elementary. I walk them to school when I don't have school and they do. That's how I found the tree. It's at least triple Callan's height. Weeping willows are my favorite trees.

Wawa is exactly one mile from home. I've checked the speedometer while in the car with Dad. I've ran there and back many times. Brandon's house is about as far from Wawa as we are, in the opposite direction. Maybe there will be a weeping willow near Brandon's house that I can hide out underneath.

We head straight to the back yard when we get there. There's a keg of beer. I recognize a few of the guys from school but can't place names. I'm surprised I don't know any of the girls; they must be valley girls. P-W high school is divided. Whitemarsh kids hang out together and kids from Plymouth hang out together. We call the Plymouth chicks the valley girls. I went to Whitemarsh Junior High, but don't discriminate with whom I hang out with. Cliques are stupid. One of my best school friends, Donny, is from Plymouth. Penney still goes to Catholic school in Conshy, and I have friends like Nina, Ellie and Simone who live in Roxborough, so I hang out in Roxborough too. I know most of the juniors since my brother and two best friends are in 11th grade. Actually, I have more friends in that grade than in my own. Yep, they are valley girls, Callan seems to know all of them and he's from Plymouth.

"Hey Lina, want a beer?" David asks me.

"Yeah, sure," I say, because that's why we came. I'm a bit nervous because I haven't eaten in days and don't want to get drunk and make a fool of myself. He pours me a cup from the keg, hands it to me, and we go to sit on the ground with Callan, Karl, Ronnie, and a few of the girls I don't know. I take a sip, acting real cool, like I do this all the time. I'm the youngest one here. The girls are giggling about something, like girls do. They look more stupid than I feel.

"Here," Callan hands me the bowl that's going around the circle. It's a little wooden guitar-shaped bowl with a moveable lid that covers the bowl part.

"Thanks." It's hashish, not weed. I want to say that I like the guitar bowl but am too self-conscious and will probably sound like an amateur. I take a hit, slide the cover to keep the hash from burning too fast and pass it on. That's how Callie handed it to me, with the lid closed. David sat next to me, thank God. I take a swig of beer. It tingles going down my throat and tastes awful. In minutes, the hash starts to hit, and I relax. I giggle to myself at saying Callie, even if it was in my own mind. "Sugar Magnolia" by the Grateful Dead plays in the background. I polish off my beer and get up to get another one.

David and I started heading home when the sun went down. I'm glad I didn't finish the second beer; I'm already feeling tipsy. The night has a cool autumn breeze and I wish I brought a jacket. I'm glad that Kane wasn't there because I may have punched him in the face. I don't care how big he is.

"You ever miss Mom?" I ask Dave as we are walking home. I'm glad to have him all to myself with no friends around. I also want to ask him if he ever confronted Kane, but don't know how to approach that subject.

"Yeah," he says, real sad-like, looking at the ground. "You?"

"Yeah," this makes me blue too. I don't know why I started this conversation. Probably the buzz. "I wish they never divorced."

"Yeah, me too. It's so fucked up. I hate Saul."

"Yeah." We continue to walk in silence, but it's not awkward, there's comfort in it.

"You think they'll ever get back together?" I ask when we're about halfway home.

"Are you stupid? Her and that asshole planned to take everything from Dad, and he caught her."

"What?" I've no idea what he's talking about.

"He had Ben put in a recorder in the garage. All her phone conversations with that asshole were recorded. She was busted," he said. I had no clue.

"Oh, man," I say. What a load of information. "I still miss her though."

Now I'm getting choked up, but I'm not going to cry like a big baby in front of David.

"Hey," David stops, looks at me, and gives me a hug. "Me too, Lina, me too." We stand on Joshua Road embraced in our sadness while cars stream by.

"Thanks for letting me hang out with you guys tonight."

"No prob, you're all right," he elbows me in the ribs. I crack a smile. "Watcha doin' Friday night?"

"I dunno, probably hangin' out with Penney. Why?"

"I'm jammin' with some guys; getting together a band. Dad agreed that we could use the garage." I like hearing David play. He's really good, much better than I could ever be. He has talent. All I'm good at is reading. And not eating. "You guys can hang with us. The more the merrier." He smiles at me, and my insides warm up. I feel full. I'm so grateful to have him in my life. It's cool that we can talk about how we feel and what's going on in the family. These are things that friends just don't get because they are not in it. He's so smart, writes so well, and is a great pianist. He may get high a little too often, but I'm so proud of him.

"Cool, I'll ask Penney," I say, elated. I wish I could be in his band. As we near the corner from Joshua Road onto Sugar Maple, the gloom hits me again, but I try to fight it off.

"Remember when we used to smoke cigarettes, and then use the pine needles on our hands and chew gum to hide the smell before we went in the house? Remember that Dave?" I ask, forcing out a laugh.

"Yeah, sure do. No more Snoopy Sniffer to bug us," he says, pushing out a fake laugh.

"Yeah, that's for sure." I grab some pine needles off the tree and rub them on my fingers for old times' sake as we walk through the front yard.

Chapter 16

The House of Doom

Mom's apartment is small and warmly decorated. It has high ceilings with wood beams that are cool to look at when you're sleeping on the floor. We all slept over when she first moved, but it was too cramped and chaotic. David, Carmen, and I slept on the floor in the living room with our sleeping bags. The floor has deep shag beige carpeting, so it wasn't too uncomfortable. Anna slept with Mom so Mom could keep an eye on her in case she got shaky or had a seizure, and Lucy got the couch. We did that a few times, until the arguments over who slept where got to be too much. Now we take turns. This weekend it's my turn with Mom.

"Let's go out for Chinese. What do you think, Lina?" I know she is trying to get me to eat and will be watching me. I agree, just to make her happy, to make her think that I'm all better. I'm almost at my next goal of 105. Three pounds away. I can afford to eat some Chinese food tonight.

"Sounds good to me." I love Chinese food. We've gone to the Golden Dragon once before and it was pretty good. It's not far from here. It's about a ten-minute drive on Ridge Pike.

We order the pu pu platter to share. Mom eats the beef teriyaki, the chicken wings, and the spare-ribs. I eat the egg rolls, tempura shrimp, and fried wontons. It's fancy heating our food over the flame with our chopsticks. The next course is wonton soup.

"So, how's school going?"

"It's fine," I tell her in between slurps of my wonton soup, avoiding eye contact. School pretty much sucks. I'm way ahead of everyone in my classes. I've been cutting class, showing up for the tests and maintaining A's and B's. I wonder how I ever got put in those stupid classes. I think they tracked me wrong, but that is really the least of my concerns. "How's work?" Mom has two jobs now. She waitresses at Ralph's Diner for the dinner shift and kept her night shift at Dunkin'.

"It's okay. Pays the bills. I'm thinking of going to school for Cosmetology. What do you think?"

"That's a good idea, you're good at cutting our hair," I tell her, but she hasn't cut my hair since I was a kid. I won't let anyone touch my hair since Uncle Johnny chopped it all off. It's finally down to my shoulders again. We talk about her new friends and some boys that I think are cute. I keep my crush on Callan to me, myself, and I. We're almost full by the time our meals come. Mom asks the waiter to pack up the rest for us to take home.

"Oh my God, it's pouring out," I exclaim when we push open the restaurant's big glass door. The car is way across the parking lot near the street.

Mom bolts out the door past me. "Make a run for it!" I'm two steps behind her. She tries to jump over a huge puddle and doesn't make it. Her right leg slides forward and she practically does a split. Her take-out bag flies in the air as she goes down. I jump to catch it but end up tripping over her and landing right in the puddle on top of my shrimp chow mien. We're on the ground, in the dark, soaked. Our food is ruined. We look at each other and laugh so hard that we are crying.

Drenched, we walk with our arms on each other's

shoulders for support and make our way to the car. Mom and I are friends again. I don't even think of getting rid of what I ate today.

Once we are changed and dry, Mom makes some hot cocoa. Not the packet stuff. Real hot cocoa, with milk, cocoa powder, and sugar. And she even tops our mugs with mini marshmallows. The best.

"So, tomorrow I want to take you to see a house I'm thinking of getting for us," she tells me, while warming her hands around her mug.

I'm shocked and don't know what to say. I never thought of moving. "Where is it?"

"In Philadelphia."

"Oh," I mutter, trying to hide disappointment and fear. My only experience with Philadelphia is Aldine Street in the Northeast. That's where Dad's parents live. It's okay to visit, but I never thought of living there.

Saul shows up in the morning and comes with us. Ugh. Pretend. Don't show feelings.

The home is on the boulevard in Northeast Philly. I think. It looks like the route we take to get to Grandmom's house.

"You ready?" Saul asks as he opens my door. I don't care for his chivalry. I can open my own damn door. He is trying to score brownie points with me.

"Yep," I say, showing the least amount of emotion as possible. I don't mean to be a cold bitch. I know he is trying to help Mom, and she and Dad are divorced now, but I can't help myself.

"You have the key?" Mom asks him, giving him the flirty eye. She must think that I don't notice how her behavior changes when she is around him.

"Yes, stopped by the realtor's this morning," he says and shows her the key to the house.

"Well, let's show Lina. C'mon in," she gestures as he opens the front door. Before I even look inside the house, I know

Cristina Utti

I hate it. I do *not* want to live here. Cars zoom by the front yard, which is all of about five feet. I don't want to be this far away from my friends, the few that I have. But I take a tour for Mom's sake because she is so excited.

"This is the living room. We can fix it up and paint it a nice color." We move through the house to the back. "The kitchen is big. Big enough for all of us. What do you think?"

"It's nice." What am I supposed to say? The staircase heading to the second floor is between the living room and the kitchen. The carpeting on the steps is ugly olive green, dirty and worn, and smells like cat piss. The banister is nice. It's wooden. I admire it for a moment. Our banister at home is metal. I never saw a wooden banister in a home.

"We have three bedrooms. You girls can have this one." She shows me the bedroom to the right at the top of the steps. It's the same place my bedroom is at home. It's not a bad size. The carpet is an off-white and looks fairly new. There is one widow at the end of the room. I walk over to it to check out the view. No escape tree like at home. This bedroom has a beautiful view of an alley. "And this room is for the boys. It's just perfect!" She is so excited. The smaller room is already carpeted in blue low pile carpeting, just for the boys.

"It's nice," I say.

"There's only one bathroom, but that'll be okay, right Lina? There were twelve of us growing up and we only had one bathroom; we managed." I say nothing. I don't know what to say.

"Is that your room?" I ask, heading toward the only door left up here.

"Yes, this'll be my bedroom," she says as she opens the door for me to take a peek. It is small. It is the smallest bedroom up here, and I feel bad for Mom. Saul is right behind me, and I feel like smacking the smirk right off his ugly face. He gives me the creeps.

"Is there a basement?" At home we have a big basement. That's where we hang out with our friends when we want some privacy.

"It's only a cellar, like Grandmom's. Do you want to see it?"

"Nah, it's okay." I'm not interested in cellars.

"Well, what do you think? You want to move here? We can all be together again!" I shrug and don't look at her in the eyes. I don't know how I feel about this. Guilty mostly, because I hate it and Mom is so happy to have found a home that we can all live in with her. No apartments take five kids. If I tell her how I feel and we don't move here, that will be all my fault too. I don't like it here, it's creepy and I'm getting bad vibes. I don't want to go to school in this area. I don't want to leave my friends.

"Can we talk about it later?" I don't want to talk about anything in front of *him*.

"Sure, Lina," Mom nervously says and puts her arm on my shoulder. I get a flashback of the fun we had last night. I wish every day could be like last night; just me and Mom having fun.

We drive home in silence. Not complete silence. I'm the only person that is silent. They speak Italian, thinking I don't understand. I don't know why Mom does this. She knows I understand everything they are saying. He is putting up the money for the house. After the paperwork from the divorce is all settled and she gets her share from the marriage, she will pay him back. This is their agreement. I want nothing from him, nor do I want any part of this arrangement. When we get home and after he leaves, I'll tell her that I do not want to live in Philadelphia.

* * *

Mom drops me off back home on Sunday night. I lean toward her and give her a peck on the cheek. "Bye Mom," I say, doing my best to act like everything is okay.

"Bye Lina. Have a good night with your father." The guilt trip. I live here. What does she want from me? My legs feel like lead as I walk up the back steps.

"Hi Lina, I made mashed potatoes for you," Anna tells me, all excited. She hardly ever tries to cook. I see the box of Hungry Jack flakes on the counter. They're not homemade, but it's a start.

"Hi," I give her a hug, and take a peek at the mashed potatoes. "They look delicious."

"Are you hungry? I know you like potatoes, and Dad made fish."

"Yeah, actually, I'm starved." I tell her, although I'm scared to eat. I feel a binge coming on. I have to eat; they're all trying so hard to be nice to me. I want to tell them about the house I saw when we are at the dinner table then decide this probably is not a conversation to have with Dad sitting right here. The potatoes are way too salty and will make me swell up like a balloon, but I eat them anyway to make Anna happy. The fish was fried. Fried food is a no-no. I know everyone has their eyes on me, so I eat. I try to act normal, but fear fills me. I have to get rid of it. I'm not going to go to the bathroom because they are watching.

"Dad, I'm taking a walk, okay?"

"Yeah, sure hon," he says. He doesn't even ask where I'm going. I run up to my bedroom to get the money I have stashed and start the mile hike to Drug Emporium. As soon as I walk in the store I see a guy at the register. It's always so embarrassing. I need a box of 60. Who needs this many laxatives?

Walking home goes much faster because I'm filled with relief. Soon the salty potatoes and the fish and the guilt and everything else will be washed away. It's not good that today's Sunday, but, oh well.

Chapter 17

Guilt and More Guilt

After being up half of the night going to the bathroom, I thought I'd make it to school today. I have to wear loose jeans because my stomach is so bloated. Stop at the bathroom again.

Empty.

Barely making down the steps, I stop in the piano room because my muscles are cramping up in my thighs and calves. The pain brings tears to my eyes, but I deserve this. Anna must've heard me because now she is sitting next to me rubbing my legs. I don't have the strength to get off the floor.

"Jesus Christ, Lina. Not this shit again," Dad says to me. He thought I was better.

"Dad," Anna says in a reprimanding tone as she is rubbing my calves to help me with the cramping. My electrolyte balance is way off. I'm dehydrated.

Dad's brow furrows, and the lines in his forehead deepen. "I've got to go to work, I can't keep losing days," he says to us.

"Go to work, Dad. I'll stay here with her," Anna tells him. I'm messing up their day but am too sick to care about anything but making it to the bathroom and for my muscles to stop cramping.

"You have to go to school. You've missed enough school."

Dad's right. She missed a lot of days because of her epilepsy and just got her seizure medication right. She is actually taking it now.

"Okay, okay," she says and starts walking out of the piano room, eyes never leaving me.

I see the concern in her eyes. They turn a dark green when she is worried. "I'm fine," I say and try to get up from the floor. "Go on, Dad's right. You've missed enough school." Ever since we found out that she has epilepsy, the doctors have been testing her blood levels weekly. They check for the hormone prolactin and how much of the medication remains in her system so they can get her meds right. It took a while, but they figured out that Dilantin works for her and keeps the seizures under control. I guess Anna thought she was all better, because she began to refuse to take the meds. Then the seizures started again. Grand mal. Every day.

I had a talk with her a few weeks ago. I explained the importance of the medication. I explained how it takes a while to maintain a balance of it in her bloodstream and that's how it helps control the seizures. She's the only one out of the five of us that has medical problems. First, she was born with the blocked nasal passage, now this. I know she feels bad about herself. Her thinking was that if she just ignored it, it would go away. I talked to her for hours. I explained that getting epilepsy was not her fault. I tried to put a positive spin on it, telling her how lucky she is that there is medication to control it. Years back, there was nothing that they could do for someone with epilepsy. I researched it. They used to think that people with epilepsy were possessed by demons. I didn't tell her that, but I sure am glad that we weren't born in that time period. I think the conversation helped, because she has been taking her meds lately. It's been like this for months. Back and forth to the doctor. Back and forth to the hospital when she has a grand mal seizure and gets hurt. It makes me sad. I feel like an ass for making myself sick on purpose.

My right leg stiffens. My toes curl under and my thigh muscle tightens. This is why Penney didn't want to be friends with me anymore. The pain shoots a flashback to that day. She just left me there at the mall. I couldn't even walk around the mall with her because the bottoms of my feet hurt. I stayed in the mall bathroom for hours because I was scared that I wouldn't make it out of the mall without messing myself. The mall is four miles away. I would have never made the walk home. I finally got the guts to call Dad, and he came to get me. Penney doesn't see how fat I am. She just got mad at me. I try to stretch it out, but the cramping is unbearable. I start crying instead. Anna rushes back to me to massage my leg.

"I have to go to work," Dad says again, as if that will make this horrible scene go away. "Why the hell can't you just eat normally like the rest of the world?"

"I'm sorry," and I cry some more.

"Don't cry Lina, I'll help you," Anna soothes me.

"My legs hurt," I continue to blubber. I feel bad because Dad spent a lot of money sending me to counselors to help with my eating problem. All they want me to do is get fat. They think gaining weight is the solution to the problem. They talked about calories and three meals a day with snacks in between. If I eat that much, I'd commit suicide if I didn't explode first. They don't get it. I *need* to be empty. It's the only way I can survive.

"You can go ahead to school Anna. I'll be okay." I'll get through this. I just need some water. I know this will pass. Then I will be empty again and feel great.

"I'm not leaving you here like this. What if something happens?"

"Nothing is go–ah, oo, my leg," I grab my leg as the muscles contract.

"Try standing up and stretching it," Anna helps me to my feet. "There, is that helping?"

I lean on Anna's shoulder, and stretch out my calf. "Thanks."

"I have to go to work. I've lost too much time already," Dad grumbles. He has lost a lot of work lately between David not wanting to wake up in the morning and Anna having seizures. His hair has gone white since Mom left. He probably has a white hair for each day he missed of work.

"Go to work, we'll be okay," Anna tells him.

"Jesus Christ. It's getting later and later," he says as he glances at his watch. "Now I'm going to hit traffic. You'll both be losing another day of school." Dad glares at us. I'm disgusted with my own self, so I know how he feels. "I'll see you after work." Dad says as he is leaving the room. I haven't heard David yet this morning, so I guess he is ditching work again. "Anna, can you make sure Lucy and Carmen get on the bus?"

"Yeah, sure, don't worry, Dad," Anna says.

"Hope you feel better." Dad gives me a long, forlorn look. I don't even know how to feel better.

***

"Do people ever die of unrequited love? My heart is broken; the septum came crashing down. If the wall is fractured, can the heart function properly? The right-side pumps blood out to pick up oxygen, and the left side receives it back and sends it to the body. I would say she swims in my veins and the sadness has infected my body, but that would be incorrect. She swims in my arteries. She is in my arteries because she is in my heart, and the arteries take the blood from the heart and carry it through the body. The veins bring it back to the heart, and she is not coming back. Knowledge of the human anatomy is imperative, and this, along with my grief, never leaves me."

I found this written on a yellow legal pad that was sitting on Dad's desk. I went in there looking for a pen to do my homework so my whole day wouldn't be a loss. I never realized he was so bereft.

Now my heart contains the intrinsic knowledge of how people die from a broken heart.

Lies.

Betrayal.

Adultery.

Blame.

Guilt.

I looked in the mirror this morning and saw vacant eyes looking back at me. The eyes of a dead person.

I think of Dad and all he has done for me. I realize that love is not a contract, nor a piece of paper. It is the palette for the colors. It is the beautiful art we make by meticulously adding and mixing just the right amount of colors together and applying them to canvas with differing intensity and strokes to create something beautiful. That's what Dad does every day. My palette was destroyed. My colors all blended together to make a shit brown. Dad told me that in theory, all colors blended together make white and the absence of color is black. There are a lot of theories. In theory, once people take wedding vows, they are supposed to stay faithful and stay together all their days on this earth, no matter what.

Theories are just that, theories. I head to the bathroom again. There's nothing left in me. I think of the shit brown I've made of my life.

Anna's watching television. I tell her that I am going to bed. I try to sleep, but Dad's in my head. My mind keeps flashing back to that night that I tried to talk to him. I went into his studio when he was working and asked him if we could talk. Everyone was in bed already, everyone but me. He pulled out the black leather swivel chair next to his desk for me to sit in. I sat in it and looked at the floor. He always sees me as the big girl, but all of the sudden I felt so tiny and lost in that seat that my body barely filled. Dad pulled up the high stool that's kept in the corner of the room, the one he uses when he's painting and gets tired of standing and took a seat next to me. He put on the calmest fatherly face that he could muster. I could tell he was hoping that I wasn't going to tell him about girl problems or that I was pregnant.

He leaned toward me. "What's the matter, hon?"

"Dad, something's wrong with me," I chirped out, eyes fixed on the floor.

"What do you mean? I don't see anything wrong with you," he said, dismissing any type of problem. I guess he caught himself because he then immediately asked, "What do you think is wrong?"

I shrugged. "I don't know. Something is wrong with me. I can't stop eating." I spit it out, finally. Then, I cried like a big baby.

"Oh. Lina, you are growing. Your body is changing; it's normal. It's okay to eat when we are hungry," he told me. I guess he hoped this was helpful.

"But that's the problem, Dad. I eat when I'm not hungry and then can't stop." At that, he just sat there, looking at me like I was crazy.

"Do you want to talk to a doctor? We can find a doctor for you to talk to," he said to me after a few moments of awkward silence.

I couldn't look him in the eye. "I dunno," I said to him, because I don't know how to fix this.

"Don't worry hun, it will be okay. If you really feel like something is wrong, we'll go talk to a doctor."

"Okay. I love you Dad." I gave him a big hug. I come up to the bridge of Dad's nose now. I wished I could go back to the days when I sat on his knee while he sang "The Most Beautiful Girl" to me.

"I love you too," he said. "Do you feel better now?"

"Uh huh," I mumbled into Dad's shoulder.

"Okay then, up to bed, or you'll have another problem when you can't wake up for school in the morning." He nervously chuckled.

I went to bed that night with hope. Hope that someone could fix me, or at least explain why I couldn't stop eating.

Since that night, he has taken me to doctors and counselors. I know it costs him a lot of money. We don't have health insurance because he is self-employed. As I lay here in my bed, hoping the pain will go away, I realize that the pain is deeper than cramps. It's in my heart because I keep hurting the people who love me.

Chapter 18
Suicide Attempt?

It's been a long time since I've written. Mom got this apartment so I could move in with her. This was the great plan to help me with my problem. I missed her so much, and she kept blaming me for not wanting to move to Philly that I agreed to move in here with her. It's not like I had a real choice in the matter, they just made me feel like I had a choice. We live on the borderline of Plymouth and Norristown, so I had to change schools. I've no friends and don't fit in.

I thought having Mom all to myself would be great. I was so sick of Anna, Lucy, and Carmen not listening and telling me 'you're not my mother, I don't have to listen to you' that I couldn't wait to get out of there. No more responsibilities, no more waiting for the bathroom, no more Anna being jealous of everything I do. I get to be the only child.

It's not all it's cracked up to be. All of the messes are mine because there's no one else to blame. And there's no one to talk to. At least back home I had David, and Carmen is so darn cute, that I started to drag him out with me everywhere I went just for company since Penney ditched me. Well, almost everywhere. Not when I was meeting up with Dee to smoke, which I didn't do much anyway, because it gives me the munchies and I'm too close to my goal to stop now. I was four pounds from my next goal of 100 when we moved in here. One hundred is perfect. Then I will be light and strong enough to handle anything. Some days living here with Mom are okay because she works double shifts and I can sit here alone with my thoughts.

Today I pick a skirt to wear to hide my thighs. I know I've gained weight. I step on the scale in the bathroom. 108. I feel like I am going to die. I've gained four pounds since living here. I choose a light gray sweater and my brown boots since it's cold outside. I grab my blue jacket off the silver coat hanger stand by the door. I'm always cold lately.

"Lina, you wearing that to school?" Mom sarcastically questions.

I glare at her. She's always so judgmental. "Yeah, why?"

"Just wondering. Did you eat breakfast?"

"No, I'm running late." I need to get out of here as fast as possible. Dee said she'd meet me in the morning before school. Her brother, Clam (his real name is Alan, but everyone calls him Clam), is driving her over to my high school before school starts to sell me 30 Black Beauties. I need help curbing my appetite around Mom. She is always trying to stuff food into me. I have to get rid of these extra pounds. She watches my every move. If I don't eat, she gets offended. So, I eat dinner with her, and then get rid of it as soon as I can. I flush the toilet and run the water in the sink so she can't hear me. Then I brush my teeth and spray perfume. I have it down to a science, but it hasn't been working. I keep gaining weight.

"Bye, Mom. See you after school," I give her a kiss on the cheek.

"I'm working late tonight, make sure you have your key," she reminds me. I double-check my knapsack.

"Got it, see ya tonight."

I catch the bus right out front of the apartment complex. As I get on, I can feel the stares. I'm sure everyone is staring at my puffy face, or my fat calves. I move to the

Cristina Utti

back, well, third from the back; the cool kids take the back seats. I sit alone looking out the window, as if I am real interested in what's out there. From the corner of my eye, I see two girls pointing at me and smirking. They are preps, wearing collared shirts and shiny bows in their hair. It's obvious they try to look alike and dress alike. Immature if you ask me. I can't stand them, so I ignore them. My outfit looks stupid, but I'm too fat to wear anything else, and at least I'm not trying to look like other people.

I keep my focus on my goal. A perfect 100, not one ounce more. I want to do a water fast but can't get away with not eating while living with Snoopy Sniffer.

As soon as I get in the building, I head to the water fountain, pop two Black Beauties and wait for the buzz. First period is algebra. I'm in an accelerated class where I can work at my own speed. I started in this school in November, right after my fifteenth birthday. It's January and I'm almost finished the entire years' worth of work. I astonish myself with this because I was never good at math. Maybe I just didn't need someone breathing down my neck. I've learned algebra on my own. It's my favorite class because no one bothers me, and I don't have to talk to anyone. As I try to concentrate, I can feel my double chins.

"Can I use the restroom?" I ask Mr. Grey. He hands me the pass. I'm not like some of these girls who use the excuse that it's their time of the month and ask to go to the bathroom every single day. A lot of girls do that to the male teachers. I don't even remember the last time I had my period. I rush down the dreary brown tiled hall to the water fountain, pop a few more and then go use the bathroom, so it wouldn't be a lie to Mr. Grey. Hopefully, they will kick in before lunch.

At lunch I sit alone or with Rosalyn. I'm pretty sure she has a food problem too. I hate having to come to lunch. It feels like everyone is staring at me to see what I'm eating. My stomach growls.

Breaking Infinity

"Sounds like someone is hungry," Rosalyn jabs me in the ribs playfully.

I look to see what Mom packed. "Yeah, I guess." I know why she has been packing me lunch. To fatten me up. She hates that I am thinner than she was when she married Dad. For years, she told me she was only 117 lbs. when she got married. Well, ha! I have her beat! I'm hungry, and she packed my favorite, peanut butter and banana. I guess a few bites won't kill me.

I take a bite, chew thirty times, then another bite, then another. Before I know it, the entire sandwich is gone. Well, not gone. It's in my stomach. Making me fat. Another trip to the drugstore is due. The rest of my classes are a blur, my head clogged with planning how to get rid of this food. I get off the bus and instead of heading home, I turn to the right, and walk down New Hope Street to CVS. It's about a half-mile walk, but I need the exercise anyway. I have only the dollar Mom gave me to buy a snack or drink at lunch, so I'll have to swipe them.

I walk through the automatic doors feeling guilty as hell, but I have no choice. I have to get rid of that sandwich. Seven Black Beauties did nothing for me; I still ate lunch. I can't stand this food in my system. I feel fat cells bursting. I walk up and down the aisles, as if I'm a real shopper. As I walk down the aisle labeled Antacids/Laxatives, I check the big mirror hanging in the corner of the store. I look extra fat. I'm glad I wore my jacket this morning. It has big pockets.

The only size boxes they have here are 30 count and 90 count. I know 30 aren't enough; I ate the entire sandwich and some of Rosalyn's chips. So, I grab the 90 without even looking at it, and put it right in my pocket. Heart thumping and hands shaking, I put on an innocent face, making sure my eyes are wide with an innocent-like expression. I walk back toward the front of the store keeping my right hand in my right pocket to be sure the box is snug and will not fall out.

I know I can't walk out without buying something, so I use my dollar for a pack of Bubble Yum, hoping this makes me look like a regular customer, not a thief. When I get to the counter, I am careful not to move too quickly. My pocketbook is hanging off my left shoulder, and I made sure the dollar was still in my wallet when I was on the bus.

"Anything else?" The cashier asks me. He has brown tufts of hair falling around his slanted brown eyes and a pockmarked face. What does he even mean by that?

"Uh, no, that's it," I say, trying not to look guilty.

"That'll be twenty-five cents," he says. I hand him the dollar. When he gives me the change, my first instinct is to put it in my right pocket. I quickly transfer the coins from my right hand to my left, praying I don't look obvious.

"Thanks," I say and almost run out the front door. Cringing as I walk through the double doors, waiting for the beeper alarm for thieves to sound. Nothing. I made it! My heart feels like it will burst out of my chest. I'm not sure if it's from nerves or the pills I've been popping all day.

I walk into the apartment; almost forgetting that Mom's working late. I'm glad, I can eat all I want, get rid of it, and then take the laxatives. I make some pizza, eating it so fast that I don't even taste it. Then I have a bowl of frosted flakes, then two, then three. I search the cabinets…I take out the peanut butter, Nutella, strawberry preserves, hot fudge, and ice cream and make myself a three-scoop sundae.

I feel like I'm about to explode. I hurry to the bathroom to get rid of it because I have to clean up before Mom gets back. It never all comes out. I can feel my stomach still bulging out when I've vomited all I can. I open the box of laxatives and take 45, 15 at a time. That ought to do it. Then, I pop a few more Black Beauties so I have energy to do my homework.

Today was exhausting.

Three hours later, and I feel nothing. I take a few more of the little black pills. I thought I had more. There are only three left, so I take the rest of the laxatives. It takes two handfuls to swallow all of them, and it makes me feel nauseous. I need to put something in my stomach so I don't throw up and lose them.

I recheck the kitchen. Everything is cleaned up and put away. Mom will think I didn't eat dinner, then get on my case. I toast a piece of potato bread with American cheese, making sure to leave behind crumbs as evidence. I promise myself to stop eating after the open face sandwich but can't stop. I find the jar of hot fudge and eat it right from the jar. I have to stop. I can't throw up because I'll lose all of the pills I took, and I can't get anymore. I wash the spoon because it's gross eating right from the jar. I don't want Mom to see it. I pour a big glass of iced tea and slug down what's left of the pills from this morning.

* * *

It's dark when Mom gets home.

"Lina?" she calls. I hear her in the living room. I can't get out of the bathroom. She must see the light on in here from underneath the bathroom door. "Lina, I'm home." She always checks the kitchen to see if I ate. I hear her go in there, and I puke again. I flush the toilet and wipe out the white sink. "Hey, are you okay?" she asks me through the door.

"I'm sick," I tell her. Before I know it, she is behind me holding my hair up as I vomit into the toilet again. She rubs my back, like she did when I was small and didn't feel well. This makes me vomit some more. I look at the floor and see there's dry vomit on the pink shag rug that lies between the toilet and sink.

"You okay?" she asks. It's a stupid question. Of course I'm not okay or I wouldn't be here on the bathroom floor. I vomit again. I stand up and push her away so I can sit on the toilet.

"I'm fine, just sick," I tell her as I grab the trashcan to puke into.

"You want me to get you anything?" I shake my head and lean over the trashcan vomiting again. I try to stand up and fall back down, hitting my head on the toilet.

"*Oh Madonna*! Did you take something?" She grabs my shoulders and shakes me and looks in my eyes. "This isn't the flu. I've seen that look in David," she shakes her head back and forth and I vomit again. It's green fluid. "Lina, tell me what you took!"

"I'm, I'm," I can't make a sentence. She tries to help me to my feet, but I collapse on the floor. My legs are cramping up. My chest hurts.

"*Oh Madonna mia*! Lina, what did you take? *Cose c'e di spagliato?*" I push myself up, barely able to lift my head up enough to vomit over the seat and into the bowl.

Then, blackness.

* * *

"What happened to her?" Dad asks as he storms into the ICU. I don't want to hear them fight. I can't talk with this tube down my throat.

"I, I don't know. I got home from work and she was sick," Mom stammers. "They pumped her stomach. She took a bunch of pills."

"Pills? What kind of pills?" He demands answers, and she has none.

"I'm going to have to ask you to keep your voice down," said a man behind us holding a chart.

"Are you her doctor?" Dad asks him, just as loud as he has been yelling at Mom.

Breaking Infinity

"Yes, she is under my care."
"What is wrong with my daughter?"
"Perhaps a suicide attempt. She overdosed."
"Suicide? Why would she want to kill herself? Overdosed on what?"
"We found narcotics and laxatives in her system. We aren't sure what else she may have taken. We are still running tests. Let's go down the hall, there's a lounge where we can talk. Even though she is in a comatose state, she still may be able to hear us." I do hear them. I do know that they are here. I can't move. There are tubes all over me.

I look at the machine that tracks my heart rate. I watch the rise and fall of the red line; thirty-two beats a minute. Maybe I'm dying. "I'm not leaving her," Mom tells them.

"She was in your care! Where the hell did she get pills?" Dad says to her. I want to tell him that it's not her fault. It's my fault. I need to lose a few pounds. Mom runs out of the room and down the hall. I see her run past the nurses' station.

I scream after her, "I'm sorry, don't leave me," but no sound comes out.

PART THREE

1980

Chapter 1
The Looney Bin

They put me in Eugenia Hospital. It's not really a hospital; it's a nut house. The doctors told Dad that I'm lucky to be alive, but I don't feel lucky at all. Dad looked like he was about to cry when he dropped me off here. I know it must be costing him a ton of money. The rooms are nice, and the grounds are beautiful. If the place wasn't filled with nuts, you'd think it was a resort. I have no idea what I'm doing in this place. For example, my roommate, Sandra, really believes that Hall and Oates wrote the song "Maneater" for her. She solemnly swears that she knows them personally.

"C'mon girls, time for dinner," Charlene, our hall monitor, calls as she walks through the hallways. Charlene is about fifty years old, with a blonde bob and bright green eyes. She has the evening shift on our wing.

"Why bother? Probably serving us slop again," Sandra says as she sits on the end of her unmade bed, painting her toenails with blood red nail polish. Charlene happens to be right outside our door.

"You know the rules. And make that bed before you head to the cafeteria," Charlene commands. She isn't mean, just stern. I guess the girls here need that discipline. Not me. I know how to behave.

As we get in line, I notice they are serving spaghetti and meatballs and a small salad as an accompaniment. I'm glad. They know that I don't eat meat, so I can get away with just the salad today. They think that I'm some suicidal pill popper. They have no idea.

"You're not taking the pasta?" Sandra asks.

"Nah, you want it?"

"Sure, if you're sure you don't want it. I think they're trying to starve us in this damn place." I gladly give her my portion and my juice. I stick with water.

After dinner we go to our group sessions. I'm in a group with five others. There's Chloe, a coke addict, Roseanne, who got abused by her stepfather and started drinking at twelve years old to drown her pain, Katelynn, whose own father got her hooked on heroin, and Maryanne, who just joined us yesterday. She is angry at the world and grunts or curses if someone tries to talk to her, so I don't bother with her. And, of course, Sandra. She is here because she drove her parents crazy, staying out all night partying and sleeping with everyone in town.

I don't fit in here.

Group sessions are pretty stupid. I sit here and don't say anything. I'm not sure what to share with these people. They all have some kind of drug problem. I've got a problem with food. If I share that, I'll be laughed at. I've been here two weeks now. After group, I stick by the counselor's lounge. I learned by my fourth day here that I'd rather be with the adults. I help with the rounds at night, which gives me some extra privileges.

The woodsy setting of Eugenia reminds me of home. The counselors say it's okay for me to keep up with my running routine as long as the other patients don't know. So, I get up at 4:30 to run. Louise is always here at that time. She lets me out onto the grounds which gives me a half hour of freedom.

"Lina, we need you to talk to Sharon. She's been in her room crying. There's talk of her going AWOL," Gary tells me. He is one of our weekday evening counselors. The one all the girls go gaga over.

"Um, sure. Now?"

"As soon as possible. We can't have people going AWOL." His bluish-green eyes are full of concern.

"I'll try." I can see his six-pack under his t-shirt. He wears wire rim glasses, which make him look smart. If he trusts me, I'll do my best to help Sharon. "Where's her room?"

"Room 21, West Wing," Gary tells me while he looks over some charts. He looks up at me, "Thanks, Lina," he says in his deep, rough voice. My heart melts.

The West Wing is to the left and two hallways down from the counselor's lounge. After group, we have free time until 9 p.m. Most of the girls watch TV, play cards, or just go to their rooms until lights-out. My room is in the North Wing. The North Wing rooms are a bit larger, and we all have only one roommate, hence, my buddy Sandra. The West Wingers sleep four per room. I wonder how much Dad paid for me to be here and I feel bad all over again. I hope Sharon is alone in the room. I'm better at one-on-one conversations. As I walk toward the West Wing, I contemplate how to open a conversation with her. I've only spoken to her a few times, but the counselors seem to trust me to help the other kids. This isn't the first time they've asked for my assistance.

Sirens alarm. Red lights blinking. I freeze.

An announcement blares from the loudspeakers. "This is a lockdown! Everyone stay where you are." I'm stuck in a hall. I feel lost and am about to cry. The siren keeps shrieking. Gary comes running toward me.

"She went AWOL. Lina, cover the West Wing. Make sure no one moves!"

"Will do," I wipe my eyes and get myself together as I run down the hall to check on the girls.

"What's going on?" One of the girls asks me as I enter the West Wing.

"Someone went AWOL. Just relax, we must stay put 'til they do a head count." The girl in front of me is young, maybe twelve or thirteen. She starts to cry. I put my arms around her.

"I want to go home. I hate it here!" she tells me in between sobs.

"Me too," I tell her as I smooth her long brown hair to comfort her. I wonder what happened to her and why she is here. Lock down goes on for over an hour. By a bit after ten, everyone is back in their rooms.

"You believe that shit?" Sandra asks me.

"Believe what?" I ask, trying my best to ignore her, yet not be rude.

"Sharon ran off with Ray. They both went AWOL, where the hell have you been?"

"How'd you find that out?"

"I have my connections," she tells me in a cocky manner. And I believe her. I'm sure she has her ways of getting information and knows exactly what's going on in the boy's side of this looney bin.

"I don't even know why I'm here," I mumble to myself.

"Didn't you try to kill yourself or something? Obviously, something's wrong with you. You're so fuckin' skinny. What the hell are you on?"

"Nothin'," I say under my breath and cover my head with my blanket. I want to go home. Tomorrow I'm going to ask Gary when I can get the hell out of here. I hate talking to this sex fiend, hate that they watch me eat, and hate getting weighed in front of everyone every other morning. What is up with that? This is not helping me feel any better.

"Yeah, right," she snickers.

Chapter 2

Freedom

They finally let me out of the looney bin. I had to do 90 days and weigh 108 pounds before they set me free. That's a thirteen-pound weight gain, but I did it to get the hell out of that joint. I've missed months of 10th grade. Dad comes to get me because Mom moved to Florida when I fell into a coma. Thanks Mom.

Carmen, Lucy, and Anna are all happy to see me when I get home. Dave is upstairs, so I head up to say hi to him. I knock on his door. He opens it, grabs me and squeezes me so tight that I lose my breath for a minute. When he lets go, his eyes are wet.

"Jesus Christ, Lina, what the hell were you thinking? You scared the shit out of me. We almost lost you." I didn't realize it was that bad. The only people permitted to visit in the looney bin were parents, so the only visitor I had from the outside world was Dad. I look at Dave and start crying. I don't know what the heck is wrong with me lately. Every little thing makes me cry.

"I'm sorry, I didn't mean to. I wasn't trying to kill myself. They're all nuts," I laugh through the tears.

"I knew you weren't. I knew it the whole time," he says and hugs me again. I sure missed him. He's the only one I can talk to since I lost Penney. "I think Dad's getting pizza for dinner. Are you gonna eat?"

I rub my belly, "I sure am, I'm starving." It's a big fat lie, but I will try my best to eat to make him see that I'm okay now.

I take the ride to Eliano's with Dad to pick up the pizza. "How are you feeling hon?" he asks me while he drives down Ridge Pike.

"I'm good, Dad," I tell him, smiling.

"That's good. So, you're all better now?"

"Yep, all better. Love you Dad."

"I love you too," I almost faint when he says this. I know he loves me because he is always here for me and spent tons of money to get me better, but he never ever says those three little words. "I'm glad you're home. We all missed you."

"I'm glad I'm home, too," I say, sensing his sadness. "I missed everyone so much." I want to tell him about the looney bin, but that would make him feel worse for wasting all of that money.

"You look good," he says. That means I look fat.

"Thanks," I try to sound sincere as I evaluate my enormous thighs. We pick up the pizzas and drive home in silence.

The same old shenanigans start when we get home.

"That's not fair that Dad bought mushroom pizza for you. No one else likes mushrooms," Anna claims.

"Anna!" Dad gives her a mean look.

"Well, it's true. You know we don't like mushrooms and she isn't even going to eat!"

"I got a plain one too," Dad tells her.

"Yeah, David and Carmen took it all before I even got in the kitchen. It's not fair!"

"You can take the mushrooms off." He looks over at me. I look at specks on the floor.

"You didn't have to get mushroom just for me, Dad." He already spent enough money on me.

"It's okay. Anna, cut it out, that's enough," he shoots Anna a glare.

She slumps in her seat. "Still not fair."

"I am going to eat it Anna. See? I'm on my second piece," I tell her and grab another slice. "Not my fault the boys are pigs and ate the plain one. You always get to eat all of the ice cream, so shut up."

I grab the soda and pour a tall glass. I can feel everyone's eyes on me, except Carmen. I drink it down in a few gulps and then start in on the second slice. I feel Dad's eyes on me.

After everyone is finished, the kids do their chores, and everyone retreats to their comfort zones. Anna, Lucy and Carmen go into the living room to watch television. Dave goes to his room. I drink another glass of soda. Dad pretends not to see.

"I'm fine Dad," I assure him. "I'm going up to unpack. Thanks for the pizza," I smile and give him a hug.

"You sure you're okay? You can talk to me," he holds me a few seconds longer than usual.

"I'm fine Dad, really."

He heads into his studio to work, and I head up the steps. My stomach hurts so badly from all of the soda and pizza that it's coming up on me already. I'm glad David's music is loud.

"Hey, turn that down!" I hear Dad yell through the door. I flush the toilet and run the faucet. The music stopped. I look in the mirror. My eyes are red, and my glands feel swollen.

I stand by the door for a minute to listen, not quite sure what I'm listening for. I open it and come face to face with Dad. I've failed him again.

I go to my room and close my door behind me. I wish David would turn his music back up and drown the sounds of my sadness.

Chapter 3
Hilastrophy Catastrophe

I thought things would change when I got home a few months ago. I'm learning not much ever changes. I'm still battling this eating thing, but Dad thinks I'm better. Lately, I haven't been the main concern and I like it like that. My sixteenth birthday was yesterday. Anna had a grand mal seizure and David came home drunk. Happy birthday.

Dad has a daily battle with Anna to take her meds. She should know better by now; she will be fourteen years old at the end of this month. Her seizures have lessened a little. Now she has them a few times a week instead of every day. Usually when she skips her meds. David refuses to go to school anymore, which is stupid if you ask me, since he is a senior. Dad finally gave in and signed the papers two days ago to let him quit. Now he works with Dad instead of going to school. I'm just glad the fighting stopped.

"Hey Lina, you mind watching the kids tonight?" Dad asks me.

"Is it okay for Penney to sleep over?" We've been talking again since I got home from the looney bin. She thinks I'm all better now too.

"Sure, I shouldn't be too late. Uncle Johnny and I are going out for a bit."

"No problem, Dad." Of course, Dave never has to babysit.

While I'm making scrambled egg and sausage sandwiches for the kids for dinner, David comes in through the back door. He looks wasted.

"Yo, watcha cookin'?" he asks, slurring.

"Eggs, want some? Looks like you should eat," I tell him. I think he's been drinking, probably on an empty stomach. He's been drinking a lot lately. I'm worried about him.

"Nah man, headin' out. Just stopped in to get something. Catch ya later," and he heads down the basement. I hear the outside basement door slam a few minutes later.

When Penney gets here, we hang out in the living room and watch movies with the kids. I make some popcorn and let them eat in the living room because they are behaving. Anna grabs herself a bowl of ice cream. It's mint chocolate chip, her favorite. Like I said, some things never change. I don't mind. Carmen and Lucy see her, but don't say anything. They are content with their popcorn. As long as she doesn't have a seizure on my watch, and they all get to bed at a decent time, it's fine with me.

By the time "Peter Pan" is over, David walks into the living room with Brandon and Callan trailing right behind him. I didn't even hear them come in. He knew Dad was going out tonight. They must've come in through the basement. I ignore them because I'm angry that he never has to watch the kids. They laugh and carry on, opening and closing the fridge and cabinets, and then head back down the basement. As soon as the kids go upstairs, I'm going down there to see what they are up to.

"Thank God they are finally in bed!" Penney exclaims. "Now we can chill."

"Yeah," I agree. "Let's head down to see what they are up to." As we head down the basement steps, I can smell the weed and alcohol. Ronnie is here too. David told me he wants to go out with me. I'm not interested in the least.

He is bony, with shoulder length black greasy hair. No thank you.

"Hey, what's up guys?"

"Just chillin'," says Ronnie. "Want a beer?"

"Yeah, sure." I take the can of Bud that he offers me. I only had a banana today, so I can manage the 145 calories in one can of beer. At least I'll get a buzz out of it along with the calories.

"Want one?" I ask Penney.

"Nah, I'm cool. Let's smoke." She takes out her bowl.

Hours later, everyone is gone except David, Penney, and me, of course, because we live here, and Penney is spending the night. We've been drinking and smoking for hours and can't stop laughing. I hope Dad stays out until this stuff wears off.

"Hey, we better clean this mess up before Dad gets home," I say as I'm picking up the beer cans and bottles that are on the floor and the wooden tables. Penney opens the outside basement door.

"Yeah, let's air this place out."

"Good idea," I say, and start cracking up again. She sees me laughing and she starts. It's contagious. David starts laughing too.

"Ya know what's really funny?" he asks us.

"What?" Penney and I say in unison.

"That I slipped you guys some acid," and he laughs harder than ever.

"What?" Penney and I look at each other and start laughing again. I wonder if he is serious, or just trying to pull a fast one.

After we clean up the basement, we head up to my room. We're stuck on laughing about everything, for hours. The hilastrophy catastrophe continues until daylight. When we hear Dad get home, we try to be quiet, muffling our laughter under the covers. When he peeks in the bedroom, we hold our breath and pretend that we are asleep. He stayed out all night, and we were awake all night to know it. He has been doing this a lot. He brings home donuts early some mornings, acting like he just went out to get them. He stays on the phone talking to someone into the late hours of the night. I don't care, really. As soon as we hear him go down the steps, we start laughing again.

Chapter 4
The Big Move

Even though the day of my sixteenth birthday was ruined, the weekend made up for it. Now back to reality. As I'm telling the kids to get up for school, I hear Dad and David arguing.

"C'mon, you're making me late," Dad yells down the basement steps to David.

"Shut the fuck up. I'm getting ready," he says back to Dad. He must be hung over or something. Dad does his best to ignore his foul language. If I was Dad and David talked to me like that, I'd beat the crap out of him. I'm in the kitchen pretending that I don't hear any of this. I'm making strawberry oatmeal for Carmen and Anna. Lucy is eating Rice Krispies.

Dad's yelling at him from the top of the basement steps. "Let's go. I'm leaving in five minutes with or without you." I don't know how Dad stands it. David makes him late for work every day. I would've fired him by now.

"I'll be right up asshole," Dave yells through the basement door. Okay, that's it. I've had enough of this disrespect. My blood is boiling now. He has no right to talk to Dad like that.

"You're the asshole!" I scream at David. I slam the basement door in his face just as he is about to open it.

"What the fuck!" he yells. He holds his bleeding nose and chases me down the foyer and up the steps. He grabs my leg, and I go tumbling down, landing on the cold tile floor. The two marble busts that sit upon podiums on each side of the front door are wobbling. I try to get up before one comes crashing down on my head.

"What the hell is going on?" Dad yells as he storms down the foyer. He grabs a hold of the statue bust the moment before it topples off the podium and glares at me squirming on the floor. I don't hear what David is saying to him, everything is fuzzy. I pick myself up off the floor, holding my hand to the back of my head, checking to see if it's bleeding.

"Get the hell out of my house!" Dad screams at me. I stare at him to be sure he is talking to me and not to David. He is glaring at *me*. I was sticking up for him! I run up the steps to my room and slam the door. I grab every bit of clothing I can and stuff them into my backpack. I throw my backpack over my shoulder, grab my guitar, my Christmas present from Dad last year, and run down the steps and out the front door.

I'm never coming back here.

Chapter 5
The Answer Found

I spent Christmas with Scott and New Year's Eve at a party with Dee. Clam plays guitar in a band. He's giving me lessons when he can. Because I can read music, I can play the treble clef on the guitar strings. It's not rocket science. Each string is a letter, and each fret is the next note. The first song I learned was "Angie" by the Rolling Stones. I'm no good at chords, that's what Clam's teaching me.

I haven't talked to Dad or David since I left in November. I should have known Dave would be at the party because we have the same friends. It was cool though; we talked. Dave said he was sorry about what happened, and that I should come home. I'm not angry with him anymore. Dad told me to get the hell out, so I left. He said Dad realizes that I'm okay because I haven't missed a day of school since that day I ran out of the house. Ran, then walked all the way to Hector Street in Conshohocken with all of my stuff. I spent the night at Dee's house, and the next day she introduced me to her brother's friend, Scott. Scott has his own place and said I could stay with him for a while. Dave said Dad figured I was staying with Dee and would come home when I settled down. He has enough on his plate with Lucy leaving. Dave said she went to see Mom for Christmas and decided to stay there, in Florida. Maybe too many bad memories at home for her. I know Mom will

Cristina Utti

help her. One thing Mom doesn't do is live in denial. I told Dave not to tell Dad that I'm living with a guy. I promise I'll give Dad a call soon so he doesn't worry.

Living here with Scott has been okay. Everything in this apartment is dark and brown. He has weird quirks. For instance, when I put the dishes away, he gets angry if I put the cups back in the cabinet right side up. The only music we listen to is what he likes. I knew he liked me when I met him, so I played it up. Really, I didn't know where to go. He is the only person I know that has his or her own apartment. Everyone at school thinks it's pretty cool that I don't live with my parents anymore. I think it stinks.

The most important thing I've learned while being on my own is how to get what I want. I pretend I like him and make out with him. He pushed me to do more stuff with him, and I did it because I feel guilty living here for free. He's the first person. It's not all it's cracked up to be. I guess if I really did like him that way, I wouldn't feel so disgusted about it. If I were good at pretending, I'd pretend to be his girlfriend, then it wouldn't be so bad. But I'm not. The only reason I stay is because he deals meth.

The answer to all my problems.

The first time he gave me a line of it, I was scared. Now, it's the greatest thing ever. I don't have to worry about my eating problem, because as long as I'm doing this stuff, I'm not hungry. And it gives me so much energy that I keep the place spotless for him, go to school, work a few nights a week at Burger King, and feel nothing emotionally when he wants sex. I'm a steady 105. No one pushing food down my throat. Five more pounds to go.

I decided this morning as soon as my eyes opened that I have to leave. I can't fake it anymore. Pretending I like him is just too gross.

He's usually not home when I get in from school. Today's no different. I write him a note to thank him for everything, letting me live here, etc., and pack my bags which takes all of fifteen minutes. Dee introduced me to Patty, who introduced me to Liz. I have been copping meth off of Liz because I didn't want to feel like I owe Scott any more than what I do for living here. Actually, that's a lie. That's what I told Patty. It's because I don't want my friends to know how much of the stuff I'm actually doing. Scott gives me meth, and I get more from Liz, and then I get even more from Joey (a friend who I'm kind of dating) too. That's why I got the job. I need money.

Liz has two little girls and told me I could live with her if I helped her out with the kids. That's a good deal since I have plenty of experience. Plus, she has a constant supply. I grab my guitar, my leather knapsack that is filled with my clothes, and my backpack of schoolbooks. No goodbyes.

As I'm walking, it hits me. One thing I never considered was how I'm going to get to school from Liz's house. She lives in Norristown. I'll quit school before I go back to Norristown High School. I leave Scott's and walk across town from West 10th Ave. to East 3rd, to Joey's. I walk the three steps up to his front door. There is a screen door, so I open it. Timidly, I knock on the storm door.

"Hi, is Joey home?" I ask his uncle, who answers the door. I try to sound cute, but I probably look like a vagabond with my guitar and backpack. I'm not even sure why I took the guitar when I left home. I guess because Dad gave it to me, and I couldn't bear to leave it behind. I don't even play well.

"Sure, come on in," he opens the door. The house is dark, even though it is the middle of a bright sunny day. "Joey, you have company!" he yells up the steps. I put the backpack down because it's getting heavy, then just stand here wondering what to do with my hands. I put the guitar down, and then I pick it up. I adjust the leather strap of my backpack on my shoulder. Joey comes running down the steps.

"Yo, Lina. What's up?"

"You busy?"

"Nah," he says and looks at the worn beige carpet under his feet. I know he likes me and I kind of like him too. I mean, he's okay as a friend, and nice to kiss, but I don't see myself going off into the blue yonder with him like in the fairy tales. I really don't know what else to do, so here I am. He has beautiful big round brown eyes that I could look into for hours, and thick, dark curly hair. Maybe I could actually fall in love with him if I didn't hate myself so much.

"Can we sit out on the step?"

"Sure," he opens the door for me. "It's a bit nippy out here. What's up?"

"Oh, Joey, I just don't know what to do." My eyes fill uncontrollably. "I have nowhere to live. I can't live with Scott anymore because he wants me to be his girlfriend, and I'm not going back home since Dad told me to get out."

"What do you mean?" he looks at me with those big warm eyes. All of my fears evaporate, just for a moment in time.

"Well, you know I can't go home, right?"

"I guess," he shrugs, confused. I thought he'd understand. There must be a reason why he lives with his uncle instead of his parents. He never talked about it, so I never brought it up.

"And I don't like Scott like that. I had to get outta there. So, I left." He sits here, waiting for more. He moves closer to me after I tell him that I don't like Scott. Before I know it, he is holding my hand. His hand is warm and calloused from his work. He smells like pine, which reminds me of home. The good old days. I draw it all in. "So, I was gonna go live with Liz and watch her kids and stuff, but then I can't get to school from there." I'm talking a mile a minute, trying to get it all out. My words all run together. "So, now I don't know what to do, or where to go."

"Want me to ask Uncle Jimmy if you can stay here?" He asks, just like that. Likes it's no big deal.

"I don't know. You think he'll get mad? Do you guys have room? I'll pay rent, I have a job, ya know." This all comes out in one long breath.

"Stay here, okay? I'm gonna go ask. Be right back." He stands up and opens the screen door.

"Wait a minute," I grab his arm as he is getting up. "What if he gets mad at me?"

"Just chill, okay? I'll be right back, he's cool."

Yeah, chill. I'll sit out here and freeze. I'm not lowering myself and going back home. I clean my nails. I run my fingers through the back of my hair, trying to get the knots out. I look through my backpack as if I'm looking for something. My nerves are shot. Joey shoots back through the door so quickly that I jump off the step.

"Uncle Jimmy said it's fine! You can have the extra bedroom. Thirty-five a week, is that okay?"

"Really?" I think he's kidding. Then I look in his eyes and know it's true. "Oh Joey, thank you." I give him a great big hug. His shoulders are broad, and he's strong because he does roofing. He holds me and I feel safe, the safest I've felt since Mom left.

"Come on in and talk to him, then I'll show you the room."

Chapter 6
New Horizons

Joey treated me out to dinner Saturday night for Valentine's Day since it landed on a Monday this year and I have to work after school today. It was the first time a guy ever treated me to dinner. I made sure to order a salad, eat slowly, and drink lots of water. We had a real nice time.

Things run pretty smooth around here. I get up and go to school, and Joey and his uncle go to work. Joey graduated three years ago and has been working with his uncle ever since. We're all out of the house by 7 a.m. I work nights and hang out with Patty and Dee the nights I don't work, so I'm not here too often. And for the past six weeks that I've been here, I've paid my rent on time. I'm getting antsy though. I don't have to be at Burger King until 7 p.m. tonight, and Joey isn't home from work yet, so I head over Dee's. Her dad is hardly ever home.

I knock and walk in. Even if her dad is here, he doesn't mind if I just walk in. He isn't here. Dee is in the living room cutting stuff up.

She looks up at me. "Want a line?" she asks.

"Sure," I say, but not really sure. I've been doing too much of this lately. I'm only doing it because it helps my eating problem. I can't be binging while living with other people. I grab a dollar bill from my pocket, roll it up into a makeshift straw, and sniff the stuff up through my right nostril. It burns.

"What the heck are you doing with all this stuff?"

"Sellin' it. Want to help? I'll give you a cut."

"Sure, I guess. I need money to pay my rent and stuff." Sounds like a good idea to me. I just don't want to get busted. I'm glad I'm only sixteen.

"Well, here," she hands me a razor. "Help me cut this stuff up into dime bags." We sit there and divide it into small bags.

"Where do you sell it?"

"Mostly school," she tells me. That makes sense because last year she was selling pills. When I met her, she was a bit overweight, not fat. She's just a big girl. She's lost a lot of weight in the past year. I guess her dad doesn't hawk over her eating habits like my family did when I was there. Her house is a lot smaller than mine, well, Dad's. Dee lives in a row home, but her Dad works a lot too.

"I'm not taking it to school." That's too risky. I don't have the guts for that.

"Okay. Do you still hang out at the park?"

The park is two blocks from Joey's uncle's house. "Yeah, Joey and I hang out there sometimes."

"Can sell a ton there."

"I don't have money to give you for it."

"Just take about ten of them, sell 'em for ten bucks each. They cost me about five a piece. Give me seventy, keep thirty." I contemplate this for a minute. Sounds like a good deal. That practically pays my rent and leaves me my paycheck to spend as I want.

"Okay, when do you want the money by?"

"How 'bout by Friday? Weekends are big, give me the money by then and I'll get more." Today is Tuesday, so that gives me four days.

"I'll try. If I can't get rid of it, I'll just give it back to you." The fear of having all of this on me runs through my veins. My pulse races.

"Good enough." We hang out for a while, but I have to get up and move. I head back to Joey's. I need to walk. Nervously, I keep the stuff in the front pocket of my jeans. Joey's been working long hours lately. When he gets home, I tell him about the deal I made with Dee.

"I'll get rid of it at work no problem, if you want," he offers. I guess a lot of roofers do this stuff.

I'm not sure how this will work, because I'll have to give him a cut for helping me. "Yeah, sure," I give him five bags. He gives me fifty bucks. I'm glad to be rid of them.

"Well, better get some homework done. I'm working every night after school the rest of the week." I head up the creaky wooden steps to my room. It's burning a hole in my pocket, and I can't concentrate. I take out one of the small bags and sniff a bit. I don't want it to look short. I have to get rid of this stuff. This was a bad idea. At least I'm awake enough to get my homework finished.

* * *

My shifts at Burger King are the only place I see Penney anymore. We hang out with different crowds now. Most of the people that work there are from school. Easily enough, I'm able to unload four of the baggies at work. I finished one myself. Short ten bucks now. It's not the best thing in the world, but it's cheaper than buying laxatives, and it's keeping my eating in check.

Friday after school, I head back to Dee's house to give her the money like I promised. Clam and I go down the basement and play guitar for a bit. And make out. And do some stuff. He is not even my type, whatever that is. He is taller than me, which I like. His hair is blonde and straight, like Dee's. His wallet is attached to a chain that attaches to a belt loop of his jeans. I never understood this. How much money can be in there to have to keep it chained to your clothes? I know he likes me because he always wants to spend time with me. That's why he gives me guitar lessons. I'm not sure how I feel about kissing him, or if this is cheating on Joey.

"Want to take a ride with us?"

"Yeah, sure. Where we goin'?"

"Headed to Keith's to get some for the weekend."

All of a sudden, I get a wave of consciousness. Maybe I shouldn't have kissed Clam. "Sure, let me just call Joey." Things are getting a bit serious with Joey and me, so I give him a call to let him know I'll be home later. I feel a bit guilty for making out with Clam, but it's not like I have a ring on my finger.

Keith lives at home with his mom and two brothers. It pisses me off that he deals drugs out of his mother's house. I mean, I'm into it now too, but I wouldn't do this out of Dad's house, and Dee doesn't have people stopping by her house to get stuff. You have to draw the line somewhere. I decided to reinvest the twenty I made and add twenty more. Dee and I split what we get. It's better this way. Now I won't have to owe her money back.

Chapter 7
The Standing Ovation

Within weeks, I'm making over a hundred easy and have my own connection with Keith.

I don't need to go there with Dee anymore. I'm in with the bigwigs now. And Joey said I can borrow his truck whenever I need it.

The first place I drive is home.

I pull into the driveway, proud of myself. I want to throw it in Dad's face that I don't need him, that I'm doing great since I left.

He isn't home.

"Lina's home!" Carmen yells as he opens the back door. I grab him up in a hug, taking in his little boy smell. I can't believe how tall he is.

"I missed you," I say into his hair. Anna comes strolling in. She looks older, her face no longer has the baby curves. Her thick brown wavy hair is longer. Her body is shaped more womanly than mine will ever be. It feels like I've been gone for years.

"Hi Anna," I say and give her a hug. She's restrained at first and then relaxes into my arms. "I missed you. How've you been feeling?"

"Good," she mumbles. She hates talking about her epilepsy, but I don't know what else to say to her; we never had too much in common.

"You taking your meds? Still giving Dad a hard time?"

"Nah, I'm taking 'em."

"She hasn't had a seizure in a month," Carmen chimes in.

"Shut up, stupid," Anna snaps back. I laugh. It feels good to be home.

"That's enough you two. Where's David?"

"Downstairs with his band, but he left too," Carmen says.

"His band? What do you mean he left?" I wonder who he is jamming with now. I go to the basement door, that dumb door that got me thrown out of here, and yell down the steps. Carmen tags along right behind me.

He is chock full of information. "Moved out, right after you did, but Dad lets him use the garage for his band."

"Dave, I'm home." As I head down, he is running up.

"Lina," he grabs me and gives me a great big brother hug. It feels good to be held by him. Even when we are apart, we are never really apart. It feels like our souls are one, and when we hug everything meshes together. This is what love feels like. I love Carmen, Lucy, and Anna too, but it's not the same. Maybe this is how they feel about me, since I'm older than them. Dave smells the same; lingering Newport cigarette smell and iced-tea breath. He drinks it by the gallon, especially when he is writing. It's a relief not to smell alcohol.

"Where've ya been, man?" he asks. "I asked around for you when I heard you left Scott's."

"Oh, here and there." He lets me go and looks at me, eyeing me up and down. "You're too damn skinny. You doin' okay?"

"Yeah, I'm good." I hold back a smile because that's a compliment. I see some faces in the basement that I don't know and suddenly feel like an intruder.

"You guys jammin'?"

"Yeah, just goin' over some new music we wrote. Well, that I wrote," Dave tells me. "I'm actually playing it in the talent show tonight. Imagine that," he beams.

"The talent show at school? How are you going to do that when you don't even go there anymore?" I asked, perplexed.

Smiling, he points at the band. "They do."

I'm excited for him, but don't want to stay long. I'm always on edge lately. "Cool, maybe we can catch up when I get back."

"Get back? You just got here," he says disappointedly. "I got my own crib now, won't be hanging around all night. Can't you hang out a while?"

"You can't leave, Lina," Carmen says from the top of the steps. I should have known he was still right behind me. "You just got here." I feel twinges of guilt when he says this. I've been so caught up with my friends, school, and work, that I didn't realize how much time passed since I'd seen everyone and how much I've missed them.

"I'm not leaving silly. I'm taking you guys for a ride. How'd you like to go to Dairy Queen?" I knew this would get Anna. She can't resist that invite.

"You got some wheels?" Dave asks, surprised.

"Anna," Carmen runs off yelling for Anna. "Lina's taking us to Dairy Queen."

"Yeah, a friend's. See you when we get back?"

"Definitely. Hang out with us for a while. We're actually not that bad." His eyes sparkle when he tells me this and I'm happy for him. He's glowing. His inner joy emanates throughout his whole being, and the electricity is contagious. "We've been playing some gigs on weekends too."

"Wow, that's cool. I won't be long. I just want to treat the kids." As soon as I open the basement door and see the bathroom door across the foyer, I start getting itchy. I don't want to eat ice cream because I'm finally getting a grip and have gone a whole week without a binge. If I eat it, I'll risk everything. The little baggie in my pocket calls; I go in the bathroom to answer.

The talent show is at seven, so I go back to Joey's to ask him if he wants to go. When we get to school, the parking lot is packed. We maneuver our way to the front of the auditorium to get seats close to the stage so I can see David when he comes on. The first act is some girl tap dancing. She's actually not bad. I'm not too surprised that I've never seen her before in my life. The second act is two guys from the football team doing a comedy act. The only thing funny is how stupid they are. Dave and his band are on next. Maria Torrellini introduces the band, Sideways Eight. Dave opens with a short intro on the piano. There are two guitar players, a drummer, and a bass player on stage besides Dave and Maria. She does back-up vocals. Callan is up there turning the pages of sheet music as Dave plays. They do a cover of a Van Halen song. After the clapping ceases, the band leaves the stage. Dave sits there at the piano.

"The next song is an original I wrote," he says into the mic that's in the stand to his right. "It's called 'Travel On.'" I'm shocked. I never thought he had the guts to play all by himself up there.

When he begins to sing, the lyrics are difficult to understand. This makes me nervous for him. Moving into the next bridge, his voice becomes crisp and clear. The audience is silent. I'm not sure if this is good or bad. He ends with a few bars without lyrics. When the music stops, the clapping starts. As if in a dream, I look around at all of the rising bodies, and rise myself as I continue to clap. Everybody in the auditorium is out of their seat, clapping and clapping.

Looking around with glee, I elbow the guy next to me, "That's my brother." I tell the kids behind me, "That's my brother up there!" I want to yell it to the world.

Chapter 8
The Times They Are A Changin'

A few more weeks until school lets out. I'm almost through the year, despite everything. I get in the house and run up the steps to change from my jeans into shorts and a half shirt because the day got hotter and hotter since I left for school this morning. Plus, I'd never wear shorts to school. It's not cool. Only the weirdos wear shorts to school. I throw on my cut-offs and my Clearwater Beach belly shirt as fast as I can so I can get out of here before Joey and his Uncle Jimmy get home from work. I dash back down the steps, whip open the front door, and almost slam right into him. Shit.

He is covered with asphalt. "Hey, slow down. Where are you going?" Joey asks. "Headed to Keith's. I'll be back in a bit." I give him a peck on the cheek. He's getting way too smothering lately. Just because it's Friday doesn't mean I have to hang out with him all night.

"What the hell, Lina? Why you always up at his house?"
"Oh, just chill, will ya? I'll be back."
"How about I give you a ride there?" he offers.

I'd take him up on this because even though it's easy to hitch a ride, I'm kind of tired tonight, but then he would want to hang out. I don't feel like arguing with him right now with his uncle in the living room about ten feet away. "C'mon Joey. You know it's not like that. You can't, ya know?" He knows Keith's got too much going on in that house to bring strangers by. He's getting real paranoid.

"Yeah, whatever," his big brown eyes droop like a sad puppy.

"Awe, c'mon, don't be like that. I'll be home soon."

"No, you won't. Don't even tell me that anymore 'cause you're never right back."

"Look, I gotta go. People are waiting on me. Catch you later, ok?" I head out the door without looking back so he doesn't kill me with those eyes. I wish I loved him, I really do, but I don't know how.

Two rides got me to Keith's house. The place looks abandoned. I don't know what's up with his mom, but she's never here. I knock on the front door. No answer. Maybe Joey was right. I shouldn't have come over here. I peek in the window. I can make out the couch, loveseat, and coffee table, but that's it. It's dark in there. I knock again louder. I try the doorknob and the door opens.

"Keith, you home?" I call through the living room up the steps.

"Up here, c'mon up," he calls through his bedroom door. I turn on the light at the bottom of the steps and head up the stairs.

"Did you know the front door was unlocked?" He is at the top of the staircase, waiting for me. He looks dumbfounded. "That's not too safe, considering." I sure as hell would not leave the door unlocked.

"Oh, I must've forgot to lock it when I got back," he answers distractedly.

"Whatcha doin'?" I ask as we enter his bedroom.

"Trying to get in touch with Barry. Want to watch a movie?"

"Not sure if I have time for a whole movie," I ease back on his bed and lean against the wall. His arm comes around me and it feels good. "I told Joey I wouldn't be too long, so I'll have to get back soon." I fidget back to the edge of the bed. I like him as a friend, nothing more, plus I guess Joey and I are together, whatever that means.

"No problem," he mumbles. He slides to the edge of the bed near the nightstand and cuts out some lines. He offers some to me.

"Nah, I'm good," I tell him because I know if I do some now, I'll want more, and I'm broke. I only have twenty dollars. Better off not even getting started until I get back to Conshohocken. "I get paid tomorrow."

"You know you don't have to give me money, Lina," he says. Yeah, I know better. I've been through this with Scott. If they don't want money, they want sex.

"I'm good, really. I just wanted to see you and need to pick some up for someone." Constant lies come out of my mouth. It's embarrassing all the money I spend on this shit, but I get paid Friday. "We still going halfers tomorrow?"

"That's the plan," he tells me between sniffs.

"Okay, cool. Can you pick me up?"

"Yeah, sure. What time?"

"Is noon okay?"

"Perfect," he says as he pushes his jet-black hair out of his eyes. His eyes are the opposite of Joey's. Keith's are bluish gray. I don't look in his eyes too long, or he may get the wrong idea, or worse, I'll get sucked into him. With this I settle my head on his shoulder. I'm proud of myself. I haven't given in to temptation. For now.

Chapter 9
The Big Bang

Dee offers me a ride to Keith's house after school. It's her last day of school forever, since she's a senior. This makes me sad because I don't know what I'll do next year in school. All of my friends graduated this year. I'm proud of myself that I made it through the year with very few absences and decent grades while living on my own.

As her long blonde hair blows in the warm summer air that flows in through her window, she asks me, "So are you going to senior week?"

"Nah, I have to work." The truth is I have no money. I never have enough money.

"You sure? It'll be a blast. We're heading down tonight," she tries to cajole me into going.

"Yeah, I didn't request off. Plus, I'm trying to save money." A big, fat lie. All I do is spend money.

"Alright, I'll catch up with you next week when we get back." She gives me a quick hug. I'm happy for her; she made it out of school alive. Me, I have another dreadful year to go.

"Have fun, see you next week." I hop out of her jalopy and walk down the block to Keith's. If I come here first before going back to Joey's, then I don't have to answer endless questions. As I'm walking up the sidewalk to his front door, I notice a guy I've never seen before knocking at

Cristina Utti

Keith's front door. His jeans are hanging off of his bones. His hair is matted and long, and his clothes are dirty. Approaching with caution, I stay a few feet behind him.

Keith opens the door. "What's up guys? Come on upstairs." I'm getting bad vibes from this dude. They head up the steps and I follow.

"Be right there, I have to use the bathroom." I head for the bathroom across the hall from his bedroom. I actually do need to use the bathroom; I haven't gone since lunchtime at school.

"No prob, you know where it is," he says as they walk into the bedroom and shut the door.

We are the only people in the house. That long-haired dude gives me a bad feeling. I usually don't feel this way toward new people. I give everyone the benefit of the doubt unless they prove otherwise. I wouldn't want anyone prejudging me, so I try not to condemn others before I really know them. Nevertheless, for some reason, I don't like him. Maybe if I take long enough, he'll get his shit and leave. I look in the mirror above the sink. I hop on the scale. A lovely 102 registers after it wiggles back and forth for a few moments. Two more pounds to go. I reach into my purse and fish out my hairbrush and begin to brush my hair, which is a chore. After I get through the knots in the back of my head, I flip my head over and give it fifty strokes to help the shine. I flip it back over and look in the mirror. It's all puffy. This had to take at least ten minutes. I can't stay in here forever, so I put my brush away, and head for the bedroom hoping that dude left.

I knock gently, then walk in. My eyes land right on him, sitting there on the bed, pulling a syringe out of his arm. My mouth dries up and a chill runs up my spine.

"Yo," he says when he sees me, his pupils blackened.

"Ah, um." Words cannot form.

"Yo dude, thanks," he says to Keith. "Later," he says as he shuffles past me and down the steps. When I hear the front door slam shut, the saliva comes back to my mouth.

"What the fuck Keith! What the hell was that?"

"What?"

"What do you mean what? That. That dude doing that shit in here. What the fuck? This isn't what we agreed on when we decided to sell this shit."

"Just chill, alright?"

"Chill? What if he died? What if the shit is bad? You ever think of that while you're *chillin'* all of the time?"

"If he didn't get it here, he'd get it somewhere else. What's the big deal?"

"I can't be part of this. I'm not gonna be responsible for killing people."

He shrugs. "Suit yourself." This infuriates me even more. I stare at him and wonder who this person is that I've been hanging out with for the past six months. I'm glad I didn't have sex with him. He doesn't care about people, as long as he makes money. I storm down the steps and out the door.

I walk and walk. I'm barely at Ursinus College campus, but I'm already getting tired. The sun's starting to go down, and my stomach's growling. I only have ten dollars and don't want to spend it on food when I can get a bite to eat back at the house. It's a long walk from Collegeville to Conshohocken, so I stick my thumb out.

A green pickup truck stops. I peer through the window and see a man and woman in there. Safe enough. She opens the door and moves closer to her man to let me in. I get out at the intersection where the main road divides into Ridge Pike and Germantown Pike. They are headed down Germantown Pike into Plymouth Meeting; I'm headed down Ridge to Conshy. I walk a bit and then out goes the thumb. It's getting late, and I just want to get back to Joey. Maybe I do love him.

Cristina Utti

I walk for about a half mile until someone pulls over. It's a small gold car with four guys in it. I don't care. I'm tired. If I don't get back soon, there will be another argument. It's a two door, so the guy in the front gets out to let me in the back, and the two guys in the back seat make room for me to sit between them. They initiate small talk. They work at the Limerick Power plant. I don't give a crap but keep smiling and being nice because they are giving me a ride.

"How about a little fun?" says the guy on my right, who is already squishing me with his body. He talks across me to the guy sitting on my left, as if I am not here. My heart skips a beat.

"She sure is cute," the other answers. I look straight ahead, heart in throat.

I lean forward, popping my head in between the front seats. "You can let me out at this corner," I say to the driver, trying to ignore these two. He doesn't answer me. He stares forward and keeps driving.

The guy on my right grabs my hair, pushing my head down. I reach with my arm to fight him, but he holds my arm down and is much stronger than I. I open my mouth to scream and the other man's penis gags me. I clench my teeth on him.

"You bitch," he screams as he whacks me across the head. The other guy still has a hold of my hair and shoves me back down.

"Feisty, huh? How about some of this?" I hear him say as he pushes my face into his crotch. I wiggle and squirm with all my might and shut my mouth tight so he can't shove it in. I manage to shove the front passenger seat forward a little and reach for the door. The guy on my right grabs me around the waist but I kick and flail until I can reach the door handle. I get to the handle. The guy in the front is saying something, but I can't hear anything. I open the door and it's flapping in the wind as they speed down the road. The front of my body is in the front and bottom half being held down in the back. The man in the front punches my arm back, trying to close the door. With my body back in the back seat, I push my legs forward, kicking the seat in front forward, and jump out, rolling onto the street.

"Crazy bitch," I hear them yell out the window. I get back on my feet and run into the woods on the side of the road.

I run and run and run into the woods, stopping to puke my guts up. I hide in the darkness. I'm scared they will come back for me. I stay in the woods as the sun goes down behind the trees. Now that it's dark, I head out to the street, but then I see shadows following me. I feel the aches in my knees and left elbow from landing in the street. The back of my head is pounding where the guy was pulling my hair and punching me. I feel myself running, as if I am not here at all. I see the 7-Eleven on Fayette Street and stop for refuge. It's the only place lit up on the entire street. They can't get me in a public place.

I have no idea what time it is. I want to forget what happened. I head to Marywood Park. I'm hyperaware, jumping at every shadow. I want to go back to Joey's but can't show up at this time, whatever time it is, and I have no idea what to say to him. I sit on a swing and swing lightly in the moonlight. The place is deserted. The dirt underneath me goes back and forth, back and forth. I look up at the moon. A crescent. As my pulse begins to calm, I see a dark figure walking toward me.

Show no fear. Show no fear.

Then it hits me, anyone awake this time of night knows where to get stuff. He's tall and bony. Doesn't look like he'll pose a threat.

"Hey," I say to him as he nears, to show him I'm not scared of him.

"Hey, looks like I'm not the only one out here," he says. I can't quite make out what he looks like. I know that it's not safe for me to sleep in the park, so I'll have to stay awake until the sun rises. Then I can go back and explain to Joey what happened. He'll never want me to go to Keith's again, which is fine with me. But Keith is my only contact. With Dee gone for the week, I don't know where I can get stuff, and I'm not involving Joey because I don't want our relationship to turn into another Scott thing. I need to lose weight. If I don't get some meth, I'm scared I'll binge eat, and I can't risk that at Joey's house.

"Know where to get any stuff?" pops right out of my mouth. I must be nuts.

"Yeah, sure. Got any money?"

"Ten bucks."

"If you want some shit, I'll have to go around the corner," he says looking in the direction of Fayette Street, showing the direction with his thumb.

I do want some. It's all I want right now. My pulse picks up as I reach into my pocket. "Okay." I get the ten out. "I'll walk with you." I don't trust him one bit, and it's all the money I have.

"That wouldn't be too cool. I'll be right back." I look at him. "Promise," he says, like that means anything.

"Okay, I'll wait right here then," I say, having no choice. My money is in his hands now. I regret it immediately, but I don't know what else to do with myself sitting in the park in the middle of the night with nowhere to go. God forbid I show up at Joey's at this time of night. Those guys might have been following me. I need to stay awake.

I watch him walk toward the moonlight doubting if he will be back. I'm so stupid. Stupid. I sit back on the swing and swing, watching the dirt again. Tears fill my eyes. Someone touches my shoulder and I lose my balance, almost falling off. It's him.

"Let's go to my house," he says. I sniffle and wipe my eyes.

I'm not so sure about this. "Where do you live?"

"Right here," and he points at the park house.

"You're kidding me, right?" If it is true, he can be some stalker who has been watching me out the window.

"It's my grandmother's place, c'mon," and he starts walking toward the house. I follow behind him. There's a dim light coming from the back porch. He has the key and opens the door softly.

"Come on," he motions me into the kitchen. I enter silently, feeling like an invader. "Have a seat." I'm scared shitless. I can't believe I'm sitting in this stranger's house just to get high. I take a seat at the kitchen table. The table seats four. It's clean, with doily placemats. I think of Mom. She taught me how to crochet when I was six years old. When I got good enough, we made a set of doily placemats for the kitchen table. She crocheted five of them while I made two. The chairs are cushioned. The counter is lined with glass jars of sugar, coffee, and tea. This probably is his grandmother's house. No guy I know keeps a place looking like this.

"Be right back," he says and heads into the other room. What now? He returns and goes to the sink. I've no idea what he's doing. He sits next to me with a spoon, dumps the stuff in it and squirts water in it from a syringe.

I think I'm going to pass out.

I stare at the process as if I'm not here. He ties a band around his arm, finds a vein, plunges and releases it into his arm. Rinses the syringe. Stares at me. I stare back, in disbelief. This is a bad dream. No, it's a nightmare. He tries to hand it to me. I sit here looking at him to see if he will keel over and drop dead.

"Well?" he says to me.

"You okay?"

"Great. Here," he says while he holds out the syringe for me to take. I don't take it.

"What?" he asks.
"I never did that."
"Don't you want it?"
"Well, yeah, but," I don't know what to say. I don't know what I want. I want to forget. Forget that guy's penis in my mouth. Forget their laughter. Forget my head hurts where I got whacked. Forget that Mom left, and the divorce was all my fault. Forget that I have an eating problem. Forget that Dad threw me out. Forget that I screwed up school and got put in the dumb classes. Forget that I have no home. Forget that I've no one to love. Forget that I'm fat. Forget that my hair is a rat's nest. Forget, forget, forget. "Yeah, sure." I'm scared shitless.

He does it for me. I don't even know his name.

Chapter 10

No Turning Back

I found out his name. It's Greg Jackson. We take his grandmother's car and head to Norristown, listening to Madonna. He drives down Airy Street into the darkness, pulls over and tells me to wait in the car. When he gets out, I lock all of the doors. I'm really paranoid. When he gets back, we drive back to his house, taking the back streets. I guess he's paranoid too.

The sun is coming up, and he motions with his finger to his lips to be quiet. We go into his bedroom this time. I have no money left. He does some more. I can see the rise in his jeans.

"I'll give you what you want if you give me what I want," states a voice that isn't mine.

Ugly.
Fat.
Guilty.
Empty.
This time I do it myself.
Numb.

I look over at him, spread eagle, pants already off. Waiting. I get on top of him. He grinds up against me trying to put it in. He tries to kiss me, so I move my face and go down. If there are no feelings attached, no one gets hurt.

Chapter 11
My Brother, My Savior

Joey's eyes are ice when I show up over a week later. I've lost track of time.

"You can't stay here anymore." He stares straight through me.

"I came to get my stuff," is all I say. I lost my job at Burger King for being a no show. I can't pay rent here anymore anyway. I know I can schmooze him if I really wanted to, like I did with Scott. I like Joey too much to manipulate him. "I'm sorry," I mumble.

I go upstairs to pack my belongings. My clothes fill the knapsack and my backpack, and I grab my guitar. Before I am even down the steps, I hear his truck rev up and then tear up the street.

"I'm really sorry about everything," I say to Uncle Jimmy. He doesn't respond. "Can I make a call before I go?" I ask, while he sits there staring out the window at the back alley.

"Yeah, sure. You hurt Joey real bad."

I hang my head in remorse, mostly for show. I have to think now. No time for regrets. David has a little efficiency apartment on the west side, somewhere on 5th Ave. He told me last time I was home. I was in too much of a rush to get out of there before Dad got back to wait for him to finish practicing with the band and go check out his place. I pick up the phone that hangs on the wall next to the fridge, grateful that it has one of those extra-long cords. I move as far as the cord will take me, toward the back of the kitchen so I can have some privacy. Uncle Jimmy is sitting on the couch in the living room, probably waiting for me to get the hell out of his house. I call home, praying Dad doesn't answer. Anna answers. Thank God for small miracles. She gives me David's address.

"Thanks for everything. Really, thank you." My last words in Joey's house. I put my backpack on my shoulders, grab my knapsack and guitar, and start the walk to 5th Avenue, hoping David is home.

By the time I get to the next block, it starts pouring. Great. Hopefully it's one of those summer rains that comes on suddenly and leaves just as quickly. I hold my guitar case upright so maybe only the top will get wet, and I pick up the pace. Three more blocks to go.

Apartment 2, corner of 5th and Maple St. I knock on the door, hoping this is the right place. David opens the door and stares at me. "Lina, what the heck happened to you?"

"Hello to you too. Can I come in?"

"Yeah, yeah, come on in," he opens the door and motions his arm through the air and does a little bow like I'm a princess. I get the wet backpack off my back, drop the knapsack, and open the guitar case to access the damage. "What's going on?"

"I need a place to stay."

"You're welcome to stay here but you'll have to go outside to think," he laughs.

"What?" Looking around, I see it's one room. The bed is off to the side; the front door almost hits the piano that's against the wall. The kitchen is about four by four feet, with a small round table and two chairs. His desk is shoved next to his bed. There's a make-shift bookcase made from Abbotts crates.

"The place is so small that you'll have to take big thoughts outside." He cracks up at his own joke. I don't laugh.

"I'll pay you rent," I tell him, although I've no idea how. I need a job.

"Oh Lina," he gives me a great big hug. I feel safe. The tears start coming. "You don't have to pay me rent, silly. I have to pay the rent anyway, even if you weren't here."

"Thanks," I say into his chest. Dave has always been taller than me, but as I'm in his arms I realize how tall he really is. He must be about six two. My head reaches his nose. We let go of each other and he looks me up and down.

"You look like shit."

"Well, I'm drenched." I know what he means. If I look as bad as I feel, I must be a scary sight.

He keeps staring, waiting for more. "So much has happened that I don't know where to begin."

"The bathroom is right here. How about you get changed into some dry clothes while I make us some sandwiches? You look hungry."

"Nah, thanks. I'm not hungry." I'm not hungry, I'm starving. I'm finally almost at my goal of 98 and I'd like to keep it that way. I can't eat. The next magic number is ninety-five, then everything will be okay. I don't have any stuff to control the binging and I'm broke, so I can't eat.

"I'll brew us up some coffee then, how's that sound?"

"Sounds great."

We talk through a whole pot of coffee. I learn that Dad remarried. Dave knows about my eating problem, but I'm not about to tell him that I've been involved in dealing, what I've done the past week, and what happened in that car. That, I want to forget. I can't tell him that I've been doing meth. He is doing well now, and I don't want him mixed up in that.

"Where'd you get the piano?"

"A priest didn't want it at his church anymore. Got it for the best price; free," he tells me with a huge smile.

"How's the sound?" I sit down and start to play "Wild Horses" by the Stones.

"Hey, you're not bad."

"Thanks, never be as good as you though," I say, because it's true. He's so much better than I am. When I play it sounds forced; he plays from the heart.

"You want to come hang with Sideways Eight tomorrow night?"

"Sideways Eight?"

"Yeah, remember? My band?"

Boy, have the tables turned. We all worried when he used to smoke weed and keep holed up in his bedroom. I guess he's been working on lyrics and music for years. Now he's in a band, has his own place and is doing what he loves. I don't even know what I love, except meth. "I'd love to," I say. He sits next to me on the bench and we finish the song together. He plays the low keys and I play the treble.

"We're not bad," he says and jabs me in the side, smiling. I agree, but my mind is elsewhere.

"I don't think I'm going back to school," I tell David.

"Lina, why? You're so smart."

"No, I'm not. I'll never be as smart as you are or write as well as you do."

"Don't quit school. You're only sixteen. You'll be out by the time you're seventeen."

"You did, and you're doing okay," I say as I look around. He has his own place, is playing music, and doing fine.

"But you can go to college," he tells me. This is so far from my reality it's like thinking of living on a different planet. I'm wondering how long I can stay here and be safe from hanging out with Greg, who lives only a few blocks away.

After we talked a while, David says he has to write down some lyrics while they are dancing in his head. He pours a glass of wine and works at his desk. I unpack some of my things and look for a book to read so I can give him space to write. Before I know it, I hear snoring. I look up from my book and see that he dozed off with his pen still in his hand. I'm too antsy to even think of sleep. I have no money, no stuff, am starving, and scared to eat.

As delicate as I can with my long fingers and big hands, I lift the pen from his hand and place it on the desk. I coax him to go lay on the bed, then cover him with his sheet. I wish I could sleep that hard. Once he is all settled, and I see his chest rise and fall in a regular pattern, I take a peek at what he was working on. He wasn't writing lyrics after all. His piece is called "The Equal Opportunity Murders." I have nothing else to do, so I read through it, then try my hand at poetry. I get into a flow and add two stanzas. Maybe I don't stink at poetry after all. I hope it's not some masterpiece that he's been working on that I possibly just screwed up. He could scratch my lines out if he doesn't like them. I'm tempted to wake him to show him what I wrote, but he is sleeping so soundly that I can't bear to wake him. I read it over and over.

I hope he likes what I added and can understand why I wrote it. I want to tell him what happened to me, but don't know how.

The Equal Opportunity Murders

Winded on this rainy evening
Stalking light, and barely breathing
Body tense and thoughts conclusive
Aged most tempting paths intrusive

Floating streaks of gloomy brightness
Lightning flashing by, cold without rest
Sauced in murky shadows fading—
Sparkles glitter off the pavement
Onto dim fog, soft and lambent
Demurred and fading fast

Breaking Infinity

Through the mercury cradled
Streets
Crowded with adjacent poses
Intertwined with poison roses
Sprawling leaves whose underneath things
Crackle faintly, fire-like, heavy
Sole to tar, cement curb pace
Abrupt and cry-stopping
Blade blunt, dungeon nightmare creeping
Lime lit lamplight can't replace the daylight
Sunlight real as spotlight caricatures
Macrocosmic indifference
In the essence of all substance
Real and wishing it were sleeping
Artificial candle fumes beeping

I add:
Watched neatly as the wanderers
Sighed deeply, sad and debased,
When darkness took captive passions all
And tore the ceiling from the wall
With not a deeper gasp to spare
Embarked these thoughts from here to there
Noise and clutter made each step
Obscuring matters where we crept
Undeterred and uncomfortable besides
This will be no easy ride
And I must go catch the tide
Yes, I must go to the sea...because
Something there cures what ails me
That I've kept myself so confined
In faded contemplative time
And taken it upon myself
To repose in agonizing torture
Paying for the sins of the modern world

Chapter 12
On the Move

I couldn't stay with Dave. It was too close to Greg. I wish I could go to the sea, like I wrote a year ago. I haven't written much because my life has been a mess. Dave and I stayed together for the summer. We had some good times with Sideways Eight. Dad and I got on good terms again, and I even helped out at Holy Family, the church he was painting in Norristown. I didn't do artwork, like him and Dave do, but I did learn how to varnish. I varnished the doors and all of the pews and even helped to paint the walls.

I couldn't bear to tell Dave about the drugs and being awake all night in that tiny efficiency made me crazy. I wish I could tell him. It's not that I didn't want him to know, it's because I didn't want him getting caught up in my mess. So I did the best thing I could do. I left.

I moved about a zillion times in the past year, staying wherever I could. Then, I met Phil.

He picked me up. I was living in a trailer home with Bonnie and Peter, and their two kids, Peter Jr. and Simon. They are born-again Christians who tried to help me by trying to get me to believe that God could fix me. It worked for a while. I stopped getting high, but the eating problem resurfaced. One night, I walked to the store to get some laxatives. The nearest store to them is two miles, one way. I was hitchhiking so I could get back and take the laxatives as soon as possible to get rid of the food.

That's how I met Phil. He pulled over to the side of the road, and instead of rolling down the window and asking if I wanted a ride, he got out of his car, came around to my side and opened the door for me. No one has ever done that. He was charming and handsome. The day after he gave me a ride home, he showed up with a Bible in hand and asked if I wanted to go out for coffee. I found out that he recently graduated from Drexel University. He landed his first real job in Pottsville. He asked me if I wanted to move there with him. I didn't know where the hell Pottsville was, but I said sure. What did I have to lose? I was sick and tired of living with those Bible thumpers. Every little act they do is in the name of Jesus, even washing the damn dishes. Give me a break. I stayed in Allentown with Phil for two weeks. Then we moved to Pottsville near his new place of employment.

Our apartment is nice. Actually, it's huge. We have beautiful hardwood floors. The living room is so big that we had to put the couch in the middle of the room so we could see the television. I don't like mooching off of people, so I found work right away. I have two jobs. I work at Sunrise Pizza and Lily's Diner. I work at the lunch shift at the pizza shop Monday through Friday and then waitress at the diner a few nights a week and weekends. Phil has an accounting job. We run in the mornings together and hang out every night that I am not working, watching movies or reading. He was my savior, until I met John.

John does pizza delivery for Sunrise Pizza. He lives on the north side of town. I don't have a car, so ever since my third day of work, he's given me rides back and forth, which is no big deal for him since he drives all day anyway. It started with smoking some weed with him. Now I'm back to where I was in Conshohocken a year ago. Only worse. I thought all of that was over, that I could start fresh here in Pottsville. But it has been lurking, patiently waiting. When I started again, it was like I never stopped. I wear long sleeves all of the time, especially around Phil. When we go to bed, I make sure the lights are off, so he doesn't see my arms. He has no idea. It's not like I love him. I moved here with him to get away from the Bible thumpers.

John and I have been talking for the past month about taking off, moving to Florida to get away from it. Start over. Again. We are leaving Saturday morning. The best part is that we are just friends, so there's nothing he expects from me in that other department.

I don't know what to say to Phil, so I say nothing. When he left for his morning run, I told him that I was tired and going to skip running today. I pack. I don't have much, so it doesn't take long. I call John to tell him I'm ready.

"I have to stop at the bank," I tell him as I'm loading my bags into the trunk of his Ford Escort.

I'm surprised at how much stuff I've accumulated over the past year. We drive to the bank, and I close out my account. The plan is to go halfers on an apartment in Florida. I'm glad I was able to save $500 from working so many hours.

As soon as I get back in the car, he asks, "How much money do you have?"

"I have a bit over $500. How much do you have? Apartments are cheaper in Florida than here." I know because my sister told me. When Lucy started drinking, Mom made her look for her own place to live. She's been drinking since she got there, so I guess she never dealt with what happened that day when she was little. She drowns her sorrows. I run from mine. I'm hoping that Lucy and I can help each other when I get there. I really miss her. It was wrong for Mom to throw her out because she drinks, but I suppose it's better than what she did to David. She called the cops

Breaking Infinity

on him and had him locked up for a night when Dad was away. No one ever talks about *that*.

I don't think I ever want to be a mom. I'm not even a good sister. But all of that is about to change. When I get there, Lucy and I are going to talk, and we'll help each other through. Maybe we can all get an apartment together. It's going to be great.

"I have about $600 or so," he says, eyes set dead ahead.

"That's great. We'll find something." I'm excited. I don't know anyone there except for Lucy and Mom. I can start over. We have enough stuff to make it through the twenty-three-hour drive from here to Tampa, then that's it. I'll be done with doing this stuff.

"I'm pulling over." We pull over on a side road in Centralia. We made it through one town, and he wants to get high already.

"Where are you going to get water?"

"Right here," he says as he leans over me and pulls out a small jar from the glove box. I feel paranoid doing this in the car. Half of it is mine; we bought it together. I may as well do some too; we have a long ride ahead.

We drive in silence for miles. The silence is uncomfortable.

"Mind if we turn on the radio?"

He pushes the button and "Tonight, Tonight" by Genesis is playing. I sing along. *But now I'm in too deep, you see it's got me so that I just can't sleep, oh get me out of here. Please get me out of here, just help me. I'll do anything, anything if you'll just help me get out of here.* I'm choking up. This is my life.

"You alright Lina?" he asks when the song is over.

"Yeah, just looking forward to a new life in Florida." We drive on for a few more miles down this dark, desolate road.

"Mind if we stop for a soda before we get on the highway? I'm thirsty," he says as he is already pulling into a dimly lit parking lot before I even get the chance to answer. It's a bar.

I'm jittery and need to get out of this car and stretch for a minute. "I'll run in and grab two sodas." He hands me a dollar. "Be right back," I say as I close the door. I've been in bars when I was with Sideways Eight playing gigs and in a few since I moved here, so I know most of them have a fridge with canned or bottled beers and sodas. If not, I can ask the bartender. I walk in, and there's a fridge on my left. I grab a Coke for him and a Diet Sprite for me. I pay and hurry out because a few of the guys at the bar are staring at me.

I go through the exit door expecting John to be right there, where he was a minute ago, but the car isn't here. I walk around the parking lot to see if he pulled over and parked. The Escort is nowhere in sight. My heart is pumping so fast it's about to burst right through my ribs. Everything I own is in that car. I wait.

I don't know what I'm waiting for.

Now I freak out.

I walk to the edge of the parking lot to check the road. Not a car in sight. I start walking back to Pottsville because I don't know what else to do. I walk a few feet, and realize I don't know which way to go, so I head back to the bar to get directions back to Pottsville.

I check out the guys at the bar and walk up to a man who is sitting alone at the end. He is wearing a black leather jacket and has long brown hair that sticks out under his blue bandana. His huge hand is wrapped around a mug of dark beer, probably Yuengling, which is cheap around here. With a few dollars you can get drunk because Pottsville is the home of America's first brewery. The lager sells in most bars for fifty cents a mug. I hope he isn't drunk.

"Pottsville is 'bout sixteen miles south a here girlie," he tells me.

"South?" The word etches into my brain like a shard of glass. John was driving north.

"Yeah, south. Hang a right outta the lot onto Centre Street, go 'bout half mile and hang a right on South Hoffman Boulevard. That's route 61. Take ya right into Pottsville."

"Two rights, right?" I repeat back to make sure. He takes a long swig of his beer.

"Yep."

"Thanks." I head out the door and start walking. This road is deserted. The only people in this town are probably all in that bar. I've no idea what happened to John. The only thing I can think to do is go back to Pottsville and try to find him. After walking for miles, a car comes down the road and I stick out my thumb. No luck. Keep walking. Coming up on the sign for Pottsville, a car pulls over. The guy asks me if I need a ride. I hop in and make it into town. John lives on North George Street, so I head in that direction.

When I get to his apartment, I see his car out front. I try the doors. It's locked up tight. I'm relieved and pissed off at the same time. I march up the steps to his third-floor apartment and bang on his door. He cracks it open, leaving the latch hooked. His eyes are crazed; pure pupil. He probably did all that shit.

"I want my stuff." I tell him. I'd punch him for leaving me stranded like that if he'd open the damned door. He slams the door in my face. What the hell? I bang on it. "I'm not leaving until you give me my shit back." I bang some more. I switch hands because I'm banging so hard my knuckles hurt. Then I start kicking with all my might.

Infuriated, I head back down the steps and sit on the curb. A police car passes by. I sit here. The car passes by again and this time stops. "You have to get off this corner. If I see you here when I pass by again, I'm hauling you in," he tells me.

I cross my arms. "I'm not leaving. The guy up there has all my stuff." Maybe this cop will help me. He ignores me and drives away. A few minutes pass and he's back. He pulls over next to me. I don't care. I ignore him and pick my nails.

He rolls down his window and says, "I told you, you have to leave the premises."

"I can't leave. That guy John who lives up there took all my stuff," I tell him. He looks at me like I'm crazy. I roll my eyes and explain. "We were supposed to be moving to Florida. I got out for a soda, and he took off with all of my stuff."

"Alright," he pulls over and parks. "Where does this John live?"

"Right there," I point to the building. "Upstairs, on the third floor. Apartment B." He follows me to John's apartment and bangs on the door. John doesn't answer.

"He's in there, that's his car out front," I tell him. He knocks harder this time.

In a deep voice he says, "Open up, it's the police," and takes out his gun. I don't think this is necessary. John cracks the door and peeks through the chained latch.

"Open up," the officer tells him.

"I just want my stuff back John," I say. I don't want him to get freaked out, but this is fucked up. He has everything I own, all my money, the dope, my guitar. Everything.

"I don't have your shit. I have no idea what you're talking about." He looks whacked. The police officer looks at him, then at me. I do my best to maintain my composure.

"He has all my stuff, just tell him to give me my stuff back." I plead with the officer.

"I don't have anything of hers. I have no idea what she's talking about," John tells him through his lying tongue and saucer eyes. The officer looks at him. I follow his eyes to John's arms. I'm glad I am wearing half-sleeves. I'm glad I haven't done any stuff in hours and don't look like him.

Now my anger rises. "I want my stuff back, John. Just give me my stuff!"

The policeman stands there looking at the two of us. "I'm taking you both in for disturbing the peace. You can come nicely or in cuffs," he grabs the handcuffs from his belt loop.

Thank God. Someone is listening to me.

Chapter 13
Sunbury Women's Penitentiary

I catch a glimpse of the calendar hanging on the dashboard of the police car. That's how I know what day it is. Maybe it's the 24th now, since it's after midnight. I'm not sure. The days are all running together. We sit at opposite ends of the back seat, not speaking. I'm seething. I'll explode if my mouth opens. We get to the station in no time. Thank God for small towns. After they check our licenses for identification, John and I are escorted into separate rooms, where the questioning begins.

"So explain what is going on," a police officer about six feet tall commands. He looks like he was a football player in his last lifetime. I look at the corners of the room near the ceiling for cameras. The only window is a two-way glass; I can tell because of the reflection. I feel like a real criminal. Next thing you know they will be taking my mug shot. What the hell?

"We were heading to Florida, so I closed out my bank account and packed all of my stuff. I ran in a bar to get some sodas, and he took off. I just want my stuff back." That's the story in two sentences. Well, three. There's nothing more to say.

"So, you were heading to Florida?" he asks, looking at me like I'm lying.

"Yes, Florida," I repeat. This guy is an ass. I'm getting more and more pissed off. I'm not scared of him. I don't care how damn big he is.

"And what were you going to do in Florida?" he asks.

"My mom and sister live there. We were going to visit them, then get an apartment," I tell him, trying to maintain my cool. "That's why I took all of my money out of the bank. Just tell him I want my stuff back."

"And how do you know John Waniki?" he continues, clearly ignoring me.

"We worked together at Sunrise Pizza. He used to give me rides home after work," I answer, playing along with this idiot.

"How long have you worked there?"

"I don't know, maybe six months." I'm losing my patience. What's with this damn guy? "Look, all I want is my stuff back."

"How well do you know Sal?"

"Sal who?" I ask, not even thinking.

"Salvatore Genovese, the owner of the pizza shop."

"Oh, him," I mumble and lower my head. It moves back and forth all on its own as I get a flashback. Sal liked me, wanted me to be his girl. I had no interest in all that. I just wanted to do my job, get paid, get high. He got pissed off when I showed no interest in his advances and gave Lola a raise because she kept flirting with him. I stayed platonic; he was my boss after all. He was cute, though, with his sandy brown hair and blue eyes. Definitely Northern Italian.

"Well, he owns Sunrise Pizza, I know that," I say. I know I am sounding like a smart-ass, but I can't help myself. I haven't slept in days.

"You know where he was born?"

"How the hell am I supposed to know where he was born? I'm not his mother." This dude is bringing out the worst in me.

"Don't make this worse than it already is," he raises his voice at me.

"Look, can you just ask John to give me my stuff back? That's all I want."

"Don't move. I'll be right back." He heads out the door, shutting it behind him. I'm sure I'm locked in here. I've nowhere to go anyway. I'm glad he's out of my face. I hope he's talking to John so I can get my things and can get the hell out of here.

The door opens a few minutes later, and the cop motions his fat arm at me. "Follow me."

We go into another room just down the hall. From the corner of my eye, I think I can see John being questioned in the room to my right.

"What do you know about that?" He points to a busted-up cash register.

"That?" I look at it. I worked the cash register many times at Sunrise. I put smiley face stickers on the side of it one day when a little kid left a sheet of them on a table. I spot them on this busted up register. "Looks like Sunrise's cash register busted up into about a million little pieces." Obviously.

"Listen, you city slicker, I've had enough of your mouth."

"I don't know anything about why that's here. You asked me what I know, and that's it. Looks like the pizza shop's register all busted up. Look, sir, I just want my stuff back." I'm obviously not getting through to him. I'm tired, have no money, and no belongings other than the clothes on my back. All I want is my stuff, and I'll be on my way.

"Have a seat," he orders. Now we are sitting at the table with the cash register. "What about these?" He shows me some papers that look like doctor's prescriptions.

"What about those?" I ask.

"Look, city slicker, I ask the questions. What do you know about these?"

"I don't know anything about those. I just want my stuff back." This guy is thick. He stands up and for a minute I think he is going to hit me. He glares at me. I glare right back at him, locking in a stare. I always win staring contests. I haven't been out-stared yet, and this asshole sure won't win. He blinks, then gets up and walks out of the room. I hear the lock click. I take in my surroundings, cinder block walls painted off-white, and a black-rimmed clock. It's 5:47 a.m. I get up and pace back and forth in front of the table. It's dark and eerie in here. I jump at the sound of the doorknob turning.

"Have a seat young lady," he says as he puts a stereo in front of me. What now?

"Are you going to tell me that you don't know anything about this either?"

"Should I know something about it?" comes out of my mouth before I can mind my words. I'm getting this guy more and more angry. He looks at me and takes a deep breath.

"Do you know Philip Berkle? Or do you not know anything about him either?"

"Yeah, I know him," I answer and look at the floor. I could have at least told Phil I was leaving.

"How do you know him?"

Oh. My. God. This guy is on my last nerve. All of this just because John took everything that I own. What the hell? I take a deep breath and answer this jerk. "I lived with him up until today, I mean yesterday, when I packed my stuff and left because I was supposed to be going to Florida with John."

"Is this his?"

"I don't know, it might be, it might not be. All stereos look alike to me," I tell him, which is the truth.

"Did you take this out of the apartment when you left?"

"What? No! It wouldn't even fit in one of my bags." Now I get it, he is accusing me of stealing a damn stereo. "Look, I don't want his stereo. I didn't touch that. All I want is my stuff back. If you get my stuff back from John, you will see that a stereo wouldn't fit in my backpack or suitcase."

"We got a call at 1 a.m. His place was robbed. You are telling me that you did not take this?"

"No, I mean yes. I didn't touch his stuff. I just want my things back." I'm choking back the knot in my throat because I almost said 'so I can go home' but realized I have no home. This is getting old, and I'm tired. I look at the clock, 8:12 a.m. I've been here for hours locked in rooms, answering stupid questions.

"Well, well, well. You sure think you're slick, don't you? All you city slickers are alike."

"I don't know what the hell you are talking about. I'm not even from a city!" I get up to leave. I've had it with this asshole. He grabs my right arm and pulls me back into the chair.

"Sit your ass down, girlie," he stammers. I sit and take deep breaths to calm myself. I really want to spit in his face. *1-2-3-4-5-6-7-8-9-10, breathe.*

"Look, I have no idea why you are asking me all these questions. I just want my stuff. Can you just ask John to give me my stuff back?"

"We need some answers. I will ask you calmly, again. Tell me about the cash register."

I stare at this asshole in his ugly, baggy eyes and count to ten. "I used the cash register at work when I wasn't making sandwiches. I rang up people's orders. I put the stickers on the side there, that's how I know it is Sunrise Pizza's register." I point to the stickers. "Now can you tell John to give me my stuff back?"

"You are slick, real slick," he says, again. That must be his favorite damn word in his idiotic limited vocabulary. "What about these?" He pulls out those papers again, the prescriptions.

"I don't even know what they are, I don't go to any doctor," I tell him, which is the truth. I can't remember the last time I saw a doctor. "I don't even have a doctor or know where one is here." At this, he glares at me.

"Okay then, what about the stereo, and Philip Berkle?"

"Oh my God, this again," I mumble as I put my head in my hands. I just told this jerk-off I know Philip Berkle. I look at the clock, 8:41. "I just want my stuff. I don't know how that got here."

"So, you know nothing about Philip Berkle, or the stereo?"

"No, I know Phil," I tell him, again. "I don't know why the stereo is here." I feel like slapping some sense into this idiot. The questions go on forever, all with the same answer. I want my stuff.

"Follow me," he says as he stands up and leads me into yet another room.

This room looks just like the last room. There's a wooden table in the center, a heavy metal door, and a big glass window. Probably bulletproof glass, or Plexiglass, or whatever they use in police stations. Can't trust criminals. I follow behind him.

"Have a seat," he points to the metal chairs. I don't want to sit. My butt is numb from all of this sitting. I want to run. I cross my arms and stand here for a minute, staring at him.

"I'll be right back," he tells me with a smirk, and shuts the door behind him. I pull out a seat and sit. I sit and wait for what feels like forever. I look at all four walls: same color paint, no clock. I get up and pace around and around the table. I sit down again and look at my nails. I bite my cuticles. I run my hand through my hair to get out the knots. When my hair is knot-free, I lay my head on my arms on the table. Drifting, drifting, I see the marks and am embarrassed within my own self.

As I am falling asleep, I hear the doorknob and jump up out of my seat, pushing my sleeves down, and folding my arms across my chest as if I am cold. "Come with me."

Cristina Utti

The gruffness of his voice jerks me back to reality. "In less than six months you will be eighteen years old. You are going to Sunbury Women's Penitentiary, missy. You can make one phone call." He grabs my arm and leads me out the door into yet another room. There is a large desk with a black phone sitting in the corner of it amidst piles of papers. "You can make *one* call," he repeats.

In a daze, I call my mother. She picks up on the third ring. I try to explain what happened, but the words don't come out right because really, I don't know what is happening. She tells me she doesn't want to hear my problems, and to call my father.

"Can I call my dad?" I ask Mr. Asshole.

"I'll allow it," he says. What a great guy.

I call Dad and explain how they want to send me to Sunbury Women's Penitentiary for a bunch of stuff, and how I have no idea what they are talking about. He tells me he doesn't know what to say, to call my mother. I am dripping. Melting. A puddle.

"Hey," someone's hand is on my shoulder and I jump. I sop the drips that are streaming down my face with my hands and quickly wipe the tears on my jeans. I look up at him. It's a different man. He's not in uniform. He has soft brown eyes that are looking at my arms. Shit. "Hey, Lina. It's Lina, right?"

"Yes sir," I nod stupidly, bleary-eyed.

"I'm Sal, Sal Renaldo," he says, and shakes my hand. "Would you mind following me? I want to go over a few things with you."

"Okay." I look in his eyes. Within them is the first comfort I've felt since before I was stranded at the bar. I follow behind him into another room that looks just like the one I've been in for hours. The only difference is the table is metal, not wood.

"How do you know John Wanicki?"

"We worked together at the pizza joint," I mumble.

"Were you two intimate?"

"What? No!"

"Okay, it's okay. I had to ask," he continues softly, "Where were you going with him?"

"We were going to Florida."

"Florida?"

"Yes, my mother lives there. I packed up all my stuff, closed out my bank account, and we were headed to Florida."

"Okay." He writes notes on his yellow legal pad.

"I just want my stuff back, I don't want to press charges or anything," I tell him. I know what happened, he did too much stuff and freaked. I'm not trying to get him in trouble.

"I have to go through these questions first, okay?" His voice is deep and warm, like Dad's. I nod my head.

"How do you know Philip Berkle?"

"We met in Quakertown when I was a born-again Christian. He was cute, and I didn't want to live with the born-agains anymore, so I moved to Allentown with him. Then he got a job in Pottsville, so that's how I landed up here." My mouth is just pouring out information now. I've no idea why I am telling this man all of this stuff. I guess it's because he reminds me of Dad. A soft, gentle heart.

He gazes at me curiously. "You were a born-again Christian?"

"Yeah, baptized and everything. I lived with a family, and they really didn't have room for me. I felt like I was imposing on them, so when I met Phil and he asked me to go with him, I went." I hang my head because I failed God with my born-again attempt. I failed a nice guy, and I have now been up all night and all I can think about is wanting to get high again. I've failed myself.

"So, you moved out here with him, then what?" I look at him. I don't know how to answer this. He looks at me, waiting.

"I don't know. I got a job. Actually, I got two jobs. I worked at the diner too."

"How long did you live with Philip?"

"Here, or all together?"

"All together." I think he is mocking me.

"Since I left Quakertown, it's probably been about six or eight months. I'm not sure," which is the truth. Most of it's a blur.

"Did you two get in a fight before you left?"

"What? No, we didn't fight. We never fought. There was never anything to fight about."

"What happened when you left?"

"I packed my stuff while he was out for a run, and John picked me up. I left the key on the kitchen counter, figuring I wouldn't need it anymore because I was headed to Florida," I tell him with remorse. I could have left a note. I could have just told him that I was leaving.

"So, you left the key?"

"Yes, on the counter. When can I get my stuff back? Has anyone even asked John what he did with my stuff?" My throat is getting tight. I push the thickness down. It makes my eyes water.

"We will get to that." Making his voice even softer, he states, "We have to get through the questions first."

"Okay, but I already answered everything, haven't I?"

"I know it has been a long night. Just bear with me, alright? Tell me about the cash register."

This again. "I really have no idea why it's here, or why it's all broken up. I know it belongs to Sunrise Pizza because I put those stickers on the side of it when I was at work a few weeks ago."

"What about the prescriptions?"

"I've no idea. I don't even have a doctor here, nor do I remember the last time I have been to the doctor. I moved out of my dad's house a few years ago and haven't been to the doctor since I got my braces off." It all just pours out of me.

He looks at my perfect teeth, the only thing perfect about me. "You had braces?"

"Yeah, for two years," I tell him, wondering why this is even a topic.

"Sounds like your father sure loves you."

"I guess," I shrug my shoulders. My head weighs a ton. I'm dissipating into my seat. I am invisible. I want these feelings to go away. I wonder if the stash is still in the car. I'm pissed John took my shit. Sal doesn't take his eyes off me. My eyes are melting onto my cheeks. "Can I just get my stuff back?"

"If you did, where would you go?" he questions. My shoulders move up and down on their own, my eyes search the floor for an answer. The cold, white tile leaves me no sign. He puts a warm hand on mine and looks at me. "You remind me of my daughter."

"Oh," is all that comes out of my mouth. I'm not sure if this is a good or a bad thing. Poor thing if she looks and acts like I do.

"I'll be right back, so sit tight," and he gives my hand a squeeze. "Would you like a cup of coffee?"

"Yes, please," I answer, wondering what time it is. The room is dark and there's a chill in the air. I wish I had a jacket or sweater, not only to cover up my arms, but also so I wouldn't feel so exposed.

Sal returns, coffee in hand, John trailing behind him.

"Have a seat," his arm motions to a chair opposite the table from me. I glare at John. He will not look at me. Sal hands me a Styrofoam cup of steaming coffee. "Cream and sugar okay?"

I put my cold hands around the cup to warm them and take a sip. "Yes, perfect. Thank you." Sal looks at me, then at John. The room falls silent.

"I brought you two together to get the stories straight," Sal looks in my direction, directly into my eyes. "John here claims you stole from Philip Berkle, from Sunrise Pizza, and from a doctor's office. When he noticed what you had done, he got scared and left you, and drove back to town. Isn't that right, John?" he directs toward John, who is looking at the table, then the floor, then at his hands which are in his lap.

"Yes sir," he says to the table. I can't believe he said all this shit about me.

"What the hell, John? All I want is my stuff back," comes out of my mouth before I can reflect on exactly what to say. His eyes move from the table to meet mine.

"You knew exactly what you were doing," he says as my eyes lock with his and don't let go.

"What? Why are you doing this?" My eyes water.

"When I saw your intentions…" and his eyes start filling up too.

"I'm not pressing charges. I just want my stuff back."

"When I saw what you did…" all of a sudden, he starts crying and blubbering. He must be coming down and tired of the lies. Pouring out of him are the facts, the real facts of what transpired the day before. Sal guides him into another room to get his statement, or so he can get himself together, or whatever they do in the other room. As I sit in shock of his lies, my stomach loudly grumbles. Seconds, minutes, or hours later, Sal returns. He drapes a jacket over my shoulders.

"We've gotten a complete statement from him. It matches up with the story you have been telling us," he says.

"Finally," I murmur and hold the oversized jacket that smells of cologne tight around my chest and wipe away my tears.

Chapter 14
The Freebie

John confessed that he dumped my stuff on a mountain in Centralia. The police told me that as they find my belongings, they will send them to my father's address. How nice of them. I'm sure he did not dump my money. I don't even have a penny to my name.

    They gave me meal tickets to a diner, a bus ticket to King of Prussia, and set me up in a motel for two nights and three days. Home sweet home. The faint smell of lemon cleaner lingers in the air ineffectively veiling the smell of piss and the musty odor of the carpet. The sheets have bloodstains that are not from a woman's cycle. I know all too well what they are from and so does my racing heart. I slept naked on them last night so I could wash my underwear, bra, and shirt because they are all the clothes I have. I've been in these jeans for three days now, but they will never dry overnight if I wash them and hang them over the shower curtain rail like the three pieces of my other clothing.

    I walk over to Garfield Diner on Market Street. Finding an empty booth in the back corner, I scoot in. The waitress is thin and jumpy; I bet she knows where to get some meth. *No, Lina. No.* Instead, I show her the meal ticket and make sure she will take it to pay for my meal before I order a black coffee. I don't want food but find myself ordering a single scrambled egg with cheese and dry rye toast. It tastes like cardboard. The egg is too salty. As I eat it, I feel my insides exploding. Chew thirty-three times. I'm pissed off that John took all of my money and all of my dope. Instead of sitting here homeless, using a meal ticket for a meal I don't want to eat, I could be getting high. Two bites of the toast. Chew the egg. My insides are churning. My nerves are wrecked.

I walk and walk and walk, going nowhere. The bus ticket back to King of Prussia sitting in my back pocket etches slivers and slices from my butt cheek to my brain and puts stones in my stomach.

Checking my pocket for the key to the motel room, I head back down Market Street. I would call David, but I don't have a dime. I want to talk to him but wouldn't even know what to say.

Chapter 15

The Evil Step Mother

Day two. I have to check out in the morning. The marks have left scars. I have to go home. Maybe Dad won't notice. Dad picks me up in front of JCPenney, the bus station depot at the King of Prussia Mall. When I get in the wagon, he says nothing to me. I keep my arms crossed.

"I didn't do all that stuff," I say to break the uncomfortable silence. Dad keeps looking forward like he didn't hear me. He takes a Pall Mall out of the pack from the front pocket of his shirt and lights it. "The police said they would send whatever they find to my address." He takes a long pull on his cigarette and blows the smoke out the window.

Giving me a sideways glance, he asks, "What exactly *did* happen, Lina?"

What happened? Mom left and blamed me. There is a hole in my soul. Everything is my fault. I can't stop eating or purging. I am fat and ugly, so I do speed to not be hungry and to forget, forget, forget. I can't stop that either. Four days clean and it has overtaken my mind. Just one hit is all I need to feel better. I'm a failure. I didn't make it on my own, so I am sitting in your car. "What do you mean what happened?"

"What happened in Pottsville? I thought you were living with that nice guy that graduated from Drexel," he reminds me, still looking straight ahead.

"I was, until I left." I really don't feel up to rehashing the entire drama. He waits for me to continue. "My friend John and I were going to move to Florida, near Mom, but he freaked out and left me stranded and dumped all my stuff on a mountain." This doesn't even sound believable to me. Dad looks at me for a moment with sad eyes. He stays silent for the rest of the ride.

We pull into the driveway and walk up the back steps.

"Hi," I say to Helga, the evil stepmother. I don't know her too well, just what the kids have told me; that Lucy moved out because Dad was marrying her, and that David couldn't stand her, so he moved out before she moved in. I wonder how Anna and Carmen can stand living here with her.

"What is *she* doing here?" Helga says, thumbing at me like she is hitching a ride, talking about me as if I am not standing right in front of her ugly face.

"Oh, come on, hon," is all Dad says to the witch. Obviously, he didn't tell her I was coming home.

"Lina's home!" Carmen runs to me and gives me a huge hug. I think he's grown five inches.

"You got so big," I tell him as he fills my arms. "And you smell good. Are you wearing cologne?"

His face gets all red. "Are you moving home now? Are you going to stay here with us now?"

"She isn't staying here," the evil step monster interjects. "Tony, she can't stay here. She is not going to stay in this house."

"C'mon Lina," Carmen grabs my hand and leads me into the living room away from the pending argument in the kitchen. Dad and Helga go into the studio. I hear her screechy voice yelling at him from two rooms away. I sit on my hands to stop the shaking. A door slams.

"You are not staying in this house." She points a finger at me from the entrance of the kitchen. "You are not sleeping here."

"I'll sleep outside," I tell her. The sun has long disappeared from the sky. I am tired of people's shit. "Dad, if you give me some blankets, I'll just sleep outside."

"You can't sleep outside, Lina," Carmen says.

"You are not welcome in this house," the step monster claims. What a bitch. She doesn't even know me. I don't know how Dad can stand her, or why he doesn't stand up for me, his daughter. Probably because I'm a failure.

"I'm not staying in here. I'm sleeping outside," and I head up the steps to find some blankets.

Carmen starts to cry.

"See? See Tony? She comes here and starts a bunch of shit. I'm not putting up with this." She follows me up the steps. "You are to get out of this house," she shrieks as she points her chubby finger at me. She's five feet tall and five feet wide. Ugly inside and out. I don't know what Dad sees in her.

"Lina, c'mon," Dad calls from the bottom of the stairs as I root through the closet looking for some blankets. The hallway closet is reorganized. We used to keep blankets on the top shelves, but they are no longer there. It's filled with towels of all sizes now. The blankets are on the bottom shelf. "Come downstairs," he calls up from the bottom of the steps.

"I'm not trying to start any problems. I don't have to sleep in here. I'll sleep outside."

Dad's voice softens. "You are not sleeping outside."

"I don't want you to have any troubles, really. It will be okay. It stopped raining." I stare at bitch face while I talk to Dad.

"How about I drive you to Grandmom's?"

"Grandmom's? What am I going to do there?"

"I'm sorry, hon. You just can't stay here right now," he voices sadly. "We can talk in the car on the ride, okay?"

I don't want to hurt him or cause him problems with the witch. "Yeah, sure." Like I have a choice. I put the blankets back–on the top shelf where they belong.

The forty-five-minute ride is filled with great advice. I am to find a job. I am to stop my nonsense. Clean up my act. I wish this were an act. It would be Act VIII of Lina's fucked-up life. Act I – Cause a divorce between my parents. Act II—Get fat and stop eating. Act III—Screw up high school. Act IV—Get sexually assaulted. Act V—Get addicted to meth. Act VI—Get ripped off by a friend. Act VII—Spend thirteen hours in a police station almost getting sent to Sunbury Women's Penitentiary and finding out my parents don't give a shit. Act VIII—Clean up the mess I made in all previous acts. Find an apartment, he will put the deposit, and then it is on me. I don't want to live alone. I don't want to be in Philly. I don't want Dad spending his money on a worthless daughter. I want to get high and forget, forget, forget.

"Can you drop me off at Dave's?"

"That's not a good idea. I'm taking you to Grandmom's." I guess I'm the bad influence now. Ha. That's funny.

We stop on Frankford Avenue. Dad takes me into a store to buy me clothes. No matter how much I hate trying on clothes, I have no choice. Size 3, too big. Size 1 fits, but all of the pants are too short because they are a bit snug at the thighs. I need to lose weight. I choose three size 1 jeans, promising myself that they will be loose in a few days. Dad tells me to get some tops, underwear, socks, and another pair of shoes.

"I'll pay you back when I get a job."

"Don't worry about it, Lina. Just get some clothes. You can't go looking for a job like this," he says. I tried not to look at myself when I tried on jeans. I didn't want to look at my fat legs or my puffy stomach. I catch a glimpse in a mirror at the end of the rack in front of us. I recognize the curly dark hair. There are greenish-blue eyes staring back at me that I don't recognize; they used to have more brown in them. They are round and sad. I look back, trying to figure out who this is.

Where did Lina go?

Chapter 16
The Real City Slicker

I can't believe I've been in this place for over two months now. The guys around here act like dogs in heat, barking out windows whenever they see a female. Or maybe it's just me. Either way, it's disgusting. If that's what city girls respond to, that's even worse. I miss the woods. I miss trees. The only green things around here are the occasionally planted bushes in front of a row home that may have a five-by-five yard or patch of grass out front. My street doesn't even have that. It's all brick and cement.

My apartment is the top floor of the last house on the corner of Jackson and Magee Street. I have my own separate entrance that opens to a steep stairwell with no lights that leads to my apartment door. Dad was nice enough to give me the furniture from the basement. I set up the two wooden tables, the yellow and brown plaid loveseat with a wooden base and wooden handles that match the tables, along with a matching single chair in the shape of a U in my living room. So now I'm homesick every time I'm in my apartment. The sofa wouldn't fit because it was too big to get up the steps. My kitchen is too small for a table, but that's fine because food is the enemy. Dad let me have my old bed. I have no need for bureaus, since my entire wardrobe fits in my suitcase.

Cristina Utti

I wash the clothes I have in cold water in the tub and hang them around the apartment to dry. I did find a Laundromat eleven blocks away. Grandmom and Grandpop live five blocks away and I'm not asking them if I can do my laundry there, nor am I dragging dirty clothes for eleven blocks. I don't need anyone. I can take care of myself. Using cold water is just fine too. I have no hot water until I get the gas turned on, but that's all right for now. It's August, so it's hot as hell in this apartment anyway. I take fast showers because the water gets colder and colder while I'm in there. Maybe I'll get the gas turned on in September when it starts getting chilly and I have some money.

Dad paid the deposit and one month's rent, and like he said, the rest is up to me. I promised myself that I will not ask him for one dime more, ever. I got two jobs. I'm a salesperson at Radio Shack by day, and a waitress at Seafood Shanty by night.

Two months.

I haven't gotten high in two months and two days.

I can't believe that I have my own apartment. It may not be the most luxurious, but it's mine. Temptation comes, but I fight it off with all I've got. I go to work, come straight home, and write. Mostly I write letters to the people I love.

Except for taking advantage of my shift meal at Seafood Shanty I haven't eaten much either. My size ones are loose. After the initial five-day training period, I've been making $35 - $70 a night waitressing. With my first night's tips, I went directly to Woolworth's and bought pens, notebooks, envelopes for writing letters, and stamps for sending them since I have no phone. The first letter I wrote was to Penney to tell her that I am doing well. The second letter was to David. I wrote and rewrote, not quite knowing what to say. The letter I finally decided to send is this:

Breaking Infinity

Dear David,

I love you and miss you.
I hope Sideways Eight is jamming up a storm!
Please come visit when you can.
Love you, always and forever,

Lina

Short and to the point. I hope he gets it soon and comes to visit. With the second night's tips, I bought some new clothes (kid size 12, yeah!), candles and towels. The rest is saved under my mattress for the $275 monthly rent, which includes heat, not that that matters in August. As long as I don't spend my money foolishly, I can get by.

I realize how far I really am from being a 'city slicker.' I don't know if I will ever get used to living in the city. The bus route is confusing, so I walk everywhere I need to go. The five-mile walk to work takes about an hour. Most days after my shift, or in between jobs, I thumb it because it's quicker. I learned my lesson. I never get in a car that has more than one person in it.

Today, I get my check from Radio Shack and want to get to the bank before they close so I can open an account. If my money is in the bank instead of under my mattress, when cravings come, it will be easier knowing that I can't get to my money. Getting paid biweekly is tough. The waitressing job sure helps. I get my check from James, the manager, clock out, and hit the road. It's my only night off. I'm on a mission. Today I am opening up my first checking account. I finally have a little bit of money above my rent; maybe I can get the gas turned on so I will have hot water before it gets cold. Excitedly, I rush across the parking lot to the Boulevard and stick out my thumb, so I have a better chance of getting to the bank before it closes. A blue pick-up truck pulls to the shoulder to pick me up. The man in the passenger seat rolls down the window, asking if I want to hop in. Bad vibes. "Uh, no thanks." I continue walking in a rush.

I have at least another three miles before I get to the bank. I check my watch. It's 4:45. I'm never going to make it. They close at 5 p.m. I don't have another day in the next two weeks to get to the bank. I turn around to face traffic and out goes the thumb again. Within minutes a small red truck pulls to the side of the road. I take a peek in the window. He is alone and doesn't seem much older than Dave. He assesses me too. I see him look me up and down. "Hop in. Where you headed?" he asks as I scoot into the seat.

"Hi, thanks. To Frankford Avenue." There's a PNC close to my apartment.

"No problem," he says as he fumbles with the radio, looking for a tune. "Where're ya from?" I'm not sure what he means by this. I don't know what to say but have to say something because he is giving me a ride.

"I grew up in the Conshohocken/Whitemarsh area," I tell him.

He's looking at me instead of the road. "Where's that?" If he keeps staring at me, we are going to get into an accident. I look out the window. He messes with the radio dial.

"Out past Roxborough. What about you?" I don't care where he lives. I'm not good at making idle conversation.

"Lived here my whole life," he says as U2 comes on the radio. "You party?"

I freeze.

I look down at my arms while keeping my gaze forward. The marks have cleared up. Rent money is under my mattress, paycheck burning in my pocket. Why not? I've proven to myself I can stop if I want to. It's been two months. Plus, I need to lose weight.

"Yeah, sometimes," I tell him, not sure what kind of partying he does. My body kicks into gear.
 Remembering.
Heart racing for the next hit.

Chapter 17
The Old Guy

Two months from today, I will be eighteen. Then I will be legal and have to stop. For now, I go right to the source. I don't waste my time hanging with Alex, the dude with the truck. The second night we went to cop, I met Pete. I watched as he checked me out, pretending I didn't feel his eyes searing through my clothes. "Hot Legs" by Rod Stewart played in the background as I stood there in my short- shorts, the only kind I wear. He sang along while eyeing me up and down. Alex led us into the living room, with Pete right behind me. I felt him checking out my ass.

I know what he wants.

He took out a cigar box filled with baggies. Alrighty then, this is the score. The older ones are the easiest. The game is easy; I give them what they want, I get what I want. I'm finished messing with Alex if he has to come here to get the stuff. I can get it myself. They think I'm naïve because I'm seventeen. For the past week, I head straight to Pete's after work to cop, using whatever money I have in tips. Then he says, "Come on, baby," and touches me and gives me stuff for free. I play the game; pretend I like him. Sometimes he gives me a ride back to my apartment, sometimes I stay the night, and sometimes I thumb it back when I cannot stand being there for one more second.

Tonight I've done too much. I gave him what he wanted and have to get the hell out of here. His smell grosses me out. Heading out to the Boulevard, I walk for a while before sticking out my thumb. Playing a game with myself, I count how many cars pass before someone stops. It's always a guy. Not once has a woman stopped to give me a ride.

A gold Toyota Corolla pulls to the shoulder. I open the door and peek in. An older guy, head barely above the steering wheel. He reminds me a short Santa. Harmless enough. I hop in.

I smile and cross my arms. "Hi, thanks a lot."

"No problem, sweetie. Where're ya headed?"

"Torresdale Ave." I'll let him drop me off there and walk the few blocks to my apartment.

"Torresdale? I live on Torresdale."

Like I care. "Oh yeah?" The least I can do is act interested. "Have you lived there long?"

"Since my divorce." Good, if he was divorced that means he was married. If he was married, maybe he has kids. Not that that's a prerequisite for having children, but if he has children, maybe he's a nice old man.

"I don't live far from Torresdale," comes out of my mouth before I can help myself.

"I ain't never seen you around here." Catholic school kicks in and his grammar hurts my ears.

"I work a lot."

He looks at me, sizing me up. "You live with family?"

I think about this for a minute. Maybe I should tell him I live with my husband, or boyfriend, or with someone. He seems like a harmless old man, so I tell him the truth. "Nah, got my own apartment."

He glances over at me, head just above the steering wheel. "It's good to be independent."

"Yeah." It's just wonderful. I smile to show how great it is.

"You have family nearby?"

"Kind of. What about you?" I question back, hoping if he thinks of his family, he'll remember that he's a nice guy.

"Yeah, not too far."

I keep up the conversation. "You have kids?" People with kids have to be nice, don't they?

"Yeah, two daughters and a son," he says while looking straight ahead. I get the impression that his relationship with them is not so great.

"That's nice," I say. I gaze out the window, pretending to be real interested in the sights as we turn left onto Cottman Avenue.

"You in a rush?" he asks, taking me by surprise.

"What do you mean?"

"You hungry? You look hungry."

"Maybe a little," I admit. I know I've been doing way too much when I get high and can still eat. Or maybe this stupid body is betraying me. I try to fight it. I don't remember the last time I ate. I have no food at home. I have no money. The past five days I flew out of work, making a beeline to Pete's instead of eating my shift meal.

"Want to stop at the Mayfair?"

I've never heard of the place. All I know is that the section where my grandparents live is called Mayfair. I joke to myself that he wants to take me to their house to eat. "What's that?"

"A little diner on Frankford Ave," he tells me.

I don't want him buying me anything. "Nah, I'm okay," I tell him. I don't want to owe him anything.

"You sure? I was heading there anyways, and it'd be nice to have some company." He sounds sincere. He's probably just a lonely old man.

"Okay, sure." I'll keep the old man company. What the hell, why not? The only thing I have to do is go back to my lonely, depressing apartment. "I'm not really hungry though."

"Great, we'll just get a little bite to eat, then I'll take you wherever you want to go," he smiles through his moustache.

We sit at a booth and the waitress brings us two menus. I order water, no ice, with lemon. He orders a coffee, black. I watch as he dumps sugar packet after sugar packet into his cup. "So, I'm Lina. What's your name?"

He balls up the empty packets. "Cosmo. You can call me Moe." We sit in silence, looking at the menus. I don't want to tell him I have no money.

"Are you ready to order?"

"I'm not hungry." My stomach is screaming for food. The smell of burgers from the kitchen fills my nostrils and I want to take a bite of everything. I don't even like hamburgers. Food is the enemy. I am not hungry. Not one bit. I look him in the eye to show him I'm telling the truth.

He smiles at me, his white moustache curling upward on his lip. "My treat. How 'bout a sandwich? The least I can do for your company." This strikes a chord. I reminisce of times David and I spent together and realize how lonely I feel without him.

"I ate earlier, at work." My stomach defies me, growling loudly.

"Where do you work, at a starvation camp?" he laughs, his round belly bouncing up and down. I laugh too. My stomach gave me away.

"Okay, I'll get a cup of soup. The cream of broccoli sounds good. What are you ordering?"

"The hot roast beef sandwiches are the best. And fries with gravy. Sure you don't want a sandwich?"

"Soup's fine, thanks."

The soup and sandwich arrive within minutes. The place is pretty empty at this time of night, or maybe all of the time. Glad I don't work here; I'd be more broke than I already am. He digs right into the sandwich like he hasn't eaten for days either. Gravy drips on his beard.

"I live on Magee near Ditman Street," he says as he wipes his beard. "Where do you live?"

"Corner of Magee and Jackson. Where's Ditman?" spills out of my lips while I focus on the soup. I stir it with the spoon. I open a pack of crackers, and crumble them in, just for something to do.

"Two blocks from Jackson. We're neighbors," he tells me while eating two fries at a time.

"Oh, that's cool." I stir the soup. I sip some more water.

"You gonna eat that soup or are ya waiting for it to get cold?"

"Just waiting for it to cool off a bit." Lies, lies, lies. Fear. Fear. Fear. One spoonful. Empty is full. I fill the spoon with soup from near the rim. Mom told me this is where it's the coolest, but I like it piping hot. Mom. One spoonful. I lift it to my mouth. It tastes so good, warming my insides. Mom. *I don't want to hear your problems, call your father.* As the warmth fills my mouth, my stomach cries for more. I take another spoonful, then another, then another. It fills the emptiness.

"I knew you were hungry," he smiles at me. I look down and the cup is empty. At least 500 calories. Shit.

"I guess I was," I look at his plate. It is near empty too. "Guess we both were." I smile at him and then down the rest of the water. I don't know how I will get rid of this soup. I don't have money for laxatives, am too scared to steal them, and I'm not going back to Pete's. I'll walk to work tomorrow.

"Where do you work?" he asks, reading my mind.

"Seafood Shanty and Radio Shack, matter of fact, I have to get going. I have to work in the morning."

"You have a ride to work in the morning?"

"Nah, I walk."

"Walk? You walk there? That's one long walk. I'll pick you up. What time?"

"I have to be in by ten." I don't know why I'm giving him this information. A ride would be nice, but he's kind of creeping me out. "You sure it's no problem?"

"No problem at all. I'd love to. I'm retired, gives me something to do," he gives me a wink and pays for the bill. I let him drop me off in front of my place. As I unlock the front door, I remember the soup. The whole cup, and two packs of crackers. Ride to work in the morning, if he shows. Can't risk it. I go up the steps, counting. Thirteen up. Thirteen down. Up, down, up-down, up-down, up-down, up-down until sweat pours out of my skin. Up-down, up-down, until my legs ache. Up-down, up-down, until my stomach hurts. Up-down, up-down, up-down until I am empty.

Chapter 18
Lost Soul

I sent Dad a birthday card, today, on his birthday. I guess better late than never. It is the only thing I have bought with my money in weeks.

Two days fasting, one day eating. This week I was sure to save enough stuff to get me through the double shifts, working both jobs. The nights I make tips, I head to Pete's. The nights I'm off from Seafood Shanty, Moe picks me up at Radio Shack and we hang out at his place. He makes sure I eat. Very fatherly.

Until.

We must have been talking about my rent and how I don't have the money for it. He says if I 'take care of him' he'll give me fifty bucks.

Disgusting.

But I do it.

He pulls down his pants. It's limp. And wrinkly. Gross. His gut is harder than his thing. He pulls me toward him to kiss me.

No. I keep my lips sealed tight and move my face away from his.

Kisses are saved for people I like like that. I move down. They never argue with that. He runs his fingers through my hair and moans. I don't want him to touch me. Flashbacks of the night in the car. Fifty dollars. Five baggies. It's over in minutes. I push the vomit back down and pretend I enjoyed it too.

And head to Kensington Avenue.

To forget, forget, forget.

It does not go towards the rent.

Then head back to Moe's to see if he wants to do it again. I need money. He has a great plan. He knows people. His two brother-in-laws. A few buddies. We can charge sixty and do it at his place. I still make my fifty; he keeps ten. And gets taken care of for free. Sounds like a good deal, and I am about sick of owing Pete.

I use the bathroom first to do up a bag to get through the night. We schedule them on the same nights. They wait in the living room for their turn while they joke and play cards. Higher and higher I get and in between each putrid act, I'm further and further away.

His brother-in-law is the most difficult. Takes the longest. He actually likes me, and always tries to start with all of the holding and kissing bullshit. The second time I was so high I let him put it in. Big mistake. I lay down the rules. No kissing. No hugging. No penetration. But he consistently tries. He must not get any at home. Now he wants it all the time, even offered double. I reiterate my rules. If he doesn't start getting off quicker, I'm going to charge him more. I know what he is up to, wanting to stick it in and put his stuff in me. He is wasting my time. Rules are rules. I tell him if he wants all that to go home to his wife.

Working Radio Shack by day, Seafood Shanty dinner shift, and then Moe's at night, I'm getting better at money management. My rent gets paid. I bought some new clothes and shoes, even some food to keep in the apartment just in case I get hungry every few days. I've a real handle on it now. Food is not the enemy anymore. Meth is magic. I eat only when my stomach is growling and have lost weight. Moe's scale reads 96. Next goal is 90. Then life will be good. Lines for the morning so there are no fresh marks for the workday.

Straight to the heart at night because I've got no heart.

Chapter 19

Company

"I'm so glad you came," I tell David, and give him a big hug, forcing the renegade tear back.

"I had to check out your crib and couldn't leave you alone on your eighteenth birthday. A city girl now, huh?" David says jokingly.

"Yeah, a real live city chick." If he only knew. I've nothing to be proud of except my weight. Yesterday I weighed myself at Moe's. The scale read back 93 wonderful pounds. Alleluia! Three pounds until perfection. Dave steps back and looks me up and down. "What?" I know that look, the one with the left eyebrow raised up, lips puckered downward.

"You look like shit. What the hell do you weigh, like twenty pounds?" He doesn't look happy with me, but I'm thrilled. He thinks I am skinny.

"I have no idea. I don't even weigh myself." Lies. "Do you even see a scale in this place?"

"You haven't given me the tour."

"You're looking at it, and there's the bedroom," I say, pointing to my right. "Want some coffee or something?" I ask, changing the subject.

"How 'bout we get a six-pack? We've got a lot of catching up to do. I've just gotta tell you all about the band. We're playing gigs all over the damn place."

"Really? That's cool! And, sure. There's a bar a few blocks down on Torresdale."

We head out for the walk, and he grabs two six-packs.

"I can't drink much. I have to work tonight." And they are 154 calories a bottle. Screw that. I'll have one beer for dinner before my shift at Shanty, which will call for a stop down the road to see Pete before heading back here. That'll take care of the calories from the beer. He fills me in on the happenings back at home, the kids, St. Peter and Paul, the church where he and Dad are working, and his band. He downs three beers in the time it takes me to drink half of mine.

"You think you should slow down, so I have some company when I get home from work?" I say, half-joking.

"You think you should gain about fifty pounds?" he retaliates. Enough said.

* * *

I skip the shift meal at the end of my shift and skip Pete's too. I just want to spend time with my brother tonight, so I thumb it right home only to find David passed out on my couch. Pills, empty beer bottles, and an empty vodka bottle are strewn all over the end table. What the hell? I knew he still partied a lot, but I had no idea about the pills. I shake and shake him, but he doesn't budge. Fear cloaks my heart. I catch my breath, quiet my thoughts, and look at his chest. Up and down it goes, slowly. Thank God. I don't know what I'd do if something happened to him. He is my only friend in this whole damn cruel world.

The money in my pocket calls. I was going to get through the night and not get high because David's here. I get out of my waitress garbs and throw on a pair of jeans and a cropped aquamarine colored sweater. I am always cold, and it doesn't help that I have no heat or hot water. I look in the mirror. My eyes have gotten lighter and lighter. Sometimes I don't recognize that person in the mirror. I write him a note, telling him I am going for a walk and will be right back in case he wakes before I return. I head straight to where I know and get three bags and new works. These guys want me to hang out with them, of course. My entire body goes into overdrive, but I wait until I get home to do it.

I turn the key on the doorknob as quiet as I can and make sure not to make a sound walking up the steps so I don't wake David. The door at the top of the steps gives me away with its creaking. Crap.

"Hey Lina," David is glassy-eyed, sitting on the couch where I left him.

"Hey," I'm stopped in my tracks.

"You just get home from work?"

"No, I got home a while ago and then headed out for a bit. I left you a note." The truth is burning in my soul. It killed me to hide it from him when we lived in Conshohocken. I can't lie to David anymore. Now I have to tell him. "I headed down the street to cop."

"Shit, really? Whatcha get?"

"This." I take the baggies out of my pocket. "Want to do some?"

"Shit, yeah," he says. That was a dumb question.

"I don't do lines anymore," I tell him. I didn't want to tell him, but I'm not wasting it that way. No one knows. Well, except the people I deal with on the street.

"What? What do you do with it then?"

"Boot it, but you don't have to. You can have a few lines."

"No, I want to try it too," he says, but I can feel his fear. I'm not sure this is such a good idea. I could have just gone into the bathroom to do it, but he would have known I was high, and then I would have had to spend the night in a lie, pretending I wasn't high while I stayed wide awake. Shit, shit, shit.

"Okay," and that was the end of that. He watches as I take out a spoon from the drawer in the kitchen, dump the stuff in, take out a q-tip from the bathroom cabinet, and ball up a little piece from the cotton tip to use for a filter....

Then, I do for him what Greg did for me.

Chapter 20

The Great Plan

David decided to stay for a few weeks. So I started using at work because he is sucking up all of my money. This was not such a great idea after all. The manager pulled me aside today and told me that things are not working out. I can't believe I lost my job. Radio Shack alone will not pay the rent because I can't sell items to the poor old people living on social security that come in during the day and we work on commission. Deciding to walk all the way home today, I see a help wanted sign in the window of Gino's Pizza Café and stop in to inquire. The owner, Demetri, is middle-aged and from Greece. I talk it up, telling him I have two years of experience working in a pizza place in Pottsville. I didn't say a word about Seafood Shanty. I guess stretching the truth by a year and a half doesn't hurt, because he hired me. I start tomorrow.

Of course, David doesn't want to go home. He is stuck, plus he doesn't want to leave me here alone here in Philly.

"Why don't you move in with me? Instead of you paying rent here and me paying rent there, we can get a two-bedroom and split the rent," he says, again. This has been the topic of conversation for a few days now.

"I don't know. I don't think the family really wants me that close to them," is my excuse, but the real fear is that I don't know where to get anything in Roxborough, which is where he lives now. "And what about a job? Then I'll need another job out there."

"Obviously you don't have a problem getting jobs," he states. I guess it looks easy to him because he has never had to look for work; he has always worked with Dad. I hate looking for new jobs. It feels like prostitution. Get dressed up, put on some makeup to do up the eyes, put on the fake smile and even faker words. David will never know what it's like. I haven't been to Moe's since he got here, and I'm flat broke. We used up my rent money.

"Easy for you to say." I want to say more, but I stop myself. I don't want to hurt his feelings. He has enough problems thinking that he will never measure up to Dad.

"You wouldn't have to work so hard and can go to college," he insists.

"College," I state. "Yeah, right. Why do you keep mentioning college? I didn't even make it through high school." I'm concerned with surviving, not college. I need money or won't have a place to live soon, and I can't let that happen.

He is serious, and stares at me solemnly. "'Cause you're smart, Lina."

"Yeah, I'm so smart that I landed up here, in this shithole. How am I going to go to college, David? I can't even pay my rent this month." I can't even figure out how to eat like a normal human being.

"Come live with me and go back to school." He always has things all figured out, like life is easy.

I shrug. "I don't know, maybe I can come live with you, but I'm not smart enough for college. You should probably go back home soon. I'm sure they want you there for Thanksgiving dinner tomorrow. Plus, Dad has to finish up that job and needs your help, and I have to work doubles."

"Let's get a two bedroom. I'll talk to Dad; maybe he'll help."

"I don't want his help. Besides, that bitch won't let him do anything if she knows I'm involved." Suddenly, David has nothing to say, because he knows it's true that Dad's wife hates all of us, especially me. Now he looks sad. Maybe he drank too much while I was at work. We sit in contemplative silence.

"Then I won't say anything to Dad. We can save up. I'll just switch from a one bedroom to a two bedroom. They can just switch my deposit over, and we can live together, and you can go back to school."

"Why don't you go back to school if you love it so much?" As soon as the words are out, I feel bad. The tongue is the most vicious muscle in the body, and I am constantly unleashing mine. There is an ongoing battle between the words that whip out and the things left unspoken. He sits here, hurt. "Aw, man, I'm sorry. I don't want to talk about this anymore."

"Just think about it, okay?"

"C'mon, let's stop talking about this stupid stuff. It's my last night off. It's bad enough I just lost a job."

"But you got another one and you hate waitressing anyway." He always looks at the bright side of life. I wish I were more like him.

"I've got sixty bucks so I'm heading out, okay?" He wants to come with, but I know it's easier to cop if I don't have a guy with me. It's the last of my cash because I won't be making tips at the pizza joint. I'll have to wait a few weeks for my first paycheck and not waste my money so I can pay the rent. Or, go back to Moe's.

"I'm going back home tomorrow to help Dad finish that church as soon as possible so we can get paid. I'll save all I can for the down payment for the two-bedroom."

"I never said I was moving there for sure, Dave."

He gently pushes his curls away from his eyes, looks me up and down, then hangs his head. "But you have to Lina, don't you see? You just have to." His shoulders slump, like he's really disappointed in me. His almond eyes frown downward, matching his rosy lips. Why do guys get all of the good features? Nice lips, long lashes, beautiful hair, nice legs. Even in his sadness he is beautiful.

"I'll be back," I cut him off before he can say more. I don't want to think about new jobs, or moving again, or going to college. I really don't want to think about anything.

Chapter 21

Mr. Movie Maker

We are getting quite a following at Moe's. More and more and more equals less and less and less.

Pane, Demetri's partner, took a liking to me. He's not my type. Too short and too skinny. He drives a Porsche and is the money half of the pizza shop partnership. The norm has been he drives me home after work, which is fine with me, but I'm not attracted to him in the least, and I'm sure as hell not going to kiss him no matter how many rides he gives me. All that is on my mind today is getting my rent paid. I'm already a month behind from when Dave stayed with me last month. Sharing costed me a lot of money. Not that I mind. He's always been there for me, and there's no price that can be put on that. Even if he didn't stay with me for a few weeks I would've probably spent it anyway. The gas never got turned on.

Broken promises unto thyself.

Pane's mouth keeps moving but I don't hear a word that he's saying.

"You ever think about doing movies?" he asks as we are heading for my apartment.

"Huh?" I'm pulled out of my self-loathing for a millisecond. "Movies? No, not really." Movies are the last thing on my mind. I don't know what the hell he is talking about. If I did movies, why the hell would I be working in his pizza shop?

Cristina Utti

"Why not? You have the body for it," he says while he looks over at me, checking out my legs. "Have you ever modeled?" He's giving me the creeps. I should've walked home from work, then I wouldn't be sitting here putting up with this crap. I'm really sick of guys. I don't know what the hell he is looking at anyway. My bust is about a 32 A-. That's the only place I wouldn't mind a little bit of fat.

"Actually, I have. Just for a little while," I admit, and stare straight ahead. It's not something that I like to talk or brag about. Three years ago, I was with the Main Line Modeling Agency. Had an entire portfolio put together. I did a few shows. Anna got worse and worse in her illness and started feeling awful about herself. She thought I was so much prettier because I was modeling. Frankly, I don't see it. She's beautiful and has a better shape than I will ever have.

The agency sent me on call for models and I was chosen to go to New York for "a complete makeover" at some salon. I'm glad I like to read, because in the contract in teeny-tiny writing, it stated that they had the right to do whatever they wanted with my hair. I refused to sign. No amount of money is worth cutting my hair. For the next assignment, they sent me to model for DeAngelis Photography Studio. Dad dropped me off for the photo shoot. The photographer, a fifty-year old pervert, tried to get me to take off all of my clothes. I refused. By then, Anna was slitting her wrists and cutting herself other places too. That was enough modeling business for me.

"I'm not too photogenic." Right now, I'm not too much of anything but behind on my rent.

His lips are still flapping away. "I don't believe you. You look very photogenic. You're the perfect size for films." I sure don't see it when I look in the mirror. "How about we go to my place and take some photos, just for fun?"

I look down at my fat thighs. "I don't think so."

"Are you crazy? You are perfect," he exclaims. No one has ever called me that.

"Okay, sure." The words pop out, just like that. It's nice that he thinks I'm perfect. Plus, I'm tired of being alone in my apartment. "Can we stop by my place first so I can get a change of clothes?" I smell like a hoagie from making sandwiches all afternoon.

He drives me to my apartment.

"I'll be out in a minute, okay?" I don't let him in just in case there is evidence lying around. I make sure to grab a three-quarter-sleeve shirt to cover my arms, and my favorite pair of jeans, the soft ones with the worn tears. Before hurrying back down the stairs, I double-check myself in the bathroom mirror. I don't know what he sees. I wish I could see out of other people's eyes.

His apartment is in Old City. It's huge and decked out with expensive furnishings. The black leather sofa and loveseat offset the white marble floor beautifully. I spot two bottles of red nail polish and a few nail files sitting on the end table and wonder why he is coming on to me if he has someone living with him. I'm glad I didn't kiss him. He offers me some iced tea, and I sit on a bar stool at the high pink stone kitchen counter while he excuses himself for a moment. I thought he had to use the bathroom, but he comes back with an armful of clothes.

"You want to try some of these on?"

"Uh, no, not really. For what?"

"For the photoshoot."

I wait to see if he is serious. He is. "I'm not wearing another woman's clothes." My heart is pounding. This is getting weird. "Can't we just take a few pictures? I really can't stay long."

"Sure, sure," he says, trying to appease me.

A few minutes into the session, I ease up and posing becomes second nature. I remember back to my short modeling stint before I landed up in the looney bin and pretend that I am there, really modeling.

"You're a natural," he says, clicking away. "You can make lots of money doing movies."

I stop. What is it with him? "What are you talking about?" This guy owns a restaurant. He's not a movie producer. He's getting on my last nerve with the movie crap. "Why do you keep talking about doing movies?"

"I make short flicks. The pay is good," he stammers while putting away the camera. Now he is talking dollars and cents.

"How much? What kind of flicks?"

"Seven hundred fifty for a half hour shooting," he states. My eyes bug out. That's three months' rent. "You interested? You take great shots," he says. If he only knew.

Chapter 22

The Grand Ole Movie

It's my first Sunday off since I lost the job at Seafood Shanty. I'm glad I don't have to work because I need to clean up my apartment. Tonight's the big night. The only visitors I've had in the past months have been David and Moe. Dad stops by on some Sundays on his way to or from Grandmom's if I'm not working. He always offers to buy me food. I don't want food, or anyone's help. I'm managing fine. I run the vacuum, sweep the kitchen floor, and wipe down the sink and toilet. I double, triple, and quadruple check everywhere for paraphernalia. I take down the clothes that I washed in the tub last night that are hanging over the kitchen chairs, bedroom and bathroom doors, and shower rail. They are still a bit damp, but I fold them and put them away, hoping they won't smell tomorrow.

Glancing at the alarm clock that sits by my bed, I see I have an hour until they get here, plenty of time to get back here by 7 o'clock. A hit to get through this and all will be okay. I'll stop. I promised myself. I'm eighteen now. I won't need it anymore. I'm maintaining my goal, 90 pounds, and rent will be paid. All will be better. Life will be good. I'll quit Moe's too. I layer up because it's freezing outside, and I'm always freezing inside too. Peeking out the window, I see snow flurries.

I get back in record time. 6:55.

Cristina Utti

Pane and his friend arrive on time, 7 p.m. sharp. One more second and I would have burst out of my skin. We make introductions and I excuse myself to use the bathroom. Careful, careful.

Need just enough to be here, yet not.

In slow motion, I enter the living room. It's set up with sheets on the walls and on the floor. I wonder how long I was in the bathroom. There's a naked man sprawled on the floor. There's a floodlight in the corner. Pane is behind a tripod camera.

"We can't do this with clothes on Lina." I stare at him wondering if this is a dream. "You are wasting our time." I look around my apartment. "Lina, what the fuck?" he says in his stupid Greek accent. "Are you going to get ready to shoot? What the hell were you doing in there all that time?"

"Oh, yeah. Sorry." Guilty of losing track of time, I pull down my jeans and fold them. I take off my shirt, glancing at my left arm, and then my right, hoping it isn't noticeable. I used make-up to cover the marks when I was in the bathroom. I fold the shirt neatly, smoothing the creases, and place it on top of my jeans on the floor. On the sheet. And stand here, exposed, and cold.

Camera on.

They are staring at me.

I wish I wore a bra so I could have had more time to undress. I'm going to have a damn heart attack right here.

"Come down here," the man on the floor whispers. I don't know if that's supposed to make me feel better, but it doesn't. I don't even know his name. I wasn't listening when he introduced himself. I don't want to know his name. Names are meaningless. Actions are what have meaning in our life. This action is despicable and has no name. I go to him. He is muscular and twice, maybe three times my size. He reeks of man sweat. I know what I'm supposed to do, but I can't.

Standing here with my arms crossed to cover my nakedness, I mutter, "I'm sorry, I'm a bit nervous. I have to go to the bathroom again," I lie, but it isn't a real lie. It's a half lie. I am nervous. I don't have to go to the bathroom. I have to use the bathroom. The stuff is hidden in a box of pads that I don't need because I've stopped getting my period months ago, somewhere they will never think to look if they have to use the bathroom. "I'll be quick, I promise." I escape to get deeper in my world of abeyance, feeling them watching me as I walk away in my panties.

Hands shaking, I double-check the door to be sure it is locked. I flush the toilet, and while I run water, I wet it up and my hands are shaking so bad I miss and have to poke again, and again, and do it so fast I don't check for air bubbles and am scared I will die and I don't wash it out because I don't want to squirt blood anywhere and I'm scared they will hear me and come busting in here wondering what the hell is taking me so long and I can't find the cap so I just shove it all back in a pad without the cap and hope they don't find it and shove the pad in between the other pads in the box and place the box back in the cabinet under the sink making no sound at all and put the make up over the still bleeding arm, and come out of the bathroom crossing my arms over my chest like I am cold but I am sweating.

Move through the process quickly. I lean into him, leaning on my left arm so they don't see. It's tremulous, like the rest of my body. He touches me. I move the hair out of my eyes as my head buzzes, I try to act sexy and smile for the camera. I touch him and smile some more. My face is going to crack.

The camera's rolling.

He pulls me toward him, and I feel his hardness. He kisses me and I kiss back, against my rules. But this is for the camera. He tastes of vodka. I think I'm going to throw up right this very second, then he pushes my head down.

Cristina Utti

I hold him close to hide my own nakedness, and fondle it, pretending I like it. I get flashbacks of Moe's. No name rubs my back and runs his fingers through my hair, like we are in love or something. I can't stop shaking. The moment my eyes avert to the camera, I see Pane's face, which was behind the tripod a few minutes ago. Now, it's staring at me with a sick smirk across it. I do my best to get this over with as quickly as possible, but it feels like I've been on this sheet for hours.

The camera clicks.

I wrap a sheet around me and go to my bedroom to dress. The bright numbers catch my eye. It's 7:57 but feels like eons later. I remember it's Saturday and they will be waiting for me at Moe's at 9 p.m. Pane gives me $700, says I wasted time and cost him money. I don't care. I just want them out of here so I can leave.

I take the money and put $600 under my mattress for the rent and the rest goes in my pocket. That catches me up, plus covers this month. I'll pay the landlord tomorrow morning. For now, I take the other hundred and head down Kensington Avenue to get more before I have to go to Moe's.

The guys I go to want me to stay and party, but I don't like getting high with people. I tell them I'll be back. Matter of fact, I don't like people much at all these days, not even myself. I rush back home, the dread of my appointments ringing in my head. The sheets are still on the floor and hanging on the wall. Feeling freshly repulsed, I rip them down and gather them up. I put them in the dirty clothes pile but really want to burn them.

I want to talk to Penney but have no phone.

I want to talk to David. I'm so alone.

I want all these thoughts in my head to stop. Half-hour until show time; there's no way out. I take out some more money from under the mattress and go back out. What the hell, I'll make more tonight. The vultures will be waiting.

When I get home, I check the clock. 8:46. I pace back and forth from the living room to the bathroom, to the bedroom, constantly checking the time. I made money. Now it's twenty minutes after nine. I'm late. I don't have to go. If I don't go, I may lose future prospects for making money when I need it. I won't need the money if I stop. What if I don't? I'll lose my apartment then have to do what I did with Scott. I don't want to go. I pull out the box of pads, gather my stuff and head to the bedroom. I check the door again to make sure it is locked.

Planning to take some with me to Moe's because I know I'll need more to get through the night, I look at my veins. My arms are mess, so I fit all I can into one shot to make sure there's enough to take away the pain, and so I don't have to poke twice.

Ugly.

Fat.

Shamed.

I sit on the edge of the bed. My heart speeds, my breath quickens, time doesn't matter. Everything moves slowly as I watch what I'm doing as if it's not my arm and not my hand doing this to my body. I push it in slowly because there is so much and I've never done this much at once my fingers are sweaty and slippery and I pull back and there's blood so it's still in though I don't feel it so I push it back in and finish. I pull it out and my hands are shaking so bad it drops to the floor I try to stand up to pick it up and clean it so it doesn't clog so I can use it again but my legs fail and my head spins and I fall back onto the bed.

Heart thumping out of my chest.

Darkness.

Lungs forget how to take in air.

Breathe in. Breathe out.

Heart pumping in my brain.

Cristina Utti

    Frozen but sweating, seeing myself from above, stop fighting.
    Finally at peace.

In a hole
struggling halfway
between life and death
believing in neither
interested in both
really sick
embarrassed to the point of nonfunctional ability

Chapter 23
Still Here

There are tubes in my nose and in my arm. There are wires attached to my chest. Everything is white. Dad and Dave are sitting in the corner of the room whispering. I can't hear what they're saying. I try to talk but my throat is dry, and these tubes keep pushing air down my throat leaving me speechless. I look at them, but they don't see me. I focus on my left foot and with all my strength, move it back and forth. Dad sees it and comes to the side of the bed.

He takes hold of my hand, the right one, the left one has tubes in it. "Lina?"

"Where am I?" It's barely a whisper and takes all of my energy. My head spins.

"In the hospital," he says, eyes distraught. A flashback of the darkness comes over me and I am ashamed. I wonder who saw what I couldn't pick up off the floor. I wonder who took off my clothes because all I have on is a hospital gown.

"How'd I get here?"

"Your friend Moe found you and called an ambulance." I thank God it wasn't Dad.

"What day is it?"

"Sunday, December 23rd." His eyes fill as he works to keep his composure. I cannot take in his pain on top of mine. Strength leaves my body and my eyes drift shut. I wish I didn't make it.

It's dark when I open my eyes again. A nurse is here taking my temperature. What a stupid thing to do. I don't have a fever. I just want to sleep.

Forever.

But they keep waking me up.

"How are you feeling, sweetheart?" A dark-skinned nurse stands over me waiting for the thermometer to beep. I nod my head. Feeling wonderful. Stupendous. I feel the need to urinate, that's how I feel, but there's even a tube down there.

"Ms. Ortiz, our social worker will be here in an hour to talk with you," she informs me as she pulls out the thermometer, records the temp, and sticks it back in her pocket.

I nod my head. The tube is not in my nose anymore. "Why?"

"Standard procedure with all suicide attempts," she says, and pats my hand.

"Suicide?"

She looks at me and shakes her head back and forth. We both remain silent for a moment. She waits for me to say something.

"I wasn't trying to kill myself," I mumble. Or was I?

"What were you thinking? You had enough drugs in you to kill someone three times your size. We're lucky you pulled through."

"Yeah. I'm still here." I shut my eyes.

"It'll be okay sweetie," she pats my arm. "Ms. Ortiz will be in to talk with you soon."

I pretend to be asleep so she will leave.

"Hey Linee," someone says. It's Penney's voice. I'm dreaming. She called me this the night of our hilastrophy catastrophe when we could not stop laughing. "Hey, I'm here. David called me this morning. Sorry I wasn't here sooner."

I force my eyes open. I try to wipe the sleepiness from them and feel the tube in my arm. They keep pumping stuff into me. "Penney?"

"I got your letters," she whispers. "Sorry I didn't write back."

"It's okay. I haven't been the best friend," I admit and close my eyes.

"They said you tried to kill yourself."

"It's not true." I mumble, even though I don't believe it.

"I didn't think so. You're a dumbass sometimes, but I knew you wouldn't leave me behind."

"No, I guess I wouldn't." She's the one who left me. "I'm still here."

"Yeah, thank God," she sniffles. All of the harshness between us dissolves in the saltwater of her tears. "You're not going back to Philly are you?"

"I don't know. I don't want to." I never want to go back there ever again. "The nurse told me they won't release me until I'm a healthy weight. They are trying to make me fat again."

"Fat? Lina, look at me." She puts her hand on my cheek, wipes the tears, and turns my face toward her. "Do you think I'm fat?" Penney asks, making me look at her and face myself.

I look at her. Really look, for the first time in eleven years. "No, you look good," I mumble, and she does. She looks healthy and perfect, so unlike me.

"Well, I'm least six inches shorter than you and weigh 125 pounds. Think about it."

I look in her eyes, really look at her body, her legs, her waistline, her shape. She does look good. I think of the image that stares back at me from the mirror. It's ugly, and empty. Now a river is flowing down my cheeks, like the pain of the past six years has broken free.

"You're gonna be okay, Linee. You're gonna be okay." She holds my hand.

Through the tears I choke down, my spirit is suddenly flooded with the reality of the past few years. "I don't want to die Penney. I want to live, but I don't know how."

Chapter 24
The Gift

I wake, forgetting where I am for a moment. I look around and see flowers and a card on my little rolling table. It's a silly Santa card with some corny joke about elves, signed, Love David. Inside, I find my present. It's a poem he wrote for me. On the card he wrote, "When I think of you, I think of the words brilliant, bold, affectionate, humble, sweetness, and love. I put it all together in this poem for you…"

This is the only Christmas present I got this year.

When love was a simple thing
Back in days of yonder
When love governed everything
And kept no mind wondering,
Purity was all abound
In each flitter's flutter
Of the glory in the sound
That Innocence had found
Glowing joyfully serene,
Virtuous and happy
In bright meadows by the stream
Of kindness in one's heart when goodness dreams
And O what dreams goodness inspires
In humble souls this very hour!
Dreams that solemnly lament

Breaking Infinity

Passion free and confident
Dreams of love, Dreams of desire,
Dreams of water, land, and fire
Dreams fed full of hope and cheer,
Dreams that never disappear.
Dreams of strength and of faith—
The kind no one can erase
Dreams that in their yearning bleed,
Carrying on life's fundamental seed
Made of visions divine and graceful
That through tacit consent
Becomes agreement silent
That in the hours we might bathe
In the sweetness of love
If we behave
And strive
With a little help from above

Chapter 25
Feelings

Happy Valentine's to me. I'm supposed to love myself. I'm trying. After a few weeks on IV fluids, they puffed me up to 100 pounds and moved me to a rehab facility. My stomach hurts when I eat, but I want to live. I watch the other young people that talk and act stupid; they have no clue. I don't try to help them. I pray for them. I'm learning to help myself. Ms. Ortiz meets with me on Mondays, Wednesdays, and Fridays and makes me write about my feelings. I've written it all.

Every Saturday and Sunday between one and five we have family visiting hours. Dad and Dave came twice. Mom hasn't come to see me because she's still in Florida, but she calls once in a while. All of a sudden, she wants to hear my problems. I have a lot of anger in my heart. Ms. Ortiz tells me to let go and forgive. She says that anger will only hurt me. I'm trying. Penney comes every weekend. I guess she's family too. I'm up to 107 pounds and scared to death. One more pound and I can leave, but I don't want to leave.

David and Dad cleaned out my apartment. I told David to get the $600 I put under my mattress and use it toward the down payment for a two-bedroom apartment. He told me there was only $400.00 there. I don't remember spending that much money that night, but I don't want to remember that night at all. I wonder who watches my porno flick. I get flashbacks of all those men at Moe's apartment, and want to shove all those memories deep, deep down where they'll never resurface. Ms. Ortiz tells me to write about it. She tells me the food has to stay down to nourish my body, and the feelings have to come out to nourish my soul.

Chapter 26
Decision Time

I figured there has to be something better than these dead-end jobs, and that I better do something to keep busy and keep out of my head, so I registered at Community College of Philadelphia for the Fall semester. The placement test placed me in the T.O.P. program, the transfer opportunity program. If I do well in the T.O.P. program, the next year I'll be in the Honors program, and then all the credits transfer to a four-year college. Imagine that, David was right. I guess I am smart.

Within a few weeks of moving in here with David, I had two jobs. I work at Super Fresh in the seafood department and waitress weekends and a few nights during the week at Toland's. I don't stay for the shift meal because everyone has a shift drink too. I leave right away with my tips in my purse and go over Penney's or come straight home. I'm saving up for a car to get to school.

David is intelligent, but not too smart. He keeps partying when he knows I am not doing that stuff anymore. It's not doing him any good in his life either; he oversleeps and gets Dad angry when he makes them late for work. Some things never change. I try to talk to him about his drinking and partying, but all he does is blow me off. He tells me that he is okay, even though I know he isn't. Last night when I tried to ask him to stop getting high, he said,

"I'm not you, Lina. I don't care how much I weigh." That hurt, so I just shut my mouth.

At outpatient sessions, I vent. I share with the group about how hard it is living with Dave. I share how annoying it is that he keeps drinking and getting high. We learn positive affirmations like 'One Day at a Time' and 'Live and Let Live.' Ms. Ortiz suggests I find different living arrangements. I explain to her that I can't just up and leave him. Through all of my ugliness, he saw my beauty and was the only one who believed in me. He was so happy for us to get an apartment together. I need to help him.

His constant partying upsets me. I try to let it go, but it's hard. He drinks every day and so do the people at the restaurant. I never liked drinking, but still. It's hard knowing I can't get high anymore even if I want to. I know where it takes me, and I never want to go back there. I don't get on the scale anymore either. I'm measuring myself in goals accomplished, not pounds. Mrs. Ortiz, Penney, and my family know, but no one else knows of my eating disorder. People in group wouldn't understand. To most people, being a drug addict is almost acceptable, but having a problem with food makes you a weirdo. I know I need to share about this, and I will when I am ready. Feeling especially antsy today, I head over to Penney's straight from work. She and her boyfriend have an apartment on Bell's Mill Road, about a mile from my place.

Her place is different from my apartment. It's similar to a townhome. She has the first floor and a little patch of yard in the front where she planted some geraniums. She loves red geraniums. Her kitchen is small but well lit, with a big bay window, which gives the impression of the room being bigger than it is. We sit and have some iced tea. She makes the best tea.

The first thing she says is, "You look good, Lina." I hate when people say this to me. It means I'm getting fat.

When negative thoughts come, I fight them off with positive affirmations.

I am not fat, I am healthy.

I am worthy.

I am beautiful.

I have people who love me.

"Thanks, Penney," I say, and mean it. She wouldn't tell me I look good if she thought I looked like crap. Good friends are like that; they dish out the truth even if it hurts. We sit quietly in the comfort of our friendship.

"So, what's going on? I know something's bothering you," she takes a sip of tea and doesn't look at me, knowing it will be easier for me to speak out if I don't have to look at her.

"I don't know how much longer I can live with David. He keeps getting high and asking me to cop for him. It's bad enough he is getting high around me. I don't know why he asks me to get it for him. Yesterday when he left for work in the morning, I looked through his room just to see what he was doing. I found it," I spurt out.

"Found what?"

"Meth," I say, and my heart goes into overdrive at the mere thought of it. "I almost did some. It took all I had not to. Ms. Ortiz tells me to write, so I wrote, but that didn't help. So then I ran and then I cried." I cut myself short before the tears fly out. I never thought it would be this hard.

"What's really bothering you?" Penney always cuts right to the heart of things. This is part of the reason why I love her. I look at my legs.

"I'm getting fat," I say, not looking her in the eye.

"Oh," she gets up, comes around to my side of the table and wraps her arms around me. "You know it's all about how you feel about yourself, right?"

"Yeah," I nod and hold back the lump in my throat.

"Have you talked to your mom lately?"

"Nope."

"Maybe you could write to her," she suggests.

"I don't know. Do you think she will listen?"

"Does it matter? It's all about you, Lina. You have to be okay."

I shrug my shoulders. "I guess."

"And, you have to get over feeling fat, or you will think that I'm a beached whale soon," she states in all seriousness.

"What? What do you mean?" I ask. I never see her as fat. She's perfect.

"Well, you're the first to know, I mean besides John," she says, and it hits me. I'm not quite sure, and don't want to say the words, so I wait. "I'm pregnant."

"Oh my God! Really?" This is so exciting, but Penney doesn't look excited. "You okay?"

"I guess so," she says quietly. "I don't know how to tell my parents. You know how my dad is."

"It'll be alright Penney, you'll see. I'm so happy for you." She doesn't look so happy. I want her to stay positive about this. "How does John feel about it?"

"Oh, he is just ecstatic. He wants a big family. Why does the seed have to nest in us?"

"Because we're the strong ones," I tell her, and this time I get up and give her a hug.

"Guess I'll have to stop smoking."

"Guess we both have to learn to love our bodies just the way they are or will be."

Together we lay out a plan on how we will get through this. I'm going to write a letter to my mom by the end of the week and show it to Penney before I send it off. She is going to go to her parent's house on Saturday and tell them she's pregnant. I'm going with her.

When John gets home, I give him a hug and congratulations, and he puffs his chest out like the proud man of a wonderful prize. He is happy from head to toe. I'm happy that he's happy. I'm glad I'm not all messed up on drugs and can be here for Penney. I head home to begin my letter.

While I walk home, I think. "To thine own self be true." This is another saying that I've taken to heart. I have to tell David that I'm moving out. I can't stay with him, it's too difficult to watch him getting high and drunk and not want to do it myself. We used to have fun when we jammed with Sideways Eight, but it got to be no fun at all for me. When I walk in, Dave is sitting at the table, drinking wine and sketching.

"Hey, how was your day?" I wait to hear him speak, so I can gauge just how much he drank today.

"A'right," he mumbles. Oh boy. Not a good time to talk.

"That's good. Did you eat? You hungry? I can make us some sandwiches," I ask him, hoping if he eats he will help sober up.

"I'll have a sandwich or som'in later," he says, hand still drawing.

"Can we talk?" I just can't keep it in anymore.

He looks up at me, over his glasses. "Sure, what's up?"

"I think I have to get my own place soon."

"What? Why?"

"'Cause that's what they mentioned might be a good idea for me to do." They taught me to use 'I' phrases, and not blame people for how I feel. "Maybe I can find a place closer to work, or closer to school."

"Then how-a ya gonna save for a car?" I don't want to make him sad, but I really can't stay in this environment. He doesn't think there is anything wrong with drinking and getting high. I have to save my life.

"I don't know," I shrug, and grab a seat across from him. "Guess I'll have to save every penny." He keeps on drawing, sketching a picture of Jesus on the cross. His art is different from Dad's. Dave's drawings are more abstract. I know that he 'gets' it, why I can't live here. I also know that he feels like he can never be as good as Dad, and this makes him feel bad. I wish he could see how talented and smart he is. "I know you can drink and stuff, but I can't. I'll die. You saw what happened to me before. Maybe you can stop too."

"You can stay here 'til school starts." He doesn't look up from his drawing. "It's fine Lina, I want ya to be a'right. I get it."

"Okay, maybe. We'll see how it goes. Thanks Dave," and I leave it at that for now, and head to my room to write that letter before my emotions overtake me. I don't want to leave, but I can't stay.

Chapter 27

Forgiveness

I retreat from touch, sound, and drama to evolve into what my soul was meant to be. She was the essence of my heart. I realize that love is not a contract, nor equal, nor a happy ending. Love is the slate under the chalk, it is the foundation homes are built upon. It's the place I come back to no matter where I've been, and she was not there for me no matter how much I wanted her to be. David is that, no matter how messed up he is. Bad is not an absolute; it's a relative term. I thought Mom did not love me, but she is only human like the rest of us here on earth. After a while of believing the fiction we tell ourselves, we can no longer remember the truth upon which it was based. This took me to the darkest corners of my existence.

    The letter took me five drafts until the words were right. I kept tearing up the pages, making fresh snowstorms of guilt and regret. Is it a crime when you love someone so much that you can't see clearly? The blood of loss thrown into the fire of sorrow turns into something else. I filled the emptiness with food, then the emptying of food filled me. Food was not the enemy. Repeat the same action over and over, and eventually it feels right. Eventually, there isn't even any guilt. That's where my addiction took me. It's not anyone's fault but mine that I reacted like I did. I'm not mad at Mom anymore. I know it will be okay now

Breaking Infinity

if I take one day at a time and live in acceptance. We are responsible for our own lives, the masters of our soul's fate, and if I continue to act like a fool and abuse myself, I won't have much of a fate, or a bad ending at that. We make messes of our lives every now and then, which I certainly have, but every now and then we manage to do something exactly right. I think my letter is exactly right.

    I close the notebook containing the letter, clean up the paper snowflakes, and head to the bathroom to wash up before bed. Peeking into the living room, I see David sprawled out on the sofa, a bottle of wine spilled on the carpet next to him. I grab the bottle and dump what is left of it down the kitchen sink, so he won't start right up again in the morning like he has been in the habit of doing lately, then I try to get the stain out of the rug. Cold water or vinegar usually works. I'll talk to him again tomorrow about getting some help.

Chapter 28
The Plan in Action

Sticking to the plan, I go directly to Penney's after work with the letter. Penney approves. We find a stamp; I lick the envelope and seal my fate. We walk to the blue mailbox to send it off before I change my mind. Ms. Ortiz was right about writing. Now I do my part, and we head to her parent's home to break the news about the pregnancy.

Penney's parents are not too happy for her, as she well knew before we walked into their house. They want her to get married. She doesn't want to get married, but she didn't want to have kids either. I do. I want four. Their wedding is set for next month, after Easter and before she starts to show. Our lives are in constant flux. She will become a wife and have a baby, and I will be starting college. I promise her I will take care of my body and not give her any worries. It's time for me to be here for her.

Chapter 29

Tough Times

I decided to stay here with Dave and try to get through my first semester of school. Some of the things I hear in the meetings make me so confused. They say 'people, places and things' can be detrimental to staying clean, so I wanted to move away from David because we used to party together. They use the word "acceptance" a lot. I watch him continue to get high, and I know I can't help him or change him, nor can I accept this, and it hurts. I do my best to keep him company when I can. Then they say, 'no major changes the first year,' so I decided to stay. I got through my nineteenth birthday, even ate cake and ice cream with the family. By the end of next month, I'll have a year drug free.

* * *

When I get home from school Dave seems okay. I'm glad his pupils aren't dilated because it makes my skin crawl when he is high on that meth crap. I scan the living room tables and don't see any bottles lying around. I don't have to work on Wednesday nights, so it's a good time to talk.

"Hi," I say as I walk in and see him sitting at the kitchen table. "What are ya working on?"

"Editing 'The Equal Opportunity Murder'," he says, not looking up.

"Oh, that's cool," I don't bother him. He is in a groove. "Can we talk later? I don't have to work tonight."

"Huh? Oh, yeah, sure," he says, not looking up.

I take my time in the shower, getting my thoughts together, not sure how to approach the subject. I condition my hair. While the conditioner sits, I shave my legs although I don't really have to. No one sees them in the winter. A thought occurs as I rinse the suds out of my hair. I'll tell him I'll stay if he stops getting high and stops drinking. I jump out of the shower, throw on a pair of jeans and a comfy oversized green sweater, and rush to the living room to share this revelation of a solution.

Before I can get a word out, he asks, "Yo, Lina, think you can call that dude Pete?"

"What? Actually, I was going to talk to you about that." Now I am nervous, the wine is out, and his glass is half empty. I sit down next to him at the table. "You know how I landed up in that mess in Philly and in Pottsville?"

"Yeah, what about it?"

"I never want to go back there."

"You never will. We're together now. You're in college now," he states these facts, but it doesn't change the problem. "So, can you call Pete for me? Just a few twenty bags. I got us a ride. Deb is on her way."

"You don't get it," my head drops. "I can't do that anymore."

"C'mon, Lina. You're fine. You haven't gotten high in over a year. I'm letting you stay here for nothing. You can't do me one little favor?"

The thought of it makes my heart race.

"This is exactly what I wanted to talk about. I want to stay here with you. What about if we both stay clean, together?"

"I'm fine Lina. I'm not you. I'm not going to get all caught up in that shit. I just want some for tonight. C'mon, give Pete a call for me."

I'm stuck. Heart pounding. Nerves on edge. The doorbell rings.

"I'm getting changed," I escape to my bedroom so I don't have to face his friend Debbie asking me to get stuff for her too. I pull out my sweatpants and the Community College of Philadelphia sweatshirt I bought for myself at the bookstore the day I registered for classes. It gives me strength and hope. I grab my running sneakers, gloves, and a hat, dressing in record time.

"Going for a run," I stammer as I whiz right past Debbie, not even saying hello. The sky is turning dark and a light mist falls from the sky. As soon as my feet hit the sidewalk, I break into a full speed run, pounding hard. I run and run. I run until my lungs feel like they will explode, my stomach hurts and the tears finish dropping. I stop and double over for a minute to catch my breath, and then start up again. Sweat beads down my face, icicles hang from my hair. I run because I want to get high. I run because I don't want to get high. I run because I don't know what to do with all the emotions. I run until it hurts, until I can't run anymore. Running is better than a needle in my arm. Running is better than binging and purging. Running clears my soul. The sky is black, and I can't go back home. I end up at Penney's apartment. She opens the door in her pajamas. The essence of time disappears when matters of the heart prevail.

"I can't stay there anymore," the words choke out between gulps of sadness and fear.

"Okay, okay, get in here before you freeze to death and catch pneumonia," she says and waddles to the couch.

We talk into the wee hours of the night and come up with a plan.

Chapter 30
The Agreement

Dave and I agree that I would stay until the end of the year, paying only the electric bill, which allows me to save some more money while also giving him time to get a roommate to help with the rent, or to move into a one bedroom by himself. He understands. He said he wants me to live. I tell him I want him to live too, but he doesn't think he has a problem. He enjoys his lifestyle.

I share about it in group. The nights he stays up all night. The drunken nights when he talks and talks and talks and I keep him company.

I pick up extra shifts at work to keep away as much as possible without hurting his feelings.

The only place that I can afford is in Norristown. It's a well-lit, spacious apartment with hardwood floors and sliding glass doors leading to a balcony; $500 a month includes heat and electricity. My move in date is December 15th, which works out perfectly, giving me time to get settled in before I start next semester. Dave says I can use his address for school purposes since I no longer live in Philly. I tell him I will still pay December's electric bill, even though I'm moving out before the end of the month. It's closer to my jobs, but further from school. I've managed worse. He decided that he will move into a one bedroom in the same complex after the holidays.

Chapter 31
The Baby!

Penney had her baby today. I was so excited that I called out of work for the first time ever since I began working at Toland's restaurant. I drove directly to the hospital after my last class. The baby came two weeks early, but she is perfectly beautiful, and a healthy 6 pounds 3 ounces and 18 inches long.

Penney let me hold her. This precious new human being makes me think about how precious and perfect we all are, just the way we are.

I love Penney and little Samantha.

I love myself, too.

Chapter 32
The Clean Life

The first week of school I took public transportation, but it became a real pain going from Norristown to Conshohocken to work, then back to my apartment to take a shower, then right back out for a two-hour commute to college. I don't like hanging around in Philadelphia waiting on the bus or train. Too many shady characters. Too easy to cop. Too many bad memories. The nights I have my waitressing shift, I take the train, then the bus, and then walk the mile to work in Flourtown. Going home from there, I can get the bus to the Plymouth Meeting Mall, then into Norristown, but they stop running after 9 p.m., so I walk from the mall all the way home. It's about a four-mile walk. Patrick, the cook, always offers to drive me home, but I see the way he looks at me, and I don't want to owe anyone anything, so I bus it and walk. No more thumbing it for me.

After a week of this, I managed to talk Dad into helping me get a car. I saved up a bit over $800 to put as a down payment, but they won't give me a loan for the rest of it because I have no credit. Dad reluctantly cosigned for me so I can get back and forth to school. I got a Plymouth Scamp. It's gold, smells new although it isn't, and seats only one other person, which is just perfect for me. I still don't like people too much.

Breaking Infinity

So far, the program at school is wonderful. The TOP students are together all day. It was good to see everyone again after break. There are two cohorts: fifteen of us in the afternoon classes, and fifteen in the morning classes. Only thirty students were chosen for this program. Although it is the transfer opportunity program, I have no idea where I am transferring after these two years. Still, I'm happy I was chosen to be part of it. I like that the classes are block scheduled. I've gotten myself into a good routine. I arrive at work to set up the seafood department by 6 am, leave at 10, and get to school by noon for classes until 4. This semester I have Algebra I. I guess I'll get tortured for what I slacked on in high school. I also have Intro to Psych, Social Science 1, and Philosophy in Literature. Now that I have a car, and don't have to spend numerous hours a day commuting, I signed up for the cross-country team. I hear my phone ringing as I walk down the hall to my apartment door. I walk into my apartment, feeling accomplished and proud.

"Hello?" I pick up the phone before dropping my backpack.

"Yo, wha'sup?" It's David.

"Hey, how are you?" I ask, trying to get a feel for his mood.

"Great, life is just fuckin' great." Oh boy, it's one of those days.

"What's the matter?"

"Nothin', nothin'. How's school?"

"It's great, I absolutely love it." I go on to tell him about my classes and how interesting the Lit and Psych classes are, but he keeps interrupting me and mumbling. "I can't understand you," I repeat over and over, as he repeats over and over whatever the heck he is talking about.

"Screw dis, dey are assholes," he says. I think.

"Who?"

"Them. You. Everyone."

"What are you talking about?"

"Forget it, neva mind," he slurs.

"Hey, I gotta go, I have a lot of homework to do," which I do, but the truth is I can't understand what the heck he is talking about and can't stand talking to him when he is drunk.

"Yeah, yeah, yeah, always busy," he guilts me.

"I'll call you later, promise. I really have to go." I say good-bye and get off the phone as quickly as possible. I put the phone on the receiver, slide the glass door open, go out on my balcony and breathe deeply. My heart aches for him. I'm glad I don't use anymore.

Chapter 33

The Accident

Dave was in a car accident two days ago. He kept calling me, but I didn't answer because I figured he was high or drunk, and I just couldn't deal with that. I'm very stressed with my classes. My grade in Algebra dropped to a B. I hate that class; it sucks up a lot of my time. Working sucks up a lot of my time too, and I have the car loan and car insurance to pay now on top of my other bills, so I can't cut back my hours. I don't want to go to group anymore, but I know that I have to because I've come mighty close to binging lately. I fight through it. I cry, or write, or run. I force myself to go to my group therapy because I know that I will probably never really be 'better.' When I look in the mirror, I still see obesity, even though I know in my brain that I'm not obese. Last time I got on a scale at Dad's house, it registered 119 pounds. I'm okay with that.

When I finally called him back, I found out what happened. He was heading to Philly with a few people and they got into an accident. He has a broken collarbone. I'm going to make the time to go see him tomorrow, maybe take him food shopping since his arm is in a sling.

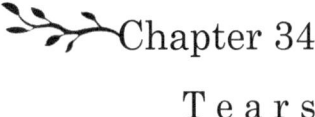

Chapter 34

Tears

The visit did not go well. He was drunk, throwing shit in my face about how he helped me out, and kept repeatedly asking me to go to Philly to get some stuff for him

I stayed for an hour, helped him clean up his apartment, then left.

And cried all the way home.

Chapter 35
Torture

The phone rings and rings when I'm home. It rings at midnight. It rings at two in the morning. It rings at three in the morning. It never stops. If I don't answer, he will just keep calling. I can't answer it because I don't know what to say to him. Why can't he just stop doing that stuff? If I could, anyone can. I'm so angry with him that it's better if I don't talk to him at all. Now I know how Penney felt.

I finally answer it. He goes on and on about nothing. The slurring and nonstop chatter break my heart. It's 4 a.m. I tell him I have to go to sleep because I have to be at work in two hours. I promise I will call him after work before I go to school tomorrow. Well, today.

When I finally get off of the phone, I shoot a prayer up to a God that I'm not sure I believe in.

Dear God, please make David stop calling me.

Chapter 36
The Uncalled Call

Dave and I talked and talked. He seems more coherent and easier to talk with during the day, but this means that he is not going to work. We had a good conversation this morning. He said that he is tired of doing that "crap" and is going to get some help. I was so relieved. I told him that I'll call around and help find him a rehab after school today.

As soon as I walk in my apartment, the phone is ringing. I know who it is before I even pick up the receiver. David's mumbling and slurring. I try to hold a conversation with him but get frustrated because he keeps repeating himself. I can't even understand what he's talking about.

I tell him that I have to get ready for work and will call him back when I get home.

I take out my math book, and start in on Algebra problems, feeling guilty as hell.

Chapter 37

W h y? W h y? W h y?

I get a call at work. I never get calls here. When Matt, the restaurant manager, approaches me and tells me that my father is on the phone, my heart begins to palpitate, and my legs turn to rubber. Not only is it a Friday night, but it's also Good Friday and people have a long weekend off from work, so we are busier tonight than on our usual Friday nights. With shaky hands, I bring four waters to the table that was just sat. I walk down the staircase from the balcony area where I'm working the tables around the bar. The steps seem to go on forever. Everything moves in slow motion. As I walk through the downstairs dining room, my mind fills with my worst fear.

I have lived with this fear for the past few years, always waiting. Why can't he just stop that crap like I did? I remember that I never called him back last night. I was going to call him before I came in to work today, but just couldn't deal with it. As these thoughts swirl around in my brain, Matt hands me the receiver. I pick up the phone

"Hello?"

"Lina, can you get out of there? Something happened to your brother."

Silence.

It takes every ounce of energy in every cell of my body to force a sound through the thick lump in my throat that is suffocating me.

"Where are you?" I finally ask, my body quivering.

"At his apartment."

My father's voice is low, soft, and deeper than usual. Although I've never heard him speak in this tone, it's not in his voice or words that I hear the sorrow; it is in the silence in between the words. I look at Matt and hand him the phone, too numb to place it on the receiver.

My only thought is to get out of here and get to my father as quickly as humanly possible. I have five tables in my station, and they are all full. I have to pick up food for my tables and get all of my customers settled before I leave. As I walk into the pantry to pick up the two salads with blue cheese dressing for table 81, the pungent smell of blue cheese makes my stomach flip.

Immediately, my body begins to shake, and my chest tightens. I can't breathe. I take a deep, forced breath and try to calm my arms and hands so I can pick up the plates. This labored effort goes on for what feels like an eternity. I cannot pick up these salads without dropping them; my body is trembling. My throat is closing up on me. I can barely get any oxygen. Water is forming in my eyes. I have to get out of here.

I leave the salads behind and walk out of the pantry to find the manager.

"Matt, I, I have to go," I muster between gulps of air.

"What's wrong?" he questions, seeing me shake.

"My brother," I cannot say another word, or I will lose it, right here in the dining room in front of everyone. We keep all of our money for paid checks until the end of the night. When we cash out at the end of the shift, we pay the checks, and the difference is ours. I don't care about the money. I hand him my tablet with the orders for my tables and all of the money in my apron.

As I walk out of the restaurant and head toward my car, the lump in my throat releases. The tears pour out of my eyes as rapidly as the rain is falling from the clouds. The heavens are crying too. As I drive from Flourtown to Norristown, the journey seems to take hours. The sounds of my own cries frighten me. They are coming from the pit of my abdomen, up through my heart, and out, forming a sound I've never heard. All of my worry has released into great sobs of pain.

God, please let my brother be okay. I'm sorry for what I asked you. My voice pleads and begs; my heart already knows.

As I pull up to the corner where David lives, all I can see are police cars; the blue and red lights come through the darkness that engulfs me. I jump out of the car to find my father. I see him standing by the front door of the brick house where David rents the top floor. Although I cannot make out his face from the corner where I am parked, I know that he is crying. I run to him. We embrace, both of us soaked from the crying heavens and our tears. No words are exchanged; for, there are no words. We stand in a world of grief, numb to the chaos of the police cars, the ambulance, and the backed-up traffic on Main Street that surrounds us.

I lose all sense of rationality. I have to get into the apartment to see my brother. I run toward his door, which is barricaded by the police.

"You can't go in there, young lady," a tall officer coldly states.

"Let me in! My brother is up there!" I yell in his face and push him. Another officer grabs me from behind as I flail and fight and curse. "My brother is in there. Let me go!"

"Miss, calm down. Step away from the premises." He holds my arms behind my back. I see my father looking at me, heart broken. I go limp.

* * *

Cristina Utti

I'm at the hospital and don't remember how I got here. We are in a white room, filled with bright white lights. David's on the bed, his body covered with white sheets up to his neck. His face is purple. My grandmother, Uncle Freddy, Aunt Lucille, and my brother Carmen are here. They all live in Philadelphia except Carmen and are now here. I've had a lapse in time. Everyone is crying, except Grandmom. She is holding David's hand.

As I stand here listening to the hustle of the hospital personnel, the beeping of various machines from the rooms of the living, and the crying of my family members, I feel nothing. I am frozen. My grandmother has no idea what is going on. I watch her holding his hand.

"Davey, everything will be okay," she repeats over and over while patting his hand. I don't have the strength, heart, or voice to tell her that he will not be okay. That he will not be anything anymore, ever again. This surreal moment breaks with an abrupt crashing sound a few feet from us. Carmen punched a hole in the wall in the hallway.

I have to call Mom in Florida and tell her. She doesn't know yet, and in this family, everything is left up to me. I do not want to call her. I know that once I speak those words to my mother, it will be real. I want someone else to call her, but everyone is falling apart. Dad is staring out into space. In my fractured, deadened state of mind, I make the call. It rings twice, and she picks up. She is happy to hear from me. This makes it even more difficult to get the words out. My mouth goes dry.

Although my clothes have dried from being out in the rain, my palms are soaked as I hold the phone. I have to tell her not once, not twice, but three times that her son died. Her scream shatters my heart and breaks the shock my body has just gone through. I feel again. The puddles on my shirt are proof.

Breaking Infinity

Looking at David in that bed, I know in my heart and soul that David doesn't yet know that his body has ceased. He isn't in his body anymore. Without his spirit in it, he looks like a wax statue of my brother. He is floating among us. I can feel him. I know he's still here. It feels as if we are sitting in the apartment, having a conversation. Then, he wisps away from me. I touch his face. It's cold. I've never realized that it is our spirit that makes us who we are, until this moment. This body in front of me is not my brother.

I will never forget this night. It will be etched in my mind forever.

Chapter 38
Broken Promises

I am back at my apartment. My car is parked out front, but I don't recall driving. I cry unceasingly. I cry myself to sleep, and cry when I open my eyes and realize I am here without David. I don't know how I will go on without him.

Every time the phone rings, I think it's him. I'm so mad at myself for being mad at him. Now he will never call me again.

I never called back.

Another broken promise on my list of broken promises.

Chapter 39

Does He Even Know?

We had to wait to have the funeral service due to Easter services.

I dress in a black skirt and a white top. I feel like I am betraying him again. When we were little, he told me he wanted everyone to wear jeans at his funeral.

Like he knew.

The needle killed him.

I caused my parents' divorce.

And I killed my own brother.

I would have worn jeans, but my jeans don't fit; they are falling off my butt.

Can't eat.

Can't feel.

It's not fair. I freeze my eyes, freeze my face, freeze my heart to face them and get through this night.

There are too many young people here.

I am the only one who knows *everyone* in this room. Even people that I haven't seen since eighth grade have shown up.

Darkness.

The casket is open.

The seating is set up in a semicircle, with rows and rows in the center, like he's on stage. There are not enough seats for all of these people. My parents are up close. My mother is crying. My father is almost as stiff as his son. The faces, the "I'm sorrys" are a world away, beyond the glass around me. My parents are seated in the chairs closest to the casket. My feet carry me towards them, to the empty seat in between them, overlooking David's body.

"How are you holding up?" Penney gives me a hug. I didn't even see her come in. This feeling has no words. Loneliness is a mirror that reflects itself. He is gone. Words are fleeting. My life will forevermore be divided in half, again, with grief being that hole in the center. I hold on to her and soak her shoulder.

"I never called him back." Wiping my eyes, choking down the pain, I turn toward my parents and try to be strong. Penney's arm guides me back to Mom and Dad. I sit in the empty seat in between them. Our hands find each other, Dad connected at the right, Mom on my left. We are one again, for this moment in grief. Guilt pulsates through my father's blood, up and through my heart, and into my mother's. We are the left behind. We are the guilty ones. We are those who could not help him. We are the ones who left, who stayed, who enabled him, who understood, who misunderstood, who got high with him, who showed him how to do what killed him.

It should be me in that casket.

I want to scream.

Silence is not golden. They lied.

"That's *my* seat."

We look up, stunned. It's the step monster, looming over me like a dark shadow in hell.

"I said that is my seat," she says again to me.

"Fuck you." I don't move. I grip my parent's hands even tighter. I'm trying to figure out how I am supposed to live without David, how to carry on in this world. I can't take this bitch right now. She stares at me. Screw this. She is not worth any ounce of emotion that I have left. I get up and go to his casket.

I kneel. I touch his arm. His face. He is cold. And puffy. Poor, poor David. Does he even know he is dead? "Stay with me always," I whisper in his ear. I know he is listening. "I'm so, so sorry." The walls close in on me. I try to hold it together but am lost.

I move past the people, the sad looks, and all of the people saying, "Lina, just want to say I'm sorry." What the hell are they sorry for? They didn't kill him, I did. I've no comment. I look with vacant eyes at these people. Friends from school are pouring through, Ronnie, Brandon, the band members, his friend Allison, his friend Deb from Conshohocken, even Mark from eighth grade. I think the entire high school is here. I spot Callan in the crowd. I go to Callan and hold him, melting into his arms.

"Get me out of here," I ask him.

"C'mon." He holds me upright parallel to his warm heart and guides me through the dark crowd, into sunlight. We walk, supporting each other. "Do you think he knows?"

"Knows what?" I ask him.

"You know, knows that he's not here anymore," Callan says, and I can't believe he spoke what has been burning in my own mind.

"No, he hasn't left yet."

Callan is crying. "I can still feel him."

"Me too, me too."

Acknowledgements

The first three people in my life have gone on from this world, yet they set the stage for who I am today. My father and my brother were always there for me during those tumultuous years of adolescence, and my mother gave me the gift of independence. They are always in my heart. I would like to acknowledge my five children, the greatest gifts in my life: Cristina, Angelina, Erica, Vincent, and Marc Utti-Hodge. Thank you for being exactly who you are and for continuously believing in me. You inspire me daily to be a better person. A special thank you to my friend Barbara Kenny for being a part of my life and for loving me just as I am. Thank you Chuck Eustace for being a good friend to my brother. A heartfelt thank you to Joan Maguire for reading early writings of my manuscript. Your life is an inspiration to me. I am grateful our paths crossed many moons ago. I would like to thank Amanda Hodge and Heather Schugar for reading the final draft and encouraging me to publish this as it is, a memoir. A special thank you to Ayesha Hamid and Steven Quigley for assisting with line editing of my early drafts. Thank you to Colleen Cummings for her patience and help with the final edits of this book. A final thanks to Krish Singh, PhD, Publisher/Owner at Auctus Publishers, who believed in my story. All of you played a huge part in this project coming to fruition. Thank you.

www.ingramcontent.com/pod-product-compliance
Lightning Source LLC
Chambersburg PA
CBHW072145100526
44589CB00015B/2107